A Home of Another Kind

A Home of Another ∽Kind∽

ONE CHICAGO ORPHANAGE AND THE TANGLE OF CHILD WELFARE

Kenneth Cmiel

THE UNIVERSITY OF CHICAGO PRESS
Chicago and London

KENNETH CMIEL is associate professor of American history
at the University of Iowa. He is the author of *Democratic
Eloquence: The Fight for Popular Speech in 19th-Century America*
(1990).

The University of Chicago Press, Chicago 60637
The University of Chicago Press, Ltd., London
© 1995 by The University of Chicago
All rights reserved. Published 1995
Printed in the United States of America

04 03 02 01 00 99 98 97 96 95   1 2 3 4 5

ISBN: 0-226-11084-2 (cloth)

Library of Congress Cataloging-in-Publication Data

Cmiel, Kenneth.
    A home of another kind : one Chicago orphanage and the
tangle of child welfare / Kenneth Cmiel.
        p.   cm.
    Includes bibliographical references (p.   ) and index.
    1. Chicago Nursery and Half-Orphan Asylum—
History.   2. University of Chicago. Chapin Hall Center
for Children—History.   3. Orphanages—Illinois—
Chicago—History.   4. Problem children—
Institutional care—Illinois—Chicago—History.   I. Title.
HV995.C42C553   1995
362.7′32′0977311—dc20
                                              95-14573
                                              CIP

for Jean–
TIBI GRATIAS AGO

CONTENTS

CONTENTS

A gallery of photographs follows page 92

INTRODUCTION

Most of us are lucky enough to spend our childhood at home. Many re-member those years warmly. And even those of us with decidedly fierce memories about growing up still usually manage to graduate to reasonably productive adult lives. While we all suffered our share of tragedies running from divorce to death, and while siblings and parents paraded the usual gamut of neuroses, most of us got on. And if we had our likes and dislikes inside the family, some quite intense, we nevertheless survived the experi-ence, got off into the world, and have probably repeated the process. As I say, most of us get on. This is a book about an institution that cared for those children who didn't.

The Chicago Nursery and Half-Orphan Asylum was founded in 1860. For over one hundred years it provided living space for kids whose par-ents couldn't support them. Specifically, it aided dependent children. Nineteenth-century welfare reformers used the categories of "dependent" and "delinquent" to differentiate needy children. The former were kids who, through no fault of their own, could not be cared for by their parents. Adult poverty, illness, or death brought dependent children to outside care. A delinquent child, on the other hand, came into contact with a wel-fare agency precisely because he or she had caused some sort of trouble. Habitual running away, petty or not so petty crime, unusually assaultive streetfighting, and in the twentieth century, truancy, drugs, and the like—such were the errant behaviors of delinquent children.

These distinctions were often practiced more in the breach than any-where else. The line between delinquent and dependent can be a quite tricky one. And certainly many institutions that supposedly cared for de-linquents wound up housing large numbers of dependents (a steady rally-ing cry for reformers over the years). The Chicago Nursery and Half-Orphan Asylum, however, rather firmly maintained the boundary. First as

I

an orphanage and later, after World War II, as a home for emotionally disturbed children, the asylum maintained its identity as a place for dependent, not delinquent, children. Only in the 1970s, when state policy made
it impossible for simply "dependent" children to be institutionalized, was
the distinction erased.

In many ways it was a typical home for dependent children. One of the
benefits of this study is that it lays out in some detail the history of such an
institution. Founded by urban elites as part of a response to the dislocation
of a bewilderingly mobile commercial society, the Half-Orphan Asylum
was one of dozens of sectarian orphanages opened in the mid-nineteenth
century. It was a Protestant institution for Protestant children, at times
housing close to 180 youngsters at a time. It served a working-class population. It was run by a volunteer board, made up exclusively of women. From
Helen Goudy in the 1870s to Clarissa Haffner in the 1950s, the Chicago
Nursery and Half-Orphan Asylum was graced with a string of energetic
and more than capable managers, none of whom were ever considered part
of the workforce.

At the turn of the century the asylum was attacked by progressive reformers. Like many institutions for dependent children, the Half-Orphan
Asylum slowly reformed itself in the early years of the twentieth century,
adopting, by half-measures, much of the progressive agenda. Professional
social workers were hired to perform tasks previously done by wealthy volunteer women. The agency gradually enmeshed itself in an increasingly
coordinated bureaucratic system designed to manage all of Chicago welfare. By the end of the 1920s, agencies like Community Fund, the Chicago
Council of Social Agencies, and the University of Chicago School of Social Service Administration began to factor in the Half-Orphan Asylum's
history.

In still other ways the story of this institution is a typical one. After
World War II, the last towering generation of volunteer women—women
such as Clarissa Haffner and Kay Milliken—turned the asylum (by then
commonly known as Chapin Hall) into a home for emotionally disturbed
children. Gradually, more psychiatric and social services were added. By
the 1960s, Chapin Hall had become what was called a residential treatment
center. The professional staff now ran the institution; the volunteer
women moved to the side. Throughout the nation, many of the old orphanages were undergoing similar transitions in those same years.

Finally, like many other private children's agencies, Chapin Hall had to
confront and negotiate the deinstitutionalization movement of the 1970s.
Chapin Hall became deeply dependent upon state money during the 1960s
and 1970s. As public policy shifted and state authorities decided that only

the most severely disturbed children would be institutionalized, agencies like Chapin Hall had to weigh their options. Should services be reoriented to meet a new and "tougher" sort of resident? Should state authorities be confronted or placated? The questions could eventually get to the soul of the operation—should it continue at all in its present form? Chapin Hall did confront this issue in 1984 and decided that it would shift from a service-providing agency to a research and development center. The residential treatment program closed and Chapin Hall moved to the University of Chicago to begin a new chapter in its history.

I have pursued four basic themes. First, I have tried to look at what social services the agency provided. What kind of care was given to the children? What did the staff and managers hope to accomplish? What were their conceptions of family? Second, I have traced the evolution of the clientele. What sorts of children lived in the asylum? Why did they come and what were their needs? What outside problems brought them to the institution? Third, I look at the relationship of the asylum to Chicago child welfare at large. How autonomous was Chapin Hall? What role did organizations like Community Fund or the state's Department of Children and Family Services have in deciding what went on inside the institution? Finally, I have traced the philanthropic history of the agency. Did it matter if the money came from private donors, from the Community Fund, or from the State of Illinois? And if so, precisely how?

A key benefit of studying a single institution is that it allows us to look at the interrelationships of all these themes at the precise point where actual services were being delivered to real children. Too much social welfare history continues to be written as if the words of a Jane Addams or the evolution of legislative policy is the sum of all social welfare. I do not want to minimize the history of elites. I never could have even imagined this book without the guidance of an extensive literature on such leaders. Still, the top-down approach does not tell the whole story. Studies of single institutions bring social welfare history to the grassroots level. This study combines a social history of those in need with a history of ideas about child care as well as the political history of child-welfare bureaucracies in a major urban center. Moreover, it tries to see how these strands fed off or conflicted with each other. Most important, I repeat, it does this by focusing on a point where social services were actually being delivered.[1]

Another advantage of studying a single institution over time is that I can look beyond the periodization that normally captures historians. Even very good social welfare history is often organized around such categories as the Progressive Era, the New Deal, or the late nineteenth century. While I have not ignored such divisions, I also have tried to indicate how the whole story is far more complicated. For example, in chapter two I argue that at the Half-Orphan Asylum, nineteenth-century styles of child welfare persisted right through 1910 and that this was very common in Chicago area children's homes. And in chapter three I try to suggest how much of the progressive agenda about child care—specifically increased foster care and the conversion of large asylums to smaller "cottage" houses—actually came in the 1920s, *after* that period normally called "progressive." Similarly, I have also tried to indicate how a successful wave of reform hit Chicago child welfare in the late 1940s while a similar effort failed in 1935–36 at the New Deal's high tide. Major shifts in Chicago child welfare do not correlate with the stereotyped periodization of twentieth-century U.S. history.

A related advantage of looking at a single institution over time is that it allows me to write far more recent history than is usually the case. While scholars like Judith Trolander, James Gilbert, John Ehrenreich, and Linda Gordon have begun to write the history of post–World War II social welfare, it still remains largely unexplored.[2] Most surveys rely on social scientific literature when approaching these years. Others wind up just not covering children's institutions after the Progressive Era.[3] Such surveys are, of course, dependent on the literature available. I hope to help fill in a bit more of the picture. Largely through the good fortune of my sources, I have been able to tell a story reaching to the present.

A final benefit to looking intensely at one institution over time is that it helps burst some conceptual categories still often used to understand American welfare. One is the public/private distinction. One theme I try to develop is that through the 1950s, the most important regulatory agency for Chapin Hall was not the state's Department of Public Welfare and certainly not the federal government, but a group of private agencies centering around the Community Fund. At the beginning of the twentieth century, progressives of various stripes created an interlocking set of private agencies designed to coordinate all the service-providing agencies of the city. These private agencies—Community Fund, the Chicago Council of Social Agencies, the University of Chicago School of Social Service Administration, and Chicago's Association of Commerce—became de facto regulators of Chapin Hall. Thus the first half of the twentieth century was marked by the private sector trying to create an effective public policy.

Recent scholarship devoted to "bringing the state back in" runs the risk of forgetting how much twentieth-century welfare was the product of forces outside the state, even after the Second World War. Standard surveys devoted to the "growth of the welfare state" run similar risks.[4] By noting the importance of private regulatory agencies such as Community Fund, I have been influenced by those historians who have systematically focused on the public-private interplay in twentieth-century institutional life.[5] It should not be surprising, as I note in the epilogue, that current state welfare agencies contract with private research firms to help figure out how to manage themselves. For better or worse, this is simply a new evolutionary twist in a long-standing pattern of U.S. social policy.

Another category I try to deconstruct is that of the social worker. People working in the field have long understood the periodic tensions between those social workers who work at service-providing agencies and those who make policy. Historians, however, generally write about the social work profession as if it was a single entity. (This practice, I add, privileges the managers over the social workers in the trenches.) Chapin Hall's history from the 1940s through the 1980s was marked by the warp and woof of dispute between those service-providing social workers employed at the institution and the social work elite trying to manage the system. The languages used differed markedly. The former spoke of the knowledge won through experience, of the importance of helping children one at a time and face-to-face. They in fact often sounded very much like the female volunteers of the late nineteenth century. The managers, on the other hand, spoke of the systemic needs of emotionally disturbed children in Chicago. Their idiom was statistical, not narrative. After studying the history of Chapin Hall, I find it quite misleading to speak of a "social work profession" without distinguishing care providers from managers.

If there are distinct historiographical advantages to tracing a single institution over time, the approach also has its limits. First, there is the problem of generalization. In broad outline, the history of the Chicago Nursery and Half-Orphan Asylum recapitulates the last 130 years of institutional care for dependent children. Yet no institution is simply a "type" and this was certainly true of the Half-Orphan Asylum. It was the only Chicago orphanage in the late nineteenth century that did not take legal control of the children it cared for. Parents retained custodial rights. And without more research it is just impossible to tell how typical funding patterns were. Where I have had outside evidence, I have tried to indicate how Chapin Hall stacked up vis-à-vis other homes for dependent children. Still, there are very few studies of children's institutions to compare it with. In general, scholarly interest in dependent children has taken a back seat to explorations of delinquency, although I hope the new scholarly interest in battered women and children will change that.[6] While I am confident that the asylum sketches the story of institutions for dependent children in its broadest features, much more will have to be done before a more complete picture can be drawn. I have no doubt that some of my hunches will be corrected by future research.

A related problem in focusing on a single service-providing institution is that I miss some of the larger social and bureaucratic politics driving such agencies like United Way, the Chicago Council of Social Agencies, or, in a later period, the state's Department of Children and Family Services. For the most part I do not look at the leadership of those agencies, nor do I explore how they made policy decisions. I have simply focused on how these larger, more powerful agencies dealt with Chapin Hall. This has its benefits, of course, showing how these managerial agencies actually dealt with a service-providing institution, whatever the rhetoric or official policy. It leaves aside, however, the internal politics of these agencies and their own intriguing place in welfare history. Here too I think future research will probably modify my own work quite fruitfully.

The limits of the documents raise still another problem. The Chicago Nursery and Half-Orphan Asylum left voluminous records; indeed, they are among the best of any comparable Chicago social service agency. Yet there are gaps. Especially in the early years, many policy decisions are never explained. There was, for instance, no discussion of why children born out of wedlock ("illegitimate" children) were not accepted in the nineteenth century, nor any record of why children could not talk at mealtime. For issues like this, top-down history, with its ability to roam to wherever adequate documentation exists, is far more informative.

More troubling gaps appear. Nineteenth-century managers' minutes have left me the decisions made by the women who ran the institution, but none of the debate leading up to them. Thus my research probably indicates a more unified sense of purpose than there actually was. Also, the families and children using the Half-Orphan Asylum are silent for a long time. In the nineteenth century there are no good records explaining why parents came to the Half-Orphan Asylum. Case records were first kept only in the 1920s. When I first read these records I was overjoyed. Here at last the clients spoke. Of course, I had to try to read through the prejudices of the social workers as well as to try and confront my own, but even with those inescapable limitations, I thought, the needy's words were there.

Upon further reading and reflection, however, I discovered that this was only partially correct. In fact, social workers in the 1920s began detailed reporting of the *parents*. The children—what they feared, what they wanted—were just not there. This only changed in the 1950s, when different assumptions about casework entered the institution. It was psychoanalysis that finally turned to the children and tried to carefully listen to what they had to say. Again, I had to try to cut through the biases of the psychoanalysts—still, the child's voice appears. Prior to that, my records limited what I could say.

These problems, while limiting, are not disabling. No history is perfect. None has the luxury of perfect sources. The advantages here more than outweigh the problems, especially given how little research has been done on either orphanages or homes for emotionally disturbed children. This study should be seen as a part of a puzzle, one that would need more social history and more elite history to fill in all the pieces. A variety of histories are needed to paint a good picture of systems of care for dependent children.

This history was commissioned by Chapin Hall. That is, it was paid for by the institution I am writing about. Nevertheless Chapin Hall is a quite different place today than it was between 1860 and 1984. It is currently a research institute, a transformation I discuss at the close of chapter six. This research institute has few ties to the earlier Chapin Hall. My independence has been complete, in fact, too complete for some who dearly hoped I would be quicker about the whole thing.

Let me make a few remarks about my use of names in the text. The official name of the orphanage, from 1860 to 1984, was the Chicago Nursery and Half-Orphan Asylum. But in the 1930s, for reasons I explain in chapter three, the institution started to be called Chapin Hall. I have followed in a general way this practice. When I am writing about the nineteenth-century orphanage I call it the Chicago Nursery and Half-Orphan Asylum. When I write about the 1930s and beyond, I tend to call it Chapin Hall. Similarly, the Chicago Council of Social Agencies (founded in 1914) became the Welfare Council of Metropolitan Chicago in the 1940s. Here too I simply shift names in the text. I hope the historical accuracy will not unduly confuse readers. And lastly, I have changed the name of every parent and child mentioned in the text.

There are many people to thank for help with this manuscript. The current staff at Chapin Hall was extraordinarily generous and supportive. Harold Richman, Matt Stagner, and most recently Susan Campbell ran all kinds of interference and did all kinds of favors. Most of all they were too damn patient with me. Also at Chapin Hall, Joan Costello taught me a number of things I wouldn't have learned elsewhere. At Iowa, colleagues Doug Baynton, Ellis Hawley, Linda Kerber, John Peters, and Shel Stromquist helped save me from myself in a variety of ways. Research assistants

William Thomas, Barbara Anderson, and Rachel Bohlmann did so too. And anyone who has worked at the Chicago Historical Society knows the magic of Archie Motley. His suggestions very materially made this a better book than it would have been without him.

Research for this book was supported by a grant from Clarissa H. Chandler, Charles C. Haffner III, Frances H. Colburn, and Phoebe H. Andrew in memory of their mother, Clarissa Donnelley Haffner.

∽ CHAPTER ONE ∽

A Nineteenth-Century Asylum

HERE ARE MANY GAPS IN THE EARLY RECORD OF
the Chicago Nursery and Half-Orphan Asylum. Whether the
institution opened in 1859 or 1860 is unclear. Whether one woman or
three founded it cannot be determined.[1] No records of the children cared
for exist until 1865. No Board of Managers' records were kept before 1867.
The gaps reflect both the uncharted nature of the nursery and the wild
expansion of the city. The asylum and Chicago grew up together, both
going through rapid and dramatic changes during the 1860s and 1870s.

Sometime between autumn of 1859 and the spring of 1860 three
women organized a day nursery for children whose mothers had to work.
They rented a cabin that had been a "ragged school" (a charity school for
paupers) located "on the sands" (the Near North lakefront where the opu-
lent Gold Coast stands today). The sands had been the center of prostitution in Chicago until 1857, at which point the city shut down the illicit
activity. City officials acted because businessman William Ogden, who had
purchased much land on the sands, wanted to begin residential development there.[2] By opening their nursery on the sands in 1859, the women
who founded the Half-Orphan Asylum were entering a neighborhood that
the *Chicago Tribune* had only recently called "the vilest and most wicked
place in Chicago."[3] But the founding of the nursery was also part of a concerted effort by businessmen, city officials, and charity women to clean up
that neighborhood.

Whatever the actual date of origin, the first mention of the nursery oc-
curs in the *Chicago Tribune* of April 25, 1860. There it is reported that the
"Chicago Nursery and Daily Home" needed an icebox and asks for the
donation of one. The institution was, the *Tribune* added, "for the benefit of
poor women who go about to earn their daily bread, who can leave their
children, on the payment of five cents each, at the Nursery, to be well cared

9

for during the day." The icebox was needed because milk did not keep on the sands.[4]

Sometime in the next year, the mission expanded. By October 1861, the institution was both a nursery and a temporary home for half-orphans. It had also acquired its name—The Chicago Nursery and Half-Orphan Asylum.[5] When exactly this change was made is unclear. It is also unclear as to why. Perhaps new dislocation brought on by the Civil War, which began in April, was a reason. Perhaps it was simply a more precise focus of the founders' goals. Any answer is speculative, however, for like so much else of the early years, documentation is lacking. Nevertheless, by the time the asylum was incorporated by the state in 1865, its object was to enable "the mothers to find employment," by housing those children "deprived by health or otherwise of the protection or support of either parent."[6] The asylum concentrated on residential care. Despite the name, the institution was not a day nursery. Moreover, it did not require that a child be literally half-orphaned. From the beginning, the Chicago Nursery and Half-Orphan Asylum took in children from homes broken by reasons other than death.

The women who founded the orphanage were solidly middle class. Mrs. Samuel Howe was the wife of a grain elevator owner who also served as director of the Chicago Board of Trade and owned, for a time, the Galena and Chicago Union Railroad.[7] Elizabeth Blakie's husband was a successful doctor. Little is known about Catherine West except that she was British. Her name fades quickly from the annals of the institution. By the time the asylum was chartered in February 1865, West was no longer active. By 1869, Blakie was also gone. Howe continued to work for the asylum through the 1870s, the only founder still an important force in the institution.

Although Howe, West, and Blakie were well-off, they were at the edges of the city's elite. That so little record remains of these women or their husbands is one indication of this. Their husbands barely turn up in the hagiographic histories of the city written between the 1880s and 1920s.[8] The names of Howe, West, and Blakie were not recorded for posterity alongside Ogden, McCormick, and Palmer. When the drive to create a more permanent and stable asylum was undertaken in the 1870s, it was carried out by women with better social connections than the original three.

The absence of documents also makes difficult any discussion of the founders' motives. Still, some reasons stand out. The phenomenal growth of the city created a real need. Chicago, like nineteenth-century Denver and San Francisco, was an "instant city," a metropolis that grew to frightening proportions overnight.[9] In 1833, Chicago was a town of 350 people, but by 1850 the population had climbed to nearly 30,000. By 1860, when the asylum was founded, Chicago's population had jumped to 109,000. The city had tripled in size in just ten years. In the next decade Chicago had again almost tripled; in 1870 the population stood at nearly 300,000. It is not surprising that the asylum grew from six to seventy-five children in the first decade. The only thing that held back further growth was lack of space.

The city's chaotic and rapid growth created problems needing immediate attention. By the 1850s, Chicago officials worried about children living and begging on the city's streets, abandoned by parents passing through on their way west. Such "arab children," as they were called, were often joined on the streets by unattended children whose parents worked. To the middle class with stable homes, this seemed the perfect environment to breed a life of crime. Institutions like the Nursery and Half-Orphan Asylum kept children off the streets and allowed poor women to work. It is "a great preventative of beggary," the *Tribune* said of the nursery in 1861, "enabling those who are willing to work to separate themselves from the great mass of idlers."[10]

The problem, moreover, was compounded by the weakness of the public sector in nineteenth-century America. Americans did not move quickly to create public welfare institutions. The officials of Chicago and Illinois were no different. Until 1865, the only public outlet for Chicago's dependent children was the state almshouse. It was notoriously ill-kept and overcrowded. A Cook County grand jury noted in 1853 that the section of the almshouse "devoted to women and children is so crowded as to be very offensive."[11] In 1865 the state opened the Soldiers' Orphans' Home for the children of Civil War casualties. No other institution for dependent children was opened by the state during the nineteenth century, although it did help fund certain private institutions.

Given the exploding population, the increase in children-at-risk, and the weakness of the public sector, it is not surprising that private organizations tried to fill the cavernous need. The Nursery and Half-Orphan Asylum was just one of the many private institutions created in mid-nineteenth-century Chicago to care for the needy. The Chicago Orphan Asylum and Catholic Orphan Asylum were founded in 1849 during the cholera epidemic, the Chicago Relief Society the next year, the Home for the Friendless in 1858, the United Hebrew Relief Organization in 1859, the Old Ladies Home in 1861, and the Uhlich Evangelical Lutheran Orphan Asylum in 1869. There were others.

The interest in special homes for dependent children was not simply a local one. As in other instant cities, Chicagoans copied institutional models from established urban areas. In the decades before the Civil War, there was tremendous growth throughout the United States of orphanages and asylums for abandoned children. The war, moreover, only intensified the trend.[12] Philanthropists, guided by environmental theories of child rearing, wanted to remove children from poorhouses, where they might be corrupted by paupers, drunkards, idlers, and other undesirable adults.[13] Between 1830 and 1850, fifty-six orphanages were founded in the United States.[14] Even more were opened after the war. Overwhelmingly, these were private institutions. Robert Bremner has estimated that through the second half of the nineteenth century, fully nine out of ten institutionalized dependent children in the United States were cared for in private institutions like the Chicago Nursery and Half-Orphan Asylum.[15]

In the years after the Civil War, two dominant sorts of institutions developed for Chicago's dependent children (hard-core delinquents and those convicted of a crime went elsewhere). The first were orphanages, homes that children under twelve went to, places like the Chicago Nursery and Half-Orphan Asylum. By 1890 there were twelve orphanages in the city.[16] The second type of institution was the industrial school. Industrial schools were for older children, roughly ten to sixteen years of age. The name "industrial school" is a bit misleading, for these institutions were in many ways similar to orphanages, except that they housed adolescents.[17]

Chicago's first industrial school opened in the 1870s. In 1879 the state legislature voted to give subsidies to industrial schools for girls; four years later for boys. Industrial schools received public support while orphanages didn't because officials worried that adolescence was the stage at which unattended girls would fall into prostitution; boys into other sorts of crime. The public subsidies ensured that industrial schools would be central institutions for dependent children. While there were only five of these institutions in the city by 1890, each housed hundreds of children. And more would be opened in the following decades.[18]

The orphanages and industrial schools for Chicago children were all located in Cook County. Almost no Chicago dependent children in the nineteenth century were sent to the state's orphanage—the Soldiers' Orphans' Home, which was in the downstate town of Normal. A few dependent children did go with their mothers to the county poorhouse through the 1890s.[19] But if a dependent child was not accepted at an orphanage or industrial school, the likely prospects were three. The child might spend more time on the streets, learning to fend for her- or himself, a depressingly common occurrence at the time. The child might work and live in one of a handful of homes for working boys and girls established in the

1870s. Only a fraction of dependent children could actually make use of this option.[20] Finally, the child might go to the Home for the Friendless. This was a temporary home for two different groups of dependents: abused mothers and their children, and children (not adolescents) without parents. The latter, after a stay of usually no more than a month, were "placed out," as it was called, sent to western states to live primarily with farming families.

To twentieth-century welfare reformers, the nineteenth-century system seemed as chaotic as the cities that spawned it. To their founders, however, the institutions seemed logically divided along religious, ethnic, and functional lines. Catholics had their own orphanages; Protestants theirs. Each had their own industrial schools. By the end of the century, Jews had also organized a parallel child welfare system. When the Half-Orphan Asylum was founded in the 1860s, none of the three existing orphanages in the city accepted children without obtaining legal control over the child's future. In the early years of the asylum, the women who ran the institution regularly referred to its special mission. It was the only refuge in Chicago in which "no surrender of a child is ever made." Thus in the Half-Orphan Asylum "the hope always remains of claiming it [the child] whenever circumstances make it possible."[21]

The creation of the Chicago Nursery and Half-Orphan Asylum in 1860, then, was part of a large-scale private response to problems that would not be addressed by a notoriously weak public sector. It was also part of a general trend among reformers to protect young dependent children from the polluting influences of the city, the poorhouse, and delinquent children. Apart from these structural reasons for the birth of the Nursery and Half-Orphan Asylum, there were also more personal reasons guiding the founders. A religious commitment and sense of noblesse oblige informed those women as it did so many other mid-nineteenth-century philanthropists.[22] The landscape of Chicago might have also contributed. There were neighborhoods defined by income prior to the fire of 1871, especially south of the Loop. But the chaotic growth of the 1850s and 1860s meant that often the rich and poor practically lived side by side. Wealthy and poor areas were frequently just a couple of blocks away from each other. Consequently, if one lived in the city, one *saw* its problems. There was no visual escape. The women who founded the asylum saw "street arab" children regularly. Poor beggars lived uncomfortably close.[23]

The asylum filled a need and it grew rapidly. In the first winter the nursery population jumped from six to twenty-five children. By 1869, seventy-five children were under care.[24] From the original three volunteers the asylum grew to twenty in 1865. By the late sixties there was a small paid staff that worked and lived at the home. Crowding was a constant problem, and the asylum moved five times in the first five years.[25] Each time it moved to a bigger house to serve more children. It remained within a two-mile radius just north of the Chicago River and close to the lake. In the 1860s this was the north side of the city.

Like the city it served, there was little settled in the Chicago Nursery and Half-Orphan Asylum during its first ten years. Its size, its mission, its location—all varied in response to the burgeoning city. Even the asylum's place within the cityscape was unclear. The many changes in location indicate not only the constant search for bigger quarters but also for the right geographical niche. From the sands at the edge of town the asylum moved in the summer of 1860 to the center of the city "for the greater convenience of the class to be benefited."[26] Several years and several moves later, though, there was some indication that an institution in the center of the city was not wanted. In 1867, when the asylum was located at Franklin and Wisconsin, the *Tribune* noted that a "very general feeling exists among the residents in the vicinity of the Half Orphan that the institution should be removed to some other location. They assert that whenever a disease breaks out [in the institution], which is not seldom, it invariably extends to families outside the walls."[27]

Finally, and not of least importance, the asylum's finances were remarkably unsettled. This was no different from any of Chicago's asylums in the 1860s.[28] When the Half-Orphan Asylum began keeping records in 1867, they were sprinkled with constant references to life-threatening money problems.[29] Indeed, the poor financial condition of the asylum led women in the late 1860s to search for stability—stability in organization, in location and mission, in clientele and finances. The nineteenth-century Half-Orphan Asylum was really created in the 1870s and 1880s.

A NINETEENTH-CENTURY ASYLUM

Refuge, religion, family—these three words sum up the goals of the asylum created during the 1870s and 1880s. The nineteenth-century Half-Orphan Asylum was a Protestant institution dedicated to the short-term care of children who had suffered the loss of a parent. Its tone was distinctly religious. It was also very consciously an *asylum*. In one sense this meant that managers tried to keep the problems of the city—crime, delinquency, epidemics, drunkenness—outside its doors. But this also meant, very explicitly to the managers and staff, that the institution was *not* a home; it was something else, an "asylum," a temporary refuge for families in distress.

That the managers viewed their orphanage as a custodial institution was in fact the flip side of their sense of family. The goal of the asylum was to keep families together over the long haul by maintaining children through a time of crisis. Late nineteenth-century managers did not think of the children as unique individuals, separate from the accident of their parents, as later managers would in the twentieth century. Instead, they thought of the children as an integral part of a family unit, a unit the orphanage was struggling to maintain.

Managerial attitudes reflected the common coin of late nineteenth-century welfare elites. Two assumptions in particular were important: Single mothers should be in the workforce, and institutions like the Half-Orphan Asylum were appropriate places for children during a family crisis. Early twentieth-century reformers who urged the states to allocate pensions for single mothers, especially widows, presented a sharply different logic: instead of using institutions for breathing space, they argued that children should be kept at home. And this would be accomplished by paying single mothers so that they could work less outside the home.

The assumptions of the 1870s Half-Orphan Asylum managers differed in other ways from ideas increasingly important after 1970. In the late twentieth century, welfare policy has aimed at the ideal of keeping women in the workforce (unlike the early twentieth century ideas but like the nineteenth-century managers of the Half-Orphan Asylum). But this is now presumed to be done while the children remain at home (quite unlike the notions of nineteenth-century managers). Largely, these two goals are met by the increased use of day care facilities.

While there were exceptions, the orphanage primarily aided the working poor—families with an adult jobholder but without enough income to keep a home together. The asylum tried to give such families the breathing space needed to get back on their feet after the loss of one of the parents.

In the late 1860s and the early 1870s, several decisions were made that set the Half-Orphan Asylum on a steady course. Not the least important of these was to construct a permanent asylum building. Through the 1860s, the orphanage had been housed in family residences. Even though the home at Franklin and Wisconsin was a large home, it was still woefully inadequate to handle seventy-five children. Moreover, other parents continued to turn up at the door asking to have their children looked after. There was simply no more room.

In 1869, the Board of Managers, together with several prominent businessmen, began looking for ways to build a spacious asylum. After some search, financial help came from Jonathan Burr, a wealthy local businessman and philanthropist. Burr donated what at the time was a very healthy sum—$17,000. This provided the money to buy the land for the asylum and to start construction.

The managers and their gentlemen advisors decided to build at what is now 1931 North Halsted.[30] In the late 1860s this represented an effort to remove the asylum to a lightly populated part of the city. The neighborhood was built up but not dense, having what we today would call a suburban feel. Most homes had spacious yards; many families grew vegetables in backyard gardens. German immigrants predominated. The area was economically mixed; small businessmen, artisans, and laborers all lived there. Disease was a major preoccupation in nineteenth-century cities, and disease was associated with overcrowded conditions. Trying to find some way to insulate the children from the city's unhealthiness led to the move to the far north side of town.[31]

Burr's bequest was large but not enough to complete the four-story building. By the summer of 1871, the building's shell was built, but it had no windows or doors, and there was no money to finish the job. Construction stopped. That is where matters stood on October 8, 1871, when the Chicago fire broke out. From its origin at about 1200 South Halsted, the fire swept east to the lake and as far north as Fullerton Avenue. For nearly two days the fire raged. As word of its approach reached the asylum, the matron, Mrs. E. C. Hobson, decided to move the children to safety. The new building, which stood west of the fire's path, was the ultimate destination. Hobson and her small staff ushered more than seventy children as well as the asylum's furniture to the uncompleted structure. They picked up almost two dozen other children on the streets—children somehow separated from their parents in the confusion. Late in the evening, word came that the fire was moving westward and that the new building was now in danger. Children and staff, now numbering nearly one hundred, again moved, this time across the west branch of the Chicago River, where they spent the night in a church. The next day, when it became clear that the fire would not consume the new quarters, everyone moved back again. The Chicago Nursery and Half-Orphan Asylum had moved into its new home.[32]

In the next few months, relief agencies readily gave money to finish the building. Here was a vitally needed institution not destroyed by the fire. The building was soon complete. With some modifications, it housed the orphanage until 1916.

One of the reasons for building a permanent asylum was the desire to keep more children. The constant growth of the city increased the demand for the asylum's services. By 1880, the number of children in the asylum reached 100; by 1890 about 150; and by 1900 nearly 170. At any given moment there might be thirty children more or less than those figures. When contagious diseases struck, no new children were admitted. In healthy times, by contrast, the population swelled.

The staff grew to accommodate the children. Already by the late 1860s there was a matron and a teacher. Through the nineteenth century these remained the most important paid positions at the orphanage. All children went to school in the asylum, hence the need for a teacher. The matron managed day-to-day affairs. Both lived in the asylum. The women volunteers of the managing board, however, made all major decisions. The matron and teacher did not make policy, they only implemented it.

In the 1870s and 1880s, cleaning staff, handymen, laundry women, cooks, servants, and nurses were added. Many lived in the asylum, adding from ten to twenty to the population noted above. The matron and the managers carefully watched the staff. The institution's bylaws did not allow these lower-level employees to strike children, to use profanity in front of them, or to bring alcoholic beverages into the asylum.

The children came to the asylum in a variety of ways. On occasion a minister, doctor, or even a neighbor of a board member might bring a needy child to the attention of the institution. The great majority of the children, however, were brought in by a parent. They simply turned up at the door and asked for help. With almost no exceptions, the applicants were working class. The sons and daughters of laundry workers, factory workers, stockyard employees, waitresses, charwomen, coopers, and cigar makers all came to the asylum, but I could find only rare examples of children from even a modest middle-class background. The Chicago Nursery and Half-Orphan Asylum overwhelmingly served working-class families in trouble.

Most often, it was the mother who brought in the child, a pattern that would continue with only minor variations all the way into the 1980s. Reliable statistics are available from the 1880s, by which time mothers brought children in by more than a two-to-one ratio.[33] Men were more likely to suffer work-related injuries or from work-derived illnesses. Also, men ran out on families far more often than women.

These women faced the worst sort of destitution. The loss of a husband in a nineteenth-century working-class family was often financially devastating. Wives with children usually did not have outside income prior to the death of a spouse. When they did work, they found themselves at the lowest end of the pay scale. In 1881, a deserted wife brought in her children. She earned $2.50 a week at the stockyards. In 1879, a widow working as a cook made $4.00 a week. In 1878 a woman employed at the Thompson Shirt Factory reported making $3.00 to $4.00 per week. It has been estimated that the median weekly wage for women in 1880 was about $5.00, easily more than the earnings of most women bringing their children to the Half-Orphan Asylum. The men bringing in children, on the other hand, usually earned $8.00 to $10.00 per week.[34]

Late-nineteenth century employers assumed that a working woman would not be the primary wage earner in a family. If a woman did work, employers reasoned, it would be to supplement the wages of either a father or husband. Consequently, women were quite simply not paid enough to support themselves, let alone any children. "In the first decade of the twentieth century," David Montgomery points out, "the Department of Labor . . . concluded that 74.3 percent of the women in factories and 66.2 percent of those in stores earned less than a 'living wage.'"[35] Women not only had to face the burden of a broken home more often than men, they also had to do so with far fewer economic resources. Quite often, the women coming to the Half-Orphan Asylum, the poorest among the working poor, were reduced to sharing a single room with a friend; they couldn't even afford the smallest and shabbiest of apartments for themselves and their children. Their poverty was truly crushing.

The men, of course, were only in a better position relatively. Some were as poor as the women. And for both mothers and fathers, the death of a spouse meant that children were deprived of care. For those who did not want their sons or daughters to end up as "arab children," the Half-Orphan Asylum was a logical solution. It gave them some breathing space to try to rearrange the household.

Although it was a "half-orphan" asylum, it appears that a large number of the children, perhaps even more than half, had both parents still living.[36] Grave sickness of one spouse brought some children to the asylum. A few men had wives who were insane. Other children came from broken homes. Almost all of the last group were brought in by mothers. They were the wives of drunks or drifters. The husband had often deserted the family. They were occasionally divorced.

That most children had a parent still living appears to have been the norm for late-nineteenth-century children's homes, regardless of whether they were called "orphan" or "half-orphan" asylums. In December 1878, to pick a date at random, fully 145 of 199 children at the Chicago Orphan Asylum were either half-orphans or from destitute families; that is, they had either one or both parents living. The same was true of Illinois Soldiers' Orphans' Home, the lone state orphanage of the late nineteenth century. In 1872, 82 percent of the children there had a parent living. And research on the St. Louis Protestant Orphan Asylum has shown that a full 95 percent of the children had at least one parent living at that time. In the late nineteenth century, full orphans appear to be a distinct minority at institutions that were called "orphanages." Readers should not take Dickensian accounts of pitiful children without parents to be an accurate representation of the average resident of the nineteenth-century orphanage. Nor should they understand the term "half-orphan asylum" as implying a sharp break with other sorts of homes for dependent children. All were largely populated by half-orphans.[37]

The children brought to the asylum were young. The institution did not take any boy older than ten. Until 1877, no girls were accepted over fourteen. In that year the Half-Orphan Asylum began refusing girls over twelve. Exceptions were made. About 3 percent of newly admitted children were over ten years of age. The managers were also hesitant to take babies under one. They posed too much of a health risk. In the 1870s, these babies comprised 3.3 percent of the population; in the next decade 5.9 percent. Most children were between one and ten years of age when they came to the Half-Orphan Asylum. The population was evenly distributed among those ages. The average age of a child entering the asylum was just under five and one-half.[38]

The entry age reflects something very common to all Chicago orphanages. Orphanages were overwhelmingly populated by children under ten. Older dependent children either went to work to support themselves or lived at one of Chicago's industrial schools, where they mixed with children who had been in some sort of trouble already. In the welfare system developed in Chicago after the fire, industrial schools were basically orphanages for adolescents.

The single largest ethnic group in the Nursery and Half-Orphan Asylum were those labeled "American," meaning at least second generation arrivals with no identifiable "foreign" characteristics. This group made up about 30 percent of the asylum's residents. Immigrants from the British Isles accounted for another 30 percent. The asylum was located in a German neighborhood, but only 11 percent of the children in the 1870s and 1880s were from German families. Swedes and Norwegians made up the only other sizable ethnic groups. In the 1870s they made up just over 11 percent of the children; in the 1880s they accounted for 21.9 percent.[39]

All the major ethnic groups were from northern Europe. All were Protestant. It is safe to say that at least 95 percent of the children in the Half-Orphan Asylum were Protestant. This reflected client preference as much as management policy. In fact, if policy was the only indicator, the Half-Orphan Asylum was more pluralistic in the nineteenth century than in the twentieth. In 1872, the Chicago Relief and Aid Society gave funds to the Half-Orphan Asylum to finish the building on the condition that children be accepted without any religious or racial qualifications. The managers agreed.[40] A smattering of Jews, Poles, Italians, and African-Americans did use the asylum in the nineteenth century.[41] On the whole, however, nineteenth-century families-in-need looked for help from the religiously and ethnically compatible. Catholics looked for Catholic orphanages; Jews took care of their own needy; and Protestants went to homes such as the Chicago Nursery and Half-Orphan Asylum. (A "white-only" policy was not considered at the Half-Orphan Asylum precisely because there were so few blacks in Chicago at that time. That would change in the early twentieth century.) Poor and working-class Protestant families from all over the city searched out the Half-Orphan Asylum because they wanted a Protestant institution for their children.

Once an application was received, each family went through a character check that took about two weeks.[42] No child was admitted unless his family was "worthy." Each application was delivered to a member of the Board of Managers who went to the applicant's neighborhood, checked references, and spoke with employers and neighbors in an effort to establish the character and finances of the family involved. This was the so-called "friendly visitor" of nineteenth-century philanthropy. She would also visit the applicant's residence to get a feel for home life and hardship. She then reported her findings to the full Board of Managers at their next meeting and they voted, as a body, on whether to take the child.

Lying was the most common reason for declaring an applicant "unworthy." Most lies were about income, but there were others. At times parents who lived together tried to place a child in the institution. They lied about being split up. Others were caught lying about their address, family background, and the legitimacy of the child. The last was not an unreasonable lie, because illegitimacy instantly disqualified a child. No reason was ever given for this in the asylum's nineteenth-century records. It was not even an issue. Other research, however, suggests that such policies were premised on the fear that illegitimacy would financially drain both family and community as well as the hope that harsh attitudes would discourage the occurrence.[43]

Apart from lying and illegitimacy, a child could be excluded if his parent was "loose," a term which applied to everything from a casual attitude toward sex to the nightly frequenting of taverns. In one instance, a boy was turned down simply because his father was a bartender. Finally, a parent's alcoholism could disqualify a child. If a sober mother was married to an alcoholic who had deserted the home, that was no bar. But if a child was in the hands of an intemperate parent, entrance to the Half-Orphan Asylum was denied. The family was "unworthy."

The character check reflects, first of all, Victorian Protestant moralism. The righteous should be rewarded; the sinful punished. It also reflects that the institution was an asylum. Some of the harshest sounding rules of the nineteenth-century indicate the strong desire to keep problems from the door. An asylum was a refuge and the morally "contaminated" had to be kept back. Their bad influence must not be allowed to pollute the "good" children. The managers did not want to bend a truculent working class to their way of thinking; they wanted children from families with values at least somewhat similar to their own.

The preoccupation with character also shows how the asylum thought in terms of families rather than individual children. The managers wanted each family to get back on its feet. As the managers themselves said, the "chief design of this charity is to 'help the poor help themselves'; giving the safety and comforts of a home to the child while the parent is left free to earn a support."[44] The Chicago Nursery and Half-Orphan Asylum was set up to help the working poor, not the chronically unemployed. This translated, in nineteenth-century terms, into a concern for "character."

Finally, the emphasis on good character was a tactical response to child-dumping. Nineteenth-century institutions were used by some parents as places to discard children. The Chicago Nursery and Half-Orphan Asylum itself experienced this in the 1870s (and would experience it again in the 1930s). By researching the parent's reliability, the asylum tried to protect itself from children delivered under false pretenses.

The "friendly visitor" also looked into the finances of the family. Each parent paid a portion of their income to help support their child in the asylum. The sum was determined by the Board of Managers and was usually someplace between 25 and 40 percent of a parent's income. The money involved was huge to the families using the Half-Orphan Asylum, but it did not come close to covering the cost of the stay. The practice, in fact, was designed by the managers at least in part to demonstrate family ties. If a parent did not pay the agreed-upon sum it reflected a lack of commitment to his or her children.

The manager's attitudes toward parental payment oscillated wildly from coldly contractual to generously kind. On the one hand, the payments were an ongoing source of tension between the asylum and the parents. These families had little, and if a parent fell behind, he or she did not see it as a sin. The managers, however, saw it differently, setting up a delinquent committee to badger parents for payments. On the other hand, if the managers perceived genuine hardship, they could be extremely generous. In 1880, a woman "in great destitution" whose husband had deserted her the year before was allowed to leave her children without cost. Earlier that year, a woman who had to go into the hospital was allowed to stop paying.[45] Such stories were common; where managers saw real need they were quite lenient. At one point in 1872, thirty-two of the ninety-six children were living at the Half-Orphan Asylum for free.[46]

The family emphasis was also reflected in the contract parents signed. Unlike other Protestant orphanages in nineteenth-century Chicago, the Half-Orphan Asylum had no legal authority over the child's future. The asylum assumed that the family would soon reassemble. But the contract also stated that parents had to visit their children at least once every two weeks. Parents who regularly neglected this stipulation indicated that their family meant little to them and that the child did not belong in the Half-Orphan Asylum. By contract, unvisited children could be sent to the Home for the Friendless, the Chicago institution for abandoned youngsters. In practice, a parent had to disappear for upwards of two years before a child was placed elsewhere.

Most children had a short stay. Just under 40 percent of the children stayed less than three months; 57 percent less than six months. A full 74 percent of the children spent less than one year in the asylum; 86 percent spent less than two years. Few children actually grew up in the Half-Orphan Asylum.[47]

The short stay reflects the basic congruence of the managers' goals and the clients' needs. The managers wanted to provide short-term care for working-class families who had lost a parent. The clients came to the asylum not because anyone forced them but because they needed help. In a few months, after the extended family was marshaled into service, after a job was secured or an apartment found, the child left.

That most children only used the asylum for a brief period corroborates some other recent research on the nineteenth-century orphanage. Scholars looking at the internal workings of the orphanages for the first time are finding that at least a fair number of these institutions were populated by half-orphans who had relatively short stays. Yet caution should be exercised here, for this research is also turning up orphanages where the average child remained institutionalized for three, four, or five years. While more research is called for, it appears right now that late nineteenth-century orphanages varied widely. The Chicago Nursery and Half-Orphan Asylum was not unusual in that some nineteenth-century orphanages were used by the working class to get through hard times. But that is not to say that other children's institutions did not keep children longer.[48]

The children slept in large dormitories. Each could accommodate up to sixty children, but at times there were more. Children were divided into three basic groups—those under six who went to the nursery, the older boys, and the older girls. The youngest children were awoken at seven in the morning, "washed, and taken to their breakfasts, after which they take a romp until they want to sit down." Then a short nap was in order, lunch, and more playtime in the afternoon. There was an afternoon nap, then dinner, and the nursery children were put to bed at 6 P.M. In 1883, a *Tribune* reporter who stopped in without warning found a cheery environment: "In the nursery department forty little ones were scampering about on the floor, rolling upon the veranda, or swinging in the hammocks, which were shaded by poplars. They were by no means timid. They tugged at the reportorial coattail and played between the legs."[49]

This is not an unattractive scene and one that was repeated whenever the press visited the Half-Orphan Asylum in the nineteenth-century. Another reporter who arrived unannounced could not get himself heard on the porch as the children were making so much noise playing. Once inside, he saw not only real affection for the matron, but kids running, jumping, and yelling with glee. "This lack of restraint," he noted, "was the best possible witness to the fact that the little waifs are well treated."[50] As another reporter said after a similar experience, it was apparent that the asylum was governed by love.[51]

From our perspective, we should be glad to see the good humor of the children. Their life was not dull regimentation, and that image, still used by social welfare historians, should be carefully reexamined.[52] But we must be taken aback by the large number of toddlers in one room. One, perhaps two women, cared for forty or more children. Grouping so many kids together encouraged the rapid spread of disease. It also left little time for the children's individual needs, something for which the Half-Orphan Asylum, like all asylums, came under attack at the turn of the century.

There were, moreover, deficiencies in the quality of care hidden to casual observers. For example, it is clear that the Board of Managers' Diet Committee functioned more to contain costs than to provide balanced meals. The scattered details left in the managers' minutes indicate grim fare indeed. In 1877, the board voted to let the children have butter once a week. In 1880, the diet was "expanded" to include fruit—once a week. Money was not plentiful and keeping costs down was essential. Still, it took some forms that, while not unusual for the times, still seem plainly bizarre to us. In the winter of 1881, in a move to save money, the board voted to serve the children weak coffee instead of milk at breakfast. Such decisions certainly contributed to the depressingly high mortality statistics of the era. Other kinds of cost cutting were also injurious to the children's health. In 1880 the school teacher told the managers she was "disgusted" by how cold the asylum was during the early fall and late spring. But when she argued for more heat, the managers' response was terse: "The matter was thought hardly practicable by the Ladies."[53]

Once a child reached six years he or she attended school. School, until the 1890s, was held on the premises. Boys and girls would get up in the morning, wash, dress, and eat, then go upstairs for classes from nine to noon. There was then lunch, followed by a play period in the yard. At two in the afternoon, school would reconvene until four. There would be time for another play period, followed by dinner. Prayers were held at 7 P.M. and the children were in bed by nine. This routine was leavened by outings to the park or a concert as well as lavish banquets on holidays. The asylum was religious but not somber.

There were minor variations for the boys and girls. In 1873, an "industrial school" was started for the girls. They learned to sew and darned the socks of the asylum. Boys, on the other hand, were allowed to find part-time work. A number of the older boys worked as "cash boys" for local merchants—children who ran money to the bank, got smaller change, and performed other tasks. It was decided in 1875 that boys who worked could attend school in the evening. American culture as a whole was much more lax about school attendance in the nineteenth century, and the Nursery and Half-Orphan Asylum was no different. As long as the child was learning responsibility, then there was no rigid reason to have him attend school during the day. The school had to conform to the child's schedule, not the other way around.[54]

There was a steady diet of religion for a child living at the asylum. Prayers were said in the morning and at each meal. A local minister came to the schoolroom each morning and led the children in prayers. Each evening at 7 P.M. there were prayers for all the children. Every Wednesday evening a minister came and conducted a formal prayer service. On Sundays, the children went to Sunday school and a local minister came to the orphanage for an evening service. In the nineteenth-century asylum, another prayer stood around every corner.

Formal prayer, however, was not the only way Protestant sensibilities ruled. Every member of the Board of Managers belonged to a Protestant church. It was, in fact, a prerequisite for membership. Local churches took the children on outings, repaired clothing, and performed other charitable work for the asylum. The staff, moreover, ideally was not hired without a peek into their souls. This did not always work out in practice, especially for the lower staff members, the laundry women and handymen. But for

the most important employees—the matron and the schoolteacher—
Protestant credentials were essential. As a consequence, daily discipline
was justified with casual allusion to religious principle, reinforcing the
messages delivered formally in prayer. At every stop, religion played an
important role in the asylum.

Many of the asylum's regulations, however, were dictated more by fear
of disease than fear of God. Disease was the asylum's biggest single problem. Epidemics came often and spread quickly. In June 1877, scarlet fever
swept through the institution. In April 1878, seventy-eight children came
down with whooping cough. Two months later it was measles. Such epidemics were often deadly. The death rate in the late nineteenth century is
staggering, although not unusual in children's institutions. In 1886, twelve
children died at the asylum; in 1888, eleven died. In 1890 there were fourteen deaths, the next year eight. In 1892, nineteen children died at the
Nursery and Half-Orphan Asylum. Overwhelmingly, these deaths occurred in the nursery, among the children under six years of age. Shock-
ingly, babies under the age of one had less than a one-in-two chance of
getting out alive.[55]

Such epidemics are not surprising given the large dormitories, the poor
diet, the fluid movement in and out of the institution, and the generally
bad living conditions in the city at large. Chicago's sewage system was rudimentary and its garbage pick-up spotty. The poorer areas, such as those
from which the asylum's clients came, were the worst. In 1887, the Board
of Health found that 85 percent of tenements and rented homes had defective sanitary facilities. Such neighborhoods suffered foul odors from garbage left on streets and from privies left uncleaned. Families still drew
water from a well, which in poor neighborhoods could not be trusted. The
epidemics that plagued the Half-Orphan Asylum were in fact citywide epidemics. In 1873, mortality of children under five accounted for 59 percent
of all deaths in Chicago; by 1893 it was still at 45 percent.[56]

The Nursery and Half-Orphan Asylum responded to the health threats
by invoking its dedication to refuge and asylum. The institution tried to
cut itself off from the city. For months at a time, in the face of epidemics,
the doors were shut to new arrivals.[57] After 1877, no child was admitted to
the asylum without a smallpox vaccination.[58] Children were turned down
if someone in their home had a communicable disease. And new children
spent two weeks in quarantine in the asylum before being allowed to move
into a dormitory.

This basic orientation reflected contemporary opinion on public
health. Until the 1890s, Pasteur's germ theory of disease had made little

headway in American medical circles. Instead, the managers supported what has been called the "dirt theory" of disease, holding that "communicable diseases originated in decayed organic matter and were conveyed by the unhygienic conditions that prevailed in the cities, especially in slum neighborhoods."[59] Such thinking put a giant priority on spotless environments. The word "asylum," then, implied a zone that attempted in a very real and physical way to be free from the city's contamination.

The health-inspired rules helped set the children starkly off from the rest of the neighborhood. The asylum children literally looked different. They wore uniforms, girls a white apron over a smock and boys blue jeans and light shirts. This dress code, condemned by twentieth-century reformers as a violation of the children's individuality, was done in an effort to keep simple clothes that would be free from any disease-carrying vermin.

Another rule generated by contemporary medical theory was the mandatory short hair. Both boys and girls were shaved almost to the scalp. It would combat not only lice, the managers thought, but more deadly illnesses as well. The initial decision was made in 1881 in the midst of a particularly bad citywide epidemic. In 1895, the rule was modified so that girls could begin growing out their hair four months before they left the orphanage.[60]

These rules appear harsh to us because they seem to violate the child's individuality. Children at the time, however, experienced the problem as "differentness." They looked "different" from the other kids in the neighborhood, and they suffered taunts because of it. They were "charity kids," and they looked the part. Still one other rule, again related to health, again causing children to appear "different," was having them go to school at the asylum. When this was raised as an issue in 1881, the Board of Managers retained the policy because they hoped to keep asylum children away from diseases transmitted through contact at the public school.[61]

Other rules seem harsh for an entirely different reason. They seemed to pull families apart instead of keeping them together. For example, parents were only allowed to visit their children on special days. The health justification for this seems very slim, but it was used nonetheless. Parents, then, were required (by contract) to visit their children, but they were restricted to just two afternoons a week to do so. The ability of parents to take their children for outings and vacations was also severely restricted. The managers retained the right to deny children leave, even with their parents, if they thought it would lead the children into an unhealthy environment. Parents, for example, were usually not allowed to take their children home for a vacation. The children could only go if the destination was outside the city. The managers feared disease. Children had to be kept clear of a polluted city.[62]

But if health was a major concern, and the reason for many of the harsher rules at the asylum, there were other regulations that simply cannot be attributed to anything other than a sterner sense of order than would be common in the twentieth century. There was, to take the most striking example, no speaking at meals. The asylum fed nearly 200 children daily. None were allowed to talk. This was never explained. It was a rule taken for granted. Perhaps some vague concern for efficiency was behind it; feeding 200 children under ten years old couldn't have been easy. Perhaps Victorian ideas about children being seen but not heard were behind it. Whatever the reasons, children at the asylum did not speak at meals until the 1920s. It must have been excruciatingly difficult for a boy or girl of six or seven to maintain that kind of silence evening after evening.

There was also no thought of doing away with corporal punishment. At no time in the nineteenth century was there any indication that the managers thought physical punishment was cruel. Opposition to corporal punishment had surfaced in various places in American culture by the mid-nineteenth century, but it was nowhere evident in the Chicago Nursery and Half-Orphan Asylum. The most common punishment was to be slapped on the hands, usually with a switch. Talking at meals, getting in fights, leaving the asylum grounds without permission, and many other infractions could result in a swat or two.

All the corporal punishment was of a relatively minor sort. And there was a good reason for this. The orphanage was set up to keep problems outside the door. Persistent trouble was resolved not by beating but by expulsion. There were always more children wanting to get into the asylum than there was room for. Dotting the records of the Board of Managers are references to children dismissed for fighting, running away, or for breaking the rules in any number of ways. One infraction would never lead to expulsion. Regular infractions almost always did. The asylum was designed to help worthy families in need. "Bad influences" were shown the door.

Keeping out health risks, keeping out "bad kids," the orphanage tried to live up to its name—it was an asylum from the problems outside. By the early twentieth century, this approach would be under attack. It is important, however, to understand the institution's goals on its own terms.

The Chicago Nursery and Half-Orphan Asylum was designed to help working poor families through temporary crises. Its end was not to reform children but to keep them from falling through the cracks in the economic system. The women who ran the asylum did not think in terms of molding children to a different way of life.[63] They wanted to help needy children from "decent" homes for a few months while the remaining parent got his or her bearings. It was an institution designed to give short-term relief, not to change lives.

Applicants were screened so that children whose parents had sharply clashing values were excluded. Parents whose children were accepted at the Half-Orphan Asylum shared with the managers attitudes about Protestant religion, parental responsibility, and steady participation in the labor market, which of course should not be taken to mean that the parents were never out of work. It was not, I want to stress, that there was a perfect mesh between parents and managers—fights over vacations and parental payments reflect that. And there must have been, I cannot help but imagine, large differences over political and labor issues. But whatever these differences, parents came to the door because they wanted a way to keep their children "right." And on this point there was agreement. Entrance requirements were such that the asylum's "control" was not dissimilar in kind from what the children faced at home. For the working poor, the Chicago Nursery and Half-Orphan Asylum was a very useful institution.[64]

But it was not a place designed to help the children of alcoholics, the chronically unemployed, or those children from hopelessly disorganized families. The children of "unworthy" families either roamed the streets, wound up in prisons, or were shipped to other, larger and more forbidding institutions, like the Home for the Friendless, where they would eventually be sent to distant states to live and work on farms, far removed from any remaining family members. This division of Chicago children's institutions between those for the "worthy" and "unworthy" is similar to what David Rosner has found in his study of late-nineteenth-century New York and Brooklyn hospitals.[65] Helping the working poor with short-term relief was the stated goal of many other private Chicago welfare organizations, including the most important, the Chicago Relief and Aid Society.[66]

That the goal of much late-nineteenth-century welfare was to help the working poor is certainly worth some notice, in part because they are probably the single most neglected group of the late-twentieth-century American welfare state.[67] In the nineteenth century, however, helping the "worthy" poor was done to the effective exclusion of many others, including children, leaving huge holes in the welfare system. In the late nineteenth century, the Half-Orphan Asylum was *always* filled to capacity. Practically every week for decades on end it turned away children who qualified for aid. And it also turned away hundreds of children who didn't qualify for help because of the behavior of their parents. Throughout the city, there was never enough room in places like the Half-Orphan Asylum for all the children in need.

ORGANIZATION AND ASYLUM, 1870s AND 1880s

The first step toward a more financially secure asylum was taken on February 25, 1868. That afternoon, a group of prominent men came by to advise the women "as to the best method of raising money and for the future support and interest of the institution."[68] The next month, the women voted to "send invitations to a number of gentlemen and invite them to form an advisory committee" to plan the asylum's future.[69] To end their money problems, the women turned to men.

This was not unusual in the mid-nineteenth century. Women rarely had training in financial matters. Illinois' Married Women's Property Act was only passed in 1860. Prior to that, women did not even have a legal right to control their own income. Given the firm gender division, it was common in all sorts of charitable institutions to have a female board that managed operations (including day-to-day finances) and a male board that managed investments. This was the pattern adopted by the Chicago Nursery and Half-Orphan Asylum. By bringing in men to solve their financial problems, the women wound up creating an organizational structure that survived until the end of the 1970s.

The precise role of each group, however, had to be negotiated. Women wanted to retain control of what they considered "their" institution. The men presumed patriarchy. Asking the men to be an "advisory committee" was in reality a strategic move by the women to retain control. Men would advise but have no power. Within a year, however, this arrangement was altered. Jonathan Burr offered money to build a permanent asylum only on the condition that a men's board be set up. As a result, a male Board of Directors was created in March of 1869.

The managers at first wanted the right to name the Board of Directors.[70] But thanks to Burr's conditions, when the bylaws were drawn up, the men had ultimate control. Not only did the female treasurer have to make quarterly reports to the Board of Directors, the men also picked which women would serve on the Board of Managers. While women were given the right to make decisions about the internal management of the asylum, they could be vetoed by the directors.[71]

The arrangement proved impractical. The men, all active in Chicago's business, legal, or medical communities, hadn't the time to oversee the Half-Orphan Asylum. Within a year, the women petitioned to change the bylaws and the men did not object. The Board of Managers was allowed to pick its own members. By 1873, the women could alter the asylum's constitution without conferring with the directors. The Board of Managers controlled the institution.[72]

By that time, the basic division of labor between the men and women was settled. The women managed the asylum; the men managed the money. In the 1870s, the women devised an elaborate committee system that efficiently divided their own labor. The most capable and hardworking women found their way to the Executive Committee. These were the officers of the asylum, women like Helen Judd Goudy, Mrs. F. H. Beckwith, Mrs. Abijah Keith, and Mrs. E. S. Chesbrough. Talented, energetic, and committed, women like these devoted the longest hours and set the asylum's course. Other women served in more limited ways on the Building Committee, the Hiring Committee, the Diet Committee, and a dozen others. Together, the Board of Managers hired staff, watched over tradesmen, raised money, bought supplies, replaced bedding, set the diet, talked with newspapermen, negotiated with parents, kept the building in repair, and performed countless other mundane tasks. Members of the Board of Managers also personally investigated every applicant.

Apart from managing day-to-day affairs, the women also set fundamental policy. They decided what kind of children to take, how many to take, and how they should be handled. Issues of money, discipline, intake, and staff were all decided by the managers. In 1870, when the permanent asylum was going to be built, the women hired the architect and oversaw all construction. No male director saw the plans or building until it was completely finished.[73] The women also organized yearly fundraising campaigns. They, not the men, raised the great bulk of the money. In short, female volunteers ran the asylum.

The Board of Directors, on the other hand, did little. They at times tried to raise money (without much success), but principally the men did no more than invest the endowment and give occasional legal and real estate advice.

The women on the Board of Managers well exemplify late-nineteenth-century volunteerism. They were not paid; they did not work full-time. As the decline of the "volunteer spirit" is something bemoaned by commentators from Mary Richmond in the 1930s to George Bush in 1980s, it is worth pausing to explain more precisely the nature of late-nineteenth-century volunteerism.

Most important, consider *how much* these women did. These volunteers were not a "women's auxiliary." They hired and fired, managed budgets, built buildings. They energetically oversaw a large, complicated institution with only the most limited input from the men.

Volunteerism was also a distinctly managerial idea. The women volunteers of the Half-Orphan Asylum made all decisions about the institution's course but they did not handle the children. Matrons, nurses, servants, and schoolteachers—all full-time paid staff—had provided the day-to-day care at least since the end of the Civil War. But the staff, without any "professional" standing, did not set policy. A profound chasm separated the managers and the matron in the nineteenth-century Half-Orphan Asylum. No one ever forgot who was working for whom.

But if volunteerism was a managerial ideal, it was also a very hands-on kind of management. The women wanted to be directly involved with the varied details of the asylum's activities. Board members, through the investigation committee, knew the problems of every family with a child at the asylum. The women managed, but they did not manage bureaucratically. They wanted to be in touch with individual cases. This very specific cultural space, managerial yet personally involved, would prove to be exactly the zone that welfare professionals tried to empty when they attacked volunteerism in the early decades of the twentieth century.

The Half-Orphan Asylum's managers were deeply imbued with a sense of Christian duty. They were also, as we shall see below, without any financial worries. Their husbands were part of Chicago's commercial elite. Volunteerism provided the perfect niche. For such women in the late nineteenth century, pursuing a career was virtually unthinkable. By running the asylum, however, they could take on all the responsibilities and headaches of managing a major institution in the fastest growing city in the nation. The women, just like their businessmen husbands, could complain about staff, worry about budgets, and be quietly proud of hard work well done. At the same time, they continued to do "women's work," caring for children, maintaining homes. Volunteerism for these women not only fulfilled their sense of Christian duty (something which should not be underemphasized). It also provided a means of asserting class status without challenging gender lines.

While the men had been brought in to put the orphanage on firm financial footing, they failed at the task. The security the institution had by the late seventies was the women's doing, not theirs. Early efforts were confused by the great fire. For several years after the fire, the Chicago Relief and Aid Society gave the Half-Orphan Asylum regular contributions. It was unclear whether those donations would be a permanent feature of Chicago philanthropy. By the middle of 1873, it was plain they would not. The directors began searching for ways to secure financial stability.[74]

In 1873, the men decided to build an endowment through a subscription drive. In the next several years some of the city's most prominent citizens contributed. William Ogden gave $2,000; Albert Munger, $500; George Pullman, $200. It was at this point that the Donnelley family first contributed to the asylum, inaugurating philanthropic ties that have lasted right up to the present. These 1870s donations, while helpful, were not the sums required to create a working endowment. The campaign was a failure.[75]

Meanwhile, the orphanage lived hand-to-mouth. One of the most striking things about the 1870s asylum is the degree to which it depended upon donations in kind. The managers rounded up large amounts of food, fuel, clothing, and furniture. The gifts came in all sizes; none was too small to note. In 1874, the Illinois Central Railroad donated fifty tons of coal, two small businesses gave fifty winter hats, and a Mrs. L. Child donated two pair of stockings. Each year, the asylum's annual report listed page after page of donations. It is impossible to estimate how much the asylum depended upon gifts in kind at this time. It is not unreasonable to guess, however, that such gifts covered 25 percent of the institution's costs.[76]

The managers in the late 1870s turned to special events, such as musicals, or strawberry festivals, to raise money. They had done this in the 1860s, and the revival might indicate a recognition of the men's failure to raise a substantial endowment. But such entertainments proved as limited in the 1870s as they had previously. They never raised much money and the time involved was enormous.[77] After their May 1880 "Frog Opera" brought in only $525, the women decided that no more entertainments would be given, "the work being arduous, and the results generally unsatisfactory."[78]

In the late 1870s, the managers also began direct fundraising. This did give the asylum some security. The women moved in well-connected circles. They had little difficulty finding donors. The sums raised were modest, but they were sums that could be counted on nonetheless. For the first time in the late seventies, the women did not have to worry that swings in the economy might topple the asylum. The wealthy just continued to give. By the mid-1880s, yearly donations made up a full 50 percent of the asylum's income.

The problem with this approach, however, was the time it took. Volunteers spent long hours tracking down businessmen to ask for donations. It made for a small but safe amount of cash each year, but it was not an endowment. Raising operating funds remained a constant and time-consuming task.

Relief came in the late 1880s from a source no one expected—legacies. As late as 1888, yearly donations still accounted for half the income. The endowment for general operating funds totaled only $38,500. By 1892, however, the endowment was $140,875.[79] In 1888, interest from the endowment raised 16 percent of the asylum's income; by 1892, it was 33 percent of total income; and by 1895, endowment interest raised 50 percent of income.[80]

No one donor gave the money. The husband of a board member left $25,000 in January 1889. A son left $30,000. John Crerar gave $50,000.[81] The fortuitous events impressed upon the directors the need to cultivate future legacies. For decades, endowment funds remained the core of the asylum's finances. It was only in the late 1960s that they diminished in importance.

THE CHARITABLE NETWORK

Until the early 1870s, the general obscurity of the women who served on the board continued.[82] After that, however, the managers (and male directors) become easier to trace. That is because they were clearly part of the city's business and social elite. By the early 1880s, most directors were members of one or more of the city's prestigious men's clubs.[83] By 1882, more than half of the board members (both men and women) were also listed in the city's social register. By 1890, thirty-three of the thirty-nine managers were on that elite list and all thirteen male directors were. The name of every officer of both boards could be found in the register.[84] The men and women who ran the asylum after 1880 were among the city's leading families, key players in its commercial growth, active in many charitable ventures, firmly entrenched in its Protestant elite.

Some of the most famous names of nineteenth-century Chicago helped manage the Half-Orphan Asylum. Mrs. Levi Leiter was a board member for several years. Her husband was the city's single most successful real estate developer, for a time Marshall Field's business partner. Mrs. S. H. McCormick, the sister-in-law of Cyrus McCormick, served on the board from 1873 to 1882. Her husband was then Cyrus' business partner. Helen Judd Goudy was the most important manager of the late nineteenth century. She served on the board for over two decades and was president of the asylum from 1879 to 1898. Her husband was one of the most successful corporation lawyers of the city. He had been the Illinois Attorney General in the 1850s and in the 1870s was the first president of the Chicago Bar Association. Ellis Chesbrough, Chicago's city engineer for almost three decades, served on the Board of Directors for many years. His wife was on the managing board from 1869 to 1884 and was president in 1878. During the 1860s, Chesbrough designed the city's water system. Mrs. J. J. Glessner served for a short period as a manager; Martin Ryerson served as a director.

The managers and directors of the Half-Orphan Asylum had other connections as well. Nearly all lived very close to each other in either downtown Chicago or on the Near North side, just over the Chicago River. While the institution served working-class families from all over the city, its management was largely a neighborhood affair. Mrs. Beckwith, the Board of Managers' recording secretary between 1880 and 1900, lived a few doors away from Mrs. McCormick on Rush Street. Henry King, a director from 1869 to 1898, lived on the same block. A few blocks away, Mrs. Chesbrough lived at 224 Ontario, Mrs. Mulliken at 267 Ontario, and Mrs. High at 285 Ontario. Around the corner and up the street, Mrs. Samuel Howe, still active in 1880, lived at 89 Pine Street. Mrs. Abijah Keith, one of the board's most energetic members, resided at 108 Pine.[85] In 1880, thirty managers lived in the Near North side while only three women lived in the fashionable South side neighborhood around Prairie Avenue. Only two resided to the west. All five officers of the Board of Managers lived either downtown or north. This geographical distribution remained steady through the close of the century. The managers and directors were drawn largely from a six-block-square area in Chicago's fashionable Near North side.[86]

The decision to locate the asylum on North Halsted in 1871 was probably related to the needs of the Board of Managers rather than to those of the clientele. Children came from all over the city; but the managers came from one neighborhood. Building the asylum on North Halsted put it within easy reach of the managers' homes, well-suited to their hands-on management style.

The Half-Orphan Asylum was not the only Chicago charity run and sponsored by a specific upper middle-class neighborhood. The Chicago Orphan Asylum, founded in 1849, was another of the city's major Protestant asylums. The bulk of its managers and directors lived in the Prairie Avenue district about 1800 South, the neighborhood where George Pullman lived. Like the Half-Orphan Asylum, the Chicago Orphan Asylum served working-class families from the whole city. And like the Half-Orphan Asylum, it appears that the question of where to put the institution was related to the home neighborhood of the managing board.[87]

Apart from commerce and geography, the board members of the Half-Orphan Asylum were linked by religion. The asylum's constitution stated that all board members must belong to a church—that it be a Protestant church was assumed. At least twenty different denominations were represented during the late nineteenth century. There were, however, two particularly important churches, St. James Episcopal and the Fourth Presbyterian. Both were on the Near North side. At least sixteen Half-Orphan board members of the 1870s and 1880s came from those denominations. The Fourth Presbyterian provided a disproportionate number of the asylum's officers. Helen Goudy was a member; so was Henry King, Mrs. Mulliken, and Mrs. Hurlbut.[88]

Many of the families active in the asylum's management contributed time and money to other philanthropic ventures. Mrs. Charles Mulliken served on the asylum's board for over ten years. Her husband was director of the Chicago Relief and Aid Society for sixteen years. He was the principal officer of the Chicago Bible Society for twelve. The father of Ellen Rogers was the first president of Chicago's Charity Organization Society. Both Henry King and Abijah Keith were officers of the Chicago Relief and Aid Society, along with notables such as Marshall Field, J. T. Ryerson, George Pullman, Julius Rosenwald, and Levi Leiter. Other families connected with the asylum supported the Chicago Historical Society. At least four board members served on the Lincoln Park Board of Commissioners.

The members of the Half-Orphan Asylum's boards were part of an informal network of wealthy and well-connected Protestants who ran many of the city's Protestant charitable institutions. Social, business, neighborhood, and religious ties were all used to organize Protestant charities. New female church members (or daughters of present members) were sized up for their potential contribution to institutions like the Half-Orphan Asylum. If they looked promising, they were asked onto the board. (This is exactly the way the Half-Orphan Asylum recruited new managers in the nineteenth century.) Similarly, businessmen could touch wealthy friends for contributions over lunch. After John Crerar left $50,000 to the Half-Orphan Asylum, the directors noted in their public acknowledgement that "Mr. Crerar was friendly to most or all of our Directors and to many of the members of our board of Lady Managers."[89]

Despite the continued growth of the city, the Protestant charitable subculture remained small enough into the 1890s that few thought formal organizations necessary. Everyone seemed to know everyone else; everyone shared the same values. The system seemed to work very well. Chicago's Protestant leadership largely agreed on questions of charity.

As a consequence, the Nursery and Half-Orphan Asylum was accountable to no outside authorities. Neither the state nor the city regulated private orphanages. The only private umbrella agency for Chicago charities, the Chicago Relief and Aid Society, did not attempt to seriously monitor the performance of asylums. Even the city's newspapers were largely supine. The Half-Orphan Asylum, despite its death rate, never had anything but good publicity in the last three decades of the century. The informal network reigned supreme—but that was soon to change.

cᴐ *CHAPTER TWO* ᴐc

A Traditional Asylum, 1890–1910

I N THE YEARS AFTER 1890, WELFARE REFORMERS appeared in Chicago with a seemingly bewildering array of new ideas about the care of dependent children. These reformers, including people as famous as Jane Addams and Florence Kelley, were often key figures in the national movement for progressive reform. While their influence might be national, they rapidly created an interlocking network of local welfare institutions. In so doing, they became a "counter-establishment" to the older and more conservative philanthropic elite that included the leaders of the Chicago Nursery and Half-Orphan Asylum. Between 1890 and 1910, as Chicago's charitable world continued to grow, it also became infinitely more complicated.

The new situation created a number of specific issues that the Chicago Nursery and Half-Orphan Asylum had to confront. With so many new children's institutions around, the managers worried about the asylum getting lost in the crowd. Managers also had to adjust to new welfare initiatives of state and local governments, some of which seemed threatening. And the managers were forced to respond to reformers who attacked the asylum as "old-fashioned" or even "cruel." Finally, thanks to heightened consciousness about public health, the women who ran the Half-Orphan Asylum began worrying about illness inside the orphanage. The number of deaths common in the nineteenth century was no longer tolerable.

The managers of the Chicago Nursery and Half-Orphan Asylum had to learn to adapt. That they would have to come to terms with outside institutions and forces was something new in their history, and troubling to the managers. The turn-of-the-century changes forced them to take stock and reassess their mission. The response had three dimensions. The managers first of all paid increasing attention to their charges' health. Second, they worked hard to reaffirm their control—control over the children, the staff, and over their policy-making prerogatives. Finally, in the course of responding, the ideological underpinnings of the asylum subtly shifted. After the turn of the century, the predominantly religious ethos began to mingle with a commitment to both civic order and tradition.

All this took place in an institution that in key ways had not changed at all from the 1870s and 1880s. The working-class parents and children coming to the door for aid were no different than before. The same ethnic mix was at work.[1] Parents continued to inundate the asylum with more applications than the institution could ever hope to handle.[2] An absolutely crushing poverty was still the norm for those families coming to the asylum. Mothers—brutally poor mothers—brought their children to the doors far, far more than men—a three-to-one ratio one year, a five-to-one ratio another.[3] And just as before, about half the children stayed for six months or less, almost all stayed under a year. Just about every child returned to a parent. The orphanage, in other words, continued to be a place for the working poor during a time of family crisis.

The turn-of-the-century adjustments at the Half-Orphan Asylum were not responses to a change in clientele but to the challenge of welfare reformers. The managers were neither opposed nor committed to progressivism. Rather, they followed a pattern of selective adaptation. If a particular reform left their control of the asylum intact it posed no problem. The women would go far. But if the reform threatened to clip the managers' autonomy it was strongly resisted. Control was central to the managers' thinking. Progressivism was useful if it served the goal; anathema if it did not.

The Chicago Nursery and Half-Orphan Asylum's response to reform provides a good example of how many orphanages reacted to the challenge at least until 1910. Most of the city's children's institutions did not turn progressive overnight. Resistance, indifference, and piecemeal reform were typical. Historians have generally written as if there were a progressive takeover of the welfare system at the turn of the century, but if we consider the full array of institutions in Chicago at the point of actual delivery of services instead of through reform rhetoric, the reality was far more complicated. Between 1890 and 1910, progressive welfare reform and actual child welfare were not the same thing.

THE CHANGING FACE OF CHICAGO PHILANTHROPY

Before looking at the Half-Orphan Asylum, it is worthwhile to step back and sketch some of the more important changes in the city's welfare efforts at the turn of the century. The most basic change was growth. In 1885, there were twenty-three asylums in Chicago; by 1900 there were fifty-eight; and by 1910 a total of eighty-seven. Just about half of these catered to dependent children.[4] The Chicago Nursery and Half-Orphan Asylum was, as late as 1890, one of only twelve orphanages in the city. By 1905, there were twenty-two.[5] It was in these years that the Half-Orphan Asylum moved from being one of Chicago's premier orphanages to being just one of the city's many welfare agencies.

The increased number of asylums was not the only expansion of charitable services. When the city's Department of Welfare published its first social service directory in 1915, it listed not only the forty-eight homes for dependent children but also thirty-seven day nurseries and twelve home-finding societies. Only five of the day nurseries had existed prior to 1890. The first settlement house, Jane Addams' famous Hull House, opened in 1889. By 1916 there were seventeen such settlements in Chicago.[6] There were also new institutions to meet more specific needs. The Ridge Farm Preventorium, for example, was founded in 1912 to protect children from tuberculosis. Children who were generally underfed or unhealthy were taken from the dense inner city to a farm in suburban Lake Forest where they were treated to fresh air and a healthy diet. Back in Chicago, the Infant Welfare Society was founded in 1911. Its nurses, working from storefronts throughout the city, distributed formula to poor immigrant women and instructed them in the care and feeding of their infants.[7]

There were also new umbrella groups designed to organize Chicago's array of institutions. In 1896 the Chicago Bureau of Charities was created to challenge the moribund Chicago Relief and Aid Society. (In 1909 the Bureau of Charities became the United Charities of Chicago.) Among the tasks it took upon itself was monitoring Chicago's various philanthropies. For the first time an outside agency would evaluate and pass public judgment on the Nursery and Half-Orphan Asylum. Another umbrella group was the Council of Social Agencies, created in 1913 as a clearinghouse for advanced opinion on social work.

In those same years government involvement grew. The well-known East Coast charity reformer, Homer Folks, reported in 1902 that Illinois was "singularly backward in making any public provision for destitute and neglected children."[8] But that was in the process of changing. By 1898, Illinois officials were speaking out about the need for a coherent state policy on dependent children.[9] In 1899, the state created the nation's first juvenile court. In 1911, Illinois became the first state to pass mothers' aid legislation, giving a small allowance to mothers and children in fatherless households. Just a few years before, the Illinois Department of Public Welfare began providing services to private agencies such as the Half-Orphan Asylum. State doctors offered free check-ups to dependent children and would test their mental abilities. The city, too, expanded services. In 1914, Chicago created its own Department of Welfare.

The public Child Welfare Exhibit that progressives put on at Chicago's Coliseum for two weeks in May 1911 gives some sense of how the meaning of "child saving" had broadened. In the nineteenth century, the term generally referred to placing children in some sort of beneficent institution or placing them out to a farm family in the west. But the Child Welfare Exhibit displayed far more. There were exhibits on food, toys, playgrounds, and model homes. There were exhibits on the public library, on settlement houses, on children's hospitals and dispensaries, on summer camps, on nurseries, on preventive health measures such as those of the infant welfare stations. Of the sixteen major exhibits, only the one on "philanthropy" even mentioned orphanages. In the glossy book published to commemorate the event, complete with a preface by Jane Addams, only two paragraphs were devoted to children's institutions.[10]

Two things were happening at once. More and more institutions were being built at the same time that progressive reformers were downplaying the place of institutions in child welfare. Most of the private orphanages and asylums created after 1885 built on patterns developed in the mid-nineteenth century, a fact usually missed by historians concentrating on "cutting edge" progressive institutions like Hull House.[11] The main providers of institutional care for dependent children continued to be private agencies with religious affiliations.[12]

But while ethnic and religious groups followed old paths, creating homes to serve their own, the new growth increasingly fragmented the system. No longer were institutions simply "Catholic" or "Protestant." Between 1885 and 1910, Swedish, German, Polish, Danish, Bohemian, and Jewish groups each built their own asylums. Methodists opened an orphanage in 1894; Baptists the next year. There were asylums for Danish Lutherans, German Lutherans, German Evangelicals, and for the children of deceased Freemasons.[13] The Chicago Home for Jewish Orphans was founded in 1893 by wealthy Reformed Jews from Central Europe. It was built on progressive principles. In 1905, Orthodox Jews from Eastern Europe created the Jewish Orphan Home over the strong objections of those progressive (and wealthier) Jews who had assumed their institution would serve all Jews.[14]

Moreover, each of these ethnic and religious groups also built increasingly specialized institutions. Homes for homeless boys, for working boys, for newsboys, for delinquent boys, for working girls, for orphans, for abandoned children, were all deemed necessary. The Chicago Nursery and Half-Orphan Asylum now had to negotiate for funds amid a packed field. One of the oldest institutions in Chicago, by the turn of the century it had to find a way to distinguish itself and maintain an identity.

The dramatic expansion of services and institutions in the decades after 1890 made Chicago's philanthropic subculture a less intimate place. Leaders no longer knew each other. That was one reason an ideological chasm opened up over what "good" charity was. After 1890, Chicago's philanthropic leaders split into distinct groups. One group included the managers and directors of the Chicago Nursery and Half-Orphan Asylum, most of the other established Protestant and Catholic institutions, and some of the new asylums. The other group was centered in the new umbrella organizations like the Council of Social Agencies, among some Catholic reformers, and in certain new Protestant-derived institutions like Hull House.[15]

Progressives had little use for institutions. They roundly attacked the nineteenth-century asylum ideal. Progressives argued that the asylum was unhealthy, a warehouse, and that it emotionally stunted its inmates. Children in particular, they claimed, were hurt by asylum living. Children needed a home. Locking children in large dormitories (or "barracks" as the progressives called them) deprived youngsters of needed warmth and succor. Instead of saving children from the ravages of the city, as the Half-Orphan Asylum managers had thought, progressives claimed that asylums in reality were creating the social misfits of the next generation.[16]

Progressives reinvigorated the movement for foster homes. As a second-best choice, they championed the cottage system. Instead of the large congregate barracks of the asylum, those children who remained in institutions would be in small-setting "cottages" that housed no more than twenty to twenty-five children. With a "housemother" instead of a "matron" in charge, a warm, home-like setting could be simulated.[17]

In the next few decades the cottage system proved very important, but in the first years of the twentieth century the more explicitly anti-institutional ideas appeared more attractive. In 1909, support seemed to reach a new pitch when the President's Conference on Dependent Children endorsed the new goals. "Home life is the highest and finest product of civilization," read the final report of the conference, which was attended by such notable Chicago progressives as Jane Addams, Louise De Koven Bowen, Charles Henderson, and Judge Julian Mack of Juvenile Court. "Children should not be deprived of it except for urgent and compelling reasons." As for those children without parents: "The carefully selected foster home is . . . the best substitute." Theodore Roosevelt—the president himself—spoke out against exactly the kind of service the Chicago Nursery and Half-Orphan Asylum was providing: "The widowed or deserted mother, if a good woman, . . . should ordinarily be helped in such a fashion as will enable her to bring up her children herself in their natural home."[18]

These ideas fundamentally challenged the presumptions of the nineteenth-century managers of the Half-Orphan Asylum. The mission of the asylum was no different than that of the progressive reformers—family stability. But each group had deeply different assumptions about how that stability was best maintained. The asylum ideal was premised on the belief that single parents, including mothers, should be in the workforce. An orphanage like the Half-Orphan Asylum was there to care for children through times of crisis, to make sure children did not fall prey to the corrupting influences of the city while a parent was looking for work or at work but without the resources to adequately care for her children. Early twentieth-century reformers, on the other hand, stressed the need to have children in a home at every possible moment. All other alternatives were second best. This "need" was tempered by deeply ideological notions of what a "good" home was. By 1920, welfare reformers would try to accomplish this goal by reducing women's participation in the labor market via mothers' pensions, stipends paid by the state to single mothers.[19]

Behind the progressive hostility to the asylum was another fundamental difference between the progressive and conservative camps. This was over the nature of charity. Progressives argued that relief, as commonly understood by people like the Half-Orphan Asylum managers, was both insulting and inadequate. It was insulting because it demeaned the client. Jane Addams, for example, argued that friendly visiting did not create sympathy between the social classes. Wealthy women visitors rarely understood working-class needs or habits. Such visits only reinforced the visitors' sense of superiority and the recipients' sense of dependence.[20]

Nineteenth-century charity was inadequate precisely because it was only designed to provide relief. It did not get at the root of the problem; it only treated symptoms. Progressives saw themselves as more systematic, more thoroughgoing, and more effective than the conservatives. The smorgasbord of welfare activities on exhibit in 1911 in Chicago's Coliseum reflected the progressive sense that child saving was far more than relief, far more than keeping a boy or girl safe when a parent died. It was everything that could shape a child.

This had implications for what went on inside asylums as well. The managers of the Half-Orphan Asylum had modestly thought of their role as "custodial" in the 1870s and 1880s. Progressives wanted far, far more active and interventionist efforts. They felt they were attacking underlying causes instead of merely providing temporary aid.

These attacks were troubling to the managers of the Half-Orphan Asylum. Like Mary Richmond, the asylum's managers sometimes worried that they were becoming old-fashioned.[21] This defensiveness was nourished by the change in media coverage during those years. Progressives were extremely adept in publicizing their views. They wrote voluminously and developed new journals to spread the message. They also created the first periodicals explicitly reaching out to social welfare workers. Finally, progressive welfare reformers convinced muckraking newspapermen to write about the evils of asylums. The old guard did none of this.

The progressives' creative and aggressive use of the media contributed significantly to the death of the informal system that had governed Chicago Protestant charity.[22] Critical stories about asylums now appeared in public print; ideas about child welfare passed through journals like *Chicago Commons* instead of by word-of-mouth in wealthy neighborhoods. The female managers of the Chicago Nursery and Half-Orphan Asylum, as representatives of the old guard of Chicago philanthropy, continued to rely on the informal neighborhood network even as it was disintegrating around them. This gave the progressive counter-establishment a strategic edge that would affect Chicago philanthropy for decades.

While the managers of the Half-Orphan Asylum resented the new progressives, there was no stony anger. Both sides listened to each other and were willing to compromise, although neither forgot that priorities and values remained far apart. Chicago philanthropy did not change overnight to the progressive system, but neither did the old guard respond with dull-witted animosity. Rather, in the years after 1890 the two groups fell into an uneasy dance. The history of the Half-Orphan Asylum during those years reflects this well.

THE CHILDREN'S HEALTH

Probably the least controversial element of the reform agenda was the heightened interest in public health. Urban progressives spent a large amount of time worrying about the water, sewage, and garbage pick-up of the city. Connected to this was a concern for the nutrition and medical care of the poorer citizens. To some degree, this reflected the recognition that the germ theory of disease had more explanatory force than the older environmental ideas about illness.[23] When translated to the more specific critique of the asylum, this progressive concern for health made the number

of deaths common in nineteenth-century asylums unacceptable. Once the
new currents were in the air, the Half-Orphan Asylum's managers needed
no convincing. They readily joined in the search for ways to reduce the
death rate of the orphanage.

The worst mortality statistics in the entire history of the Half-Orphan
Asylum came in 1892. Through that summer and fall, the managers
watched in horror while the doctors worked unsuccessfully. Nineteen children died. "Over one-half of the deaths have occurred among babies from
six weeks to six months of age," the house physician reported. "A large
number of the other children who have not recovered have been less than
one year old." He continued with some rather typical nineteenth-century
rationalization: "Three or four of the babies were hopelessly ill when admitted to the Asylum. Nearly all of the deaths were among babies who
were either suffering from hereditary disease or from malnutrition."[24]

There was certainly some truth in the doctor's statement, particularly
with regard to malnourishment. Nevertheless, such a death rate, not uncommon in nineteenth-century asylums, now horrified the managers. Out
of the catastrophe of 1892, all complacency over infant mortality disappeared.

Late that year, the first step was taken. A small, separate hospital building was erected on the grounds, designed to handle only contagious cases.
For the first time, contagious and healthy children were housed in separate
structures. Two years later, the managers began considering a new quarantine ward. New arrivals were being quarantined for two weeks in the regular hospital just one floor away from the children's living quarters.
Resident half-orphans who visited the hospital with a cold or sore tooth
were thus exposed to whatever the quarantined newcomers might be
bringing in. In 1894 it was scarlet fever, and the epidemic created the desire for a separate quarantine ward. It took several years to raise the money,
but it was finally built when the asylum underwent extensive repairs in
spring 1896.[25]

The 1896 repairs were themselves brought about by the larger concern
for health. In 1895, the Repair Committee hired a firm of engineers to look
at the general condition of the building. They reported that the plumbing
was in terrible shape, with rotten fittings that probably contributed to the
spread of disease. The water supply was unclean. This led to extensive
repairs, costing $15,000. Apart from the new quarantine ward, they
brought the asylum hot and cold running water for the first time as well as
new apartments for the servants, nurse, and matron.[26]

The progressive interest in health did not lead the managers away from
the asylum ideal. In fact, it encouraged them to reassert that ideal in more

extreme forms. The managers became determined to keep illness outside the orphanage's doors. One way they did so was by reducing the availability of children to their parents. Children who went home for weekends, holidays, or summer vacations were a major source of the asylum's epidemics. In cramped ghetto environments, such children could contract diseases that then spread through the asylum. In 1895, citing the "unlimited troubles" caused by vacations, the managers voted that no child could take a vacation with a parent. Children were allowed to leave the asylum only for urgent reasons, such as a death in the family. In 1900, the managers softened their position by allowing children two weeks of vacation with their parents but only as long as the children were taken out of the city. This had the effect of refusing to let children visit home or friends. In 1908, eight weeks of freedom were allowed, but again only if the vacation was in the country. Weekends and holidays were even more problematic. After refusing a mother's request in 1899 to take her child home between Christmas and New Year, the managers set a formal policy: "Permission for children to go out, be given as seldom as possible and those cases reported to the board."[27]

The same commitment to the asylum ideal can be seen in the decision to dismiss children with ringworm. Ringworm was caused by a parasite often found in the water supply. It spread from child to child through plates, glasses, forks, knives, and spoons. It was also extremely difficult to cure. Symptoms might disappear for weeks and then reappear. While dormant, the disease easily spread to other children. In 1902, the Board of Managers voted to remove all children with ringworm. The infected child would be treated in the hospital until the symptoms were gone. Then he or she would be asked to leave. Several months after the policy was first instated, the house physician suggested that children be readmitted if their whole family took a special examination showing that no one had the disease. While a seemingly gentler policy, it imposed a severe financial strain upon poor families. The managers, worrying about disease within the asylum, agreed to the doctor's suggestion.[28]

The managers also hoped to reassert the asylum ideal by removing the whole orphanage from the city. During the late 1870s and 1880s, the asylum's neighborhood had become a slum, losing the suburban flavor it had when the Half-Orphan Asylum was built in 1870. By the 1890s, instead of single lot homes with spacious yards, many owners had put up a second or even third home on the same lot. The neighborhood became dominated by rentals. Owners, even working-class owners, moved away if they could afford it. The mixture of economic classes, common in the 1860s, had disappeared by the end of the century. The neighborhood was poor. No longer a calm, suburban-like setting, Chicago's Near North side was, as the United Charities annual report stated in 1910, a "city wilderness."[29]

Beginning in 1902, the Half-Orphan Asylum managers began looking for ways to leave the neighborhood. "While our present quarters are very convenient and attractive, . . . the ideal home for small and growing children is without doubt farther removed from the streets, which are rapidly becoming overcrowded." The managers' motives were complicated, but a key factor was the health of the children. While the move proved financially impossible in the first decade of the century, it still reflects the commitment to the asylum ideal. To prevent disease, the institution was to be cut off from the city.[30]

The managers also fought for better health through nutrition. In March 1901, Dr. Kathrine Swartz complained to the board about the children's diet. A practicing physician, Swartz had joined the Board of Managers just the year before, the first active professional to do so. She was especially worried about the diet of children under the age of six. In the next few months a committee looked into the matter and decided that changes were needed. More fruits and vegetables were added to the diet. There was less starch. In the nineteenth century, the Diet Committee of the Board of Managers essentially functioned to contain costs; by the first decade of the twentieth century the Diet Committee was deeply committed to a "scientific" diet for the children, another part of the drive to reduce the asylum's mortality rate.[31]

Still another element in the fight against disease was the introduction of preventive care for the children. In 1897, at the house physician's suggestion, it was decided that all entering children would have a complete physical examination. The next year, county physicians for the first time administered free diptheria antitoxin. In 1900, the City Health Department notified the asylum that it would distribute free health supplies to dependent children. In that same year, arrangements for regular dental care were made for the first time in the asylum. In 1902, Northwestern University made its dental school available for free care. During the first years of the century, regular medical check-ups became routine in the Half-Orphan Asylum. Disease was now fought before it appeared.[32]

One rather startling change in the early twentieth-century Half-Orphan Asylum was the willingness of the Board of Managers to fire the asylum's physicians. A team of doctors, with one physician in charge, handled the Half-Orphan Asylum on a part-time basis. They were paid a flat monthly fee for their services. The physicians looked on it as charity work. Such a system encouraged neglect; a doctor was paid the same if he treated twenty children or two hundred. But the physicians also came from the same elite

Protestant circles that the managers did. Through the nineteenth century, the ladies remained demure before the physician's patriarchal wisdom, no matter how many children died.

That changed in the first decade of the twentieth century. Particularly important was the presence of Dr. Swartz on the managing board. She was less cowed by male physicians than her colleagues. At the same time, the Board of Directors got an unusually energetic president, Azel Hatch. A prominent Chicago lawyer, Hatch, too, was willing to challenge the male physicians. Together, Swartz and Hatch gave the board the push needed to force physicians to be more careful. In December 1902, a smallpox epidemic swept through the nursery, which was housing sixty-five children under six at the time. The managers, drawing on the expertise of Swartz, were convinced that the doctor's lackadaisical attitude at the outset allowed an isolated illness to become a major catastrophe. They summarily fired the physician. Physicians were similarly dismissed in 1904 and 1907. Sloppy work was no longer tolerated.[33]

After 1892, the death rate in the institution dropped. Never again did ten children die in one year, something common in the 1880s. Between 1894 and 1906, the asylum averaged three deaths a year. But two other changes virtually eliminated all deaths in the asylum. In 1905, children ill with contagious diseases were for the first time sent to a community hospital. An experiment at first, it quickly became a regular practice. While it did not mean that no children under the asylum's care died, it ended the rampant epidemics that had plagued the institution during the nineteenth century. Far fewer children got ill inside the orphanage after 1906. The health of the orphanage became better than that of the city at large.[34]

A few years later, there was a final change, spurred on by the city. An ordinance requiring strict quarantining of children was passed, and the Half-Orphan Asylum had to reduce its population to comply. Until that time, the managers had let the institution's population slowly rise. Between 1885 and 1890, the first six years after the 1884 expansion of the building, the average population of the orphanage was 160. During the 1890s that slowly increased. In 1898, for the first time, 200 children and staff lived in the Half-Orphan Asylum.[35]

Nevertheless, that changed in 1910 with "the increased strictness of quarantine regulations enforced by the City Health Department."[36] This immediately reduced the number of children in the asylum. In the first nine years of the century, there were on average 158 children and 28 staff people living in the building. The strict city enforcement cut down those numbers by about twenty.[37]

The managers of the asylum were not hesitant about looking for new ways to improve the health of their children. Once the issue was raised by reformers, it became a primary goal of the asylum. And the managers were successful. Yet it should be underlined that they succeeded by reinforcing the asylum ideal and by adopting the progressive public health agenda, not by accepting progressive notions of welfare reform. Welfare reformers, like University of Chicago professor Charles Henderson, claimed that illness was unavoidable in "large, barrack-like edifices" such as the Half-Orphan Asylum. The solution to the health threat was to deinstitutionalize children or to move them into smaller "cottage" homes.[38] Instead, however, the asylum's managers used the older notion of the asylum-as-refuge to drastically reduce contact between children and the unhealthy environment. Coupled with that, the managers also fixed their water pipes, began using hospitals, secured regular check-ups for the children, and kept closer watch over the physicians. By quickly adopting many public health measures, the managers were better able to insulate themselves from the progressive attack upon the asylum.

CONTROL IN THE ORPHANAGE—THE ISSUE OF AUTHORITY

In the years around the turn of the century, the asylum managers developed a passion for control. It was not so much that this was a change in outlook; the women had always wanted to run their institution. Rather, it was that the intensity with which the goal was pursued quickened. A flurry of small changes, particularly between 1900 and 1907, all reflect the new passion.

This new assertiveness was part of a changing of the guard. Many key nineteenth-century leaders retired or died at the turn of the century. Helen Goudy stepped down from the presidency in 1897. Mrs. Beckwith retired as secretary in 1901. Both had spent more than twenty years in their respective posts. Both died in 1903. Other late Victorian leaders— such as Mrs. Abijah Keith, Mrs. William Potwin, or Mrs. S. E. Hurlbut— also left the asylum's managing board at that time. In their place came younger women, all previously handpicked by the older generation to continue the asylum's work. Ellen Rogers, one of the few unmarried members of the board, served as president between 1900 and 1907. She was a transitional figure, having joined the board as a young woman in the 1880s. After her came an entirely new generation. Mrs. Cyrus Bentley, wife of a prominent Chicago banker, was president between 1907 and 1911. Other women who became influential in the asylum's affairs after 1900 include Julia Watson Thompson, Mrs. Ira Geer, Mrs. Carroll Sudler, and Mrs. Ralph

Isham. Most would have a pronounced effect on the future of the institution.

The new generation came from the same social background as the Victorian leaders. Their husbands were all part of the city's commercial leadership. Mrs. Isham was the wife of a banker; Julia Thompson, of one of the first public relations men in the nation. Nearly every manager in 1910 continued to be listed in Chicago's social register. A number of the women were the second generation of their families to serve the Half-Orphan Asylum. They entered with a strong sense of tradition.

One difference between the generations was geographic. The managers were slowly moving out of the Near North side. The trend actually began in a very small way during the 1890s. Board members left the city to live in the far north suburbs, particularly Lake Forest, one of the prettiest (and wealthiest) suburbs in the nation. Julia Watson Thompson, who lived in Lake Forest, was the first officer in the history of the asylum to live outside the city. She regularly took the train into the city to do her asylum work. This slow drift would have long-term consequences.

The new drive for control can first be seen in the wealth of organizational changes within the Board of Managers. New committees appeared for the first time since the late 1870s. In 1905, when a library was added to the asylum, a Library Committee was formed to watch over it. On the heels of a financial crunch in 1903, Mrs. Howe, Mrs. Bradley, and Mrs. Geer, three of the new generation, were constituted as a Finance Committee to keep watch over long-term monetary concerns, while the treasurer (Mrs. Geer at the time) would look after day-to-day expenditures.[39]

The new Finance Committee reflects one important dimension of the drive for control. The asylum was becoming a more complicated institution and the division of labor within the managing board had to be more carefully articulated. In 1901, the president was given the authority to admit children on a temporary basis. No longer was the whole Executive Committee consulted. In March 1905 the board decided that it was just too cumbersome to have everyone participate in the hiring of a new assistant matron, so the Executive Committee could do it alone. Two weeks later, the board decided to let the Housing Committee hire a housekeeper. Similarly, in the early years of the century, board minutes record a variety of decisions carefully delineating the exact duties of various committees. Who took care of table supplies? Did the Hospital or Education Committee supervise the nursery?[40]

Whether a reflection of a new task, a new crisis, or a new complexity, the changes—and there were dozens of them during the first years of the century—all reflected the increasing preoccupation of the board with control. No detail unchecked. Nothing left to chance. The managers wanted a hand in virtually every decision. Although vacations to the country were authorized in principle in 1900, the Board of Managers demanded that they review every request and judge its appropriateness, something they did until the late 1920s. Similarly, the managers revealed a growing statistical sophistication after 1900, particularly through the energetic work of the asylum's new director, Julia Watson Thompson. The board hoped the statistics would help them keep close watch over key long-term trends. This also meant drastically reducing staff discretion. Why create a Library Committee? Why not just leave the library to the matron? Just a few years before, that very likely would have happened. A few decades later, it would be official policy. But at the turn of the century, with the new generation at the helm, the need to control all aspects of the institution was imperative. Never before or after were the volunteer managers such a presence in all details of the asylum's management.

Manager control translated into staff subordination in many ways. In 1897, for the first time, the managers fired an employee for using foul language in front of the children. The matron was instructed that in the future she must immediately report any such language to the president or the Hiring Committee.[41] After small sums could not be accounted for in 1900, it was decided that no employee could spend money without authorization from the treasurer of the Board of Managers. In 1904, the managers voted that no child could be kept out of school without written notice being given to the Board of Managers' School Committee. The staff could no longer make such decisions without oversight. We have already noted that after 1900 the managers were willing to fire the asylum's physicians. In decision after decision, the managers tried to bring the staff under rule.[42]

Finally, the desire for firm control also extended to the children and parents. The restrictive policy on vacations has already been cited. After 1900 children weren't allowed to bring in food of any kind. One child was reprimanded for buying a pickle.[43] Nor were visiting parents allowed to bring in food, another rule passed in 1900. If parents persisted in ignoring that dictum their children were expelled. That several times in the first decade of the century children were dismissed from the orphanage because their parents brought them candy illustrates very well the degree to which the managers would go.[44] But they did still more.

Manager records reveal increasing attention to child discipline after 1895. The managers clearly thought the children were now more trouble, but it is unclear whether the new discipline was a reaction to real increases in delinquency or if it was that the managers' new concern for control made them stricter. Whatever, there are regular complaints in the man-

agers' minutes about the bad behavior of the children, something uncommon in the 1870s and 1880s. The managing board spent more time
deciding how to mete out punishments. They went back and forth over
corporal punishment, at times forbidding it, at times allowing slaps on the
hand but outlawing the switch, and still at other times agreeing that
the matron could use the switch to "uphold her authority." At one point
the board decided that disobedient children would get bread and water at
meals. At different times, the board had the matron report how often she
used the switch each month. The decision to keep such statistics for the
first time in 1894 in itself reflected the managers' belief that the children
were now more trouble. Each month, twelve, sixteen, twenty such punishments were recorded, roughly one switching for every twelve children at
the asylum.[45]

The number of runaways increased. Each month there were at least five
or six "escapees." At times there were more. In May 1901, sixteen children
ran away. Whether all this was the result or cause of the managers' new
firmness is unclear. Managers devoted much attention to the issue, but
they focused not on why the children were leaving but on what the most
effective punishment would be. Bread and water, switching, putting to bed
were all tried. Finally, in 1905, the board decided that any runaway would
be immediately expelled. No second chances.[46]

The board minutes also suggest more tension between parents and
managers. The causes of trouble were no different than in previous years,
but the incidence increased. A couple of times parents complained to the
Bureau of Charities about the asylum. The managers, however, tried to
treat unruly parents as sternly as any unruly child, as indicated by a motion
of March 20, 1906: "On any further complaints from Mrs. Benson her boy
will be dismissed. Carried." There was to be no mistake about who controlled the asylum.[47]

Controlling the children took other forms as well. As the area around
the asylum became more crowded, it was also becoming less pleasant. By
the 1890s, neighbors were complaining about the noise made by the half-
orphans, and the asylum had to worry about vandalism committed by
neighborhood children.[48] The managers responded by invoking the asylum ideal and trying to reduce the half-orphans' social contact with the
neighbors. In April 1901, in response to a complaint about the noise that
asylum children made on Burling Street, the managers voted that children
could no longer leave the grounds. Three months later, after neighborhood children induced some "asylum boys" to run away, the managers
voted that no neighborhood child could visit the asylum without the matron's permission.[49]

All this must have made life in the asylum more tiresome for the children, most between the ages of four and eight. The problem was exacerbated by the physical expansion of the asylum over the years. The addition of 1884 and the hospital building of 1896 meant that there was little yard left for children to play on. There were organized outings to Lincoln Park during the summer, but distance (about one mile), the children's young age, and their sheer numbers reduced the number of trips. In 1907, to relieve the situation somewhat, the managers built a playground in the yard.

The asylum after 1900 became a harder place for children and their parents. The rising number of runaways, the new discipline, the limited movement outside the asylum, and the more adversarial relationship between the asylum and parents all point to that conclusion. Still, this judgment should be tempered. Day-in, day-out, children were probably treated not too far from the standards of their own homes. While living in the asylum was never lavish, treats, birthday parties, holiday celebrations, and outings came almost weekly. Moreover, the managerial effort to control the staff could also benefit the children. Cause had to be shown for any corporal punishment. And no full-fledged beatings were allowed. In 1900 the matron was swiftly fired after she beat a disobedient child with a stick. The managers formally apologized to the mother.[50] And, finally, whether or not the asylum was harsher, once the new concern for health manifested itself, it was certainly safer.

Still, it is indisputable that the managers wanted to shape and control the children more than before. This was especially evident in the managers' new passion for manual training. From the 1870s, girls had been taught how to sew and cook, but while boys learned how to darn socks, they learned no more specific skills. In 1901, however, the managers decided that some carpentry and craft training were essential. They negotiated with Francis Parker School to use the facilities (for a price) and they hired Parker's industrial teacher to provide the instruction. By 1904, it was a regular feature. Several times a week, groups of boys from the asylum would walk the mile and a half to Francis Parker to be schooled in the industrial arts.[51]

Again and again, the managers argued that the manual training did more than just teach carpentry. The classes at Francis Parker, it was noted in the annual report of 1905, have provided "a great pleasure" to the boys, "as well as a means of governing them." The year before the craft classes were described as having "direct profit in the way of manual skill and indirect profit in the matter of discipline." Manual training was also moral training, a way of dealing with unruly children.[52]

This broadened into more grandiose civic themes. In the 1907 annual report, the managers described their mission as the "physical, mental, and moral training" of youngsters of "impressionable ages" whose parents, the "worthy poor," were facing financial crises. Here the work of the asylum was not described as it was in the nineteenth century—as religiously motivated and for those poor from similar religious backgrounds. Now civic themes mingled with the religious. The asylum was doing its small part to curb potential social unrest: "This Asylum has materially helped many hundreds of men and women to solve the most difficult problems of life. We, who are engaged in the work, earnestly bespeak the financial and moral support of a community, for which we are attempting to provide good and loyal citizens."[53]

If ever there was a moment when "social control" was a conscious goal of the Half-Orphan Asylum, it was during those progressive years, precisely at the time when the managers were most vigorously opposed to progressive welfare reformers. In the nineteenth century, the managers had pictured themselves as providing short-term relief. They were temporary caretakers; their image of their duties was almost passive. By the early twentieth century, however, the managers saw themselves as active participants in a larger drive to shape "responsible," "loyal" citizens. They never used explicit class terminology, but the implications were clear. The working class had to be molded. The Half-Orphan Asylum contributed to the effort.

The manual training and civic ethos provide other examples of how the managers used the larger currents of urban progressivism to fend off the more specific demands of welfare reform. If the latter called for the end to the asylum, and either the deinstitutionalization of children or the creation of the homelike "cottage" system, the managers focused on the broader, more diffuse progressive goals of citizenship.[54] Wherever progressivism did not threaten the Half-Orphan Asylum, it was easily adapted to. But wherever the progressive message told the managers that they should give up control, they resisted. That led to sustained resistance by the Board of Managers to progressive efforts to reshape Chicago's system for care of dependent children.

CONTROL OF THE ASYLUM—THE ISSUE OF AUTONOMY

Progressive welfare reformers created an array of institutions designed to bring order to Chicago's relief system. They hoped to create a formal, but essentially private, system of charitable relief. New organizations like the Chicago Bureau of Charities (founded 1894) or the Juvenile Court (founded 1899) were in theory supposed to set standards of care for the whole city. The managers of the Half-Orphan Asylum, like most conservative Chicago philanthropists (both Protestant and Catholic), resisted. Here there was little give. The Board of Managers did not want to become enmeshed in a system that would take their asylum away from them.

At key points refusal was firm and unbending. The Half-Orphan Asylum turned down repeated offers to collaborate with the Chicago Bureau of Charities. The bureau hoped to bring all of the city's eleemosynary institutions under the benevolent guidance of its own progressive staff. One thing wanted by the leaders of "Associated Charities," as the bureau was called, was to have all case investigations made by paid staff trained in the art. The Half-Orphan Asylum's Investigation Committee, the bureau thought, was no longer needed. This was a progressive response to the criticisms of nineteenth-century friendly visiting made by people such as Jane Addams. If the Bureau of Charities had its way, case investigation would no longer be done by wealthy volunteer women but by an expert staff.

As early as 1896, representatives of the Bureau of Charities had come to the Half-Orphan Asylum touting the efficiency of the Associated Charities. The managers were dubious. They refused to turn over the investigation of cases to the Associated Charities. The issue was raised again in 1900, 1902, and 1914.[55] Each time the board nixed collaboration, even when the bureau offered to do it all for free. The asylum managers took deep pride in the work of their Investigation Committee. They could not have disagreed more with Jane Addams' critique of the practice.[56] The 1911 annual report reiterated the commitment to what was called the board's "hands on" policy. The "personal nature of the services rendered" was one of the institution's best features, the report noted. Friendly visiting created "close personal relations" between the board and "the parents and guardians of our wards."[57] There was no reason to have the Bureau of Charities do that work.

Similarly, the managers were very wary about any contact with the new Juvenile Court of Cook County, created in 1899. The first such court in the nation, it was a project dear to progressive reformers. Delinquent and dependent children of all sorts would be handled through the informal workings of this quasi court. The strict rule of law would be set aside so that, in theory, children could be handled with loving discretion by sympathetic judges. Like the Bureau of Charities, this was an institution designed to make both a more humane system (taking children from cruel environments) and a more efficient system (by linking together all welfare organizations through a single channeling mechanism).

The Half-Orphan Asylum managers would cooperate, but only on their own terms. As with the Bureau of Charities, the issue of what kind of relationship to have with the Juvenile Court was raised a number of times over the years. The 1901 managers' minutes contain the representative response: "Mrs. Goodwillie moved that we comply with the requirements of the juvenile court and so come under its jurisdiction. Lost."[58] On various occasions during the next ten years, the asylum refused to accept children that the court wanted them to take. At times relations could become tense. In 1904, it took a court order for the managers to allow an "undeserving" father to visit his children in the asylum.[59]

The managers' distrust had varied sources. One was probably defensiveness. They thought they were doing a good job and resented the attacks upon the asylum ideal. And it was not as if Juvenile Court was uncontroversial. Loud, if not influential, voices in the city complained about the lack of due process children got at the court.[60] The Half-Orphan Asylum prided itself on *not* taking legal control of the children. The power of Juvenile Court judges was suspect. Second, formal alliance with the new organizations meant new obligations but no new income. Juvenile Court, for example, could not pay Chapin Hall for the upkeep of children at that time. Finally, and most important, coming under the jurisdiction of Juvenile Court or allowing the Bureau of Charities to do all investigations meant giving up crucial autonomy. It meant accepting outside decisions about whom to care for. Relying on public authorities for intake had radically altered at least one of Chicago's welfare institutions in living memory.[61] The managers were afraid they would lose control of the asylum. Progressives saw the new system as rationalizing the delivery of welfare; but the managers of the Half-Orphan Asylum saw it as a power grab. Both were right, explaining both the progressives' doggedness over the years and the conservatives' wary resistance.

The Half-Orphan Asylum did not eschew all contact with progressives. As early as 1902 Ellen Rogers, Julia Watson Thompson, and others were attending local and national progressive conferences on child welfare. They also quite willingly used services offered with no strings attached, such as the new medical services offered by the county and city. Similarly, the asylum called in city probation officers when they needed them. Finally, beginning in 1898 children whose parents had neglected them were sent to Dependent Court, established in that year. Previously, such children were sent to the Home for the Friendless, a private institution. The managers readily took advantage of the new court to dispose of unwanted residents.[62]

Disputes between the asylum and the progressive movement were subtle. It is not that there was no interaction; rather there was a pattern of interaction. Wherever association threatened the managers' control of the asylum, it was resisted. Wherever it did not, the managers were ready and willing to make use of new services.

Reformers moved from a position of extreme weakness. They had neither the power nor money to force a systemwide change in the delivery of services to Chicago's dependent children. Still, if progressives did not have legal coercive power, and if they did not control purse strings, they did have another weapon—publicity. Progressives mounted an intense ideological campaign against the asylums of the nation. They artfully waged the battle of ideas even while the political and financial struggles were uncertain.

As a consequence, the managers of the Half-Orphan Asylum found themselves on the defensive. In the early years of the century, the managers heard public criticism not only of the asylum ideal but of their own institution. In 1901, *Chicago Charities,* a progressive organ published by Graham Taylor's *Chicago Commons,* published an article critical of the Half-Orphan Asylum's handling of a particular case. In 1903, the managers were informed that the Illinois Bureau of Justice was dissatisfied with their treatment of a child. In 1904, a court order forced asylum managers to allow a father visitation rights to his children. At the same time the Bureau of Charities began to monitor the activities of all private charities in order to make sure that they met standards—meaning progressive standards. Unsuitable charities were put on a "bad" list which was made available to donors and newspapers. For the first time in its history, the Half-Orphan Asylum was being monitored in the name of the public interest. For the first time in its history, the asylum had to worry about public embarrassment.[63]

In reaction, the asylum began trying to manage its public image. The early years of the twentieth century marked the birth of the modern public relations industry, and the Half-Orphan Asylum, in its small way, reflected the trend. Managers found themselves debating how best to answer or deny charges, and trying to make sure that bad publicity did not leak out. They had not done this before precisely because bad publicity was not a problem. Bad press about Chicago's Protestant asylums did not appear in nineteenth-century papers, one aspect of the informal consensus described in chapter one. That changed rapidly after 1900. Now interested

parties on all sides actively worked to manipulate media and public percep-
tions.

Managing publicity not only meant responding to bad press, but also
attempting to prevent the negative from becoming public. The lengths to
which the asylum would go can most certainly be seen in the events following a particularly bad scarlet fever epidemic during 1906. Dozens in the
asylum fell ill; six children died. It was clear to the few in-the-know that
the cause of the epidemic was the laziness and ineptitude of Dr. Culver, the
house physician. Knowledgeable members of the managing board were
outraged, but they also struggled to protect the asylum's reputation. They
found themselves caught between wanting a thorough shake-up and wanting to keep the tragedy from the press.

The aftermath was severe, reflecting the importance of health to the
post-1900 managers. Mrs. George Isham, long a leading board advocate
for better health conditions, threatened to resign if strong action was not
taken. She was mollified. The matron was fired for not making the managers aware of the physician's incompetence. Leading board members quietly decided that Ellen Rogers, president of the asylum since 1900, would
have to step down at the end of 1906 because of her failure to monitor the
situation. Mrs. Elizabeth Bentley, a member of the new generation, took
her place.[64]

There was still one sticky issue—what to do with the doctor. No one
denied he was at fault; the question was how to prevent scandal. Discussion was restricted to a handful of key managers and directors. Even in
early 1907, almost six months after the epidemic and deaths, most of the
women on the managing board did not know of Dr. Culver's incompetence. George Isham, the president of the Board of Directors, hoped that
the doctor would quietly resign and that would be that. He wanted the new
president of the Board of Managers, Elizabeth Bentley, to privately approach Culver and tell him that his name would not be dragged through
the mud if he left. Isham (and probably his wife) wanted even most of the
managers to be kept in the dark permanently, the better to keep the matter
from the press.

Elizabeth Bentley's husband, Cyrus, disagreed. Cyrus was also on the
Board of Directors. Mr. Bentley told Isham that it was wrong for Elizabeth
to handle the matter privately, even given "the lax administrative methods
in the Board of Managers." Bentley wanted his wife protected. Precisely
because "there was danger of a large size scandal" if the circumstances
surrounding the four deaths became "generally known," it was important
that the decision be more than hers. Bentley suggested that the Executive
Committee of the managing board be told that "Dr. Culver had been dere-

lict, . . . that he had practically admitted this by tendering his resignation, and that in view of his resignation it seemed unnecessary to go into the details of his shortcomings." This way the whole board would not have to be told but the decision would not be Elizabeth Bentley's alone. Bentley also suggested that his wife write a letter to Culver explaining why he was being asked to resign and that the asylum keep a copy in case the matter became public, as a means of at least mitigating any bad publicity that might accrue.

There was one hitch. Culver hadn't yet quit. Bentley thought "there was very little likelihood" that he would refuse to do so as it would mean Mrs. Bentley would have to make a "full statement" to the whole board, "trusting that the ladies would keep the matter secret." It was clear that neither Bentley nor Isham nor the two men's wives felt the whole board could be so trusted, and they were convinced that the doctor would share their opinion.[65]

How exactly events went from there is unclear. We do know that the physician thwarted those managing his ouster by refusing to resign. In March, the whole Board of Managers voted to fire him.[66] Still, the effort to keep the matter quiet was such a success that we have no exact information on the nature of the doctor's incompetence. Any letter written on the subject has long since disappeared. The epidemic never made the Chicago newspapers. The worst fears about scandal were not realized.

The incident makes clear the extraordinary care that the asylum's leaders took to manage the institution's public image. Yet in 1907 this was something very new. As late as 1900, managers and directors of the Half-Orphan Asylum never worried about bad publicity precisely because there was no one to generate it. Newspapers all gave uniformly good press to the city's Protestant asylums. There were no watchdog organizations like the Bureau of Charities or journals such as *Chicago Charities*. Asylum managers could trust the informal consensus governing Protestant urban charity.

By 1907, that informal system was coming apart. No longer could the wealthy philanthropists rely upon the "good sense" of their neighbors who managed Chicago's newspapers. Now bad publicity could come, and it would have to be contended with. Managing a public image became still another aspect of the battle for control. Autonomy would be preserved, the managers of the Half-Orphan Asylum tacitly realized, only if bad publicity did not hound the asylum. In a city that now had so many more charities looking for money, a bad image could seriously damage the bottom line. By the early years of the twentieth century, the asylum's directors and managers were engaged in very intense, very confidential efforts to make certain that the orphanage's name would remain a good one throughout the city of Chicago.

TRADITION: THE HALF-ORPHAN ASYLUM AND THE CITY'S OTHER ORPHANAGES

Learning to manage the orphanage's public image was one way the asylum adapted to the new conditions of Chicago philanthropy. Others we have noted include: the new attitude toward health, the willingness to fire physicians and matrons, the use of Dependent Court and Juvenile Court to take unwanted children, attending national conferences to obtain information about child care, and using new services provided by the city, county, and state, such as free physical exams and mental evaluations. Many were responses to the progressive challenge. Some were efforts to adapt to the changing neighborhood in which the asylum stood. All were efforts to maintain control.

Yet there were powerful limits to change. The managers remained firmly committed to the asylum ideal. They expressed no discomfort with the children's large dormitories. They continued to speak of the "worthy poor" as they always had. The volunteer women remained adamant about doing their own case investigations. The Half-Orphan Asylum remained devoted to helping "worthy" families facing severe poverty. Children whose parents made a lower-middle-class income were denied admission.[67]

By the second decade of the century, the managers regularly called attention to the traditional character of their charity. Noting the "rapidly changing opinions and ideals . . . in regard to the care of dependent children" and the increased "suspicion of old methods," the managers asserted that "the chief note in the business and charitable world . . . has been instability." The Half-Orphan Asylum, however, pursued a steady "course of action," something now taking "courage and zeal beyond the ordinary."[68]

Even the change of leadership evoked tradition. Julia Watson Thompson praised the stability that family continuity brought: "The personnel of the Board of Managers of this Institution has often changed by the law of time in the last half century, but the spirit and character of the work of a Board where daughters come to take the place of their mothers and even their grandmothers, have remained the same from year to year, from generation to generation."[69]

Certain aspects of the traditionalism do expose some of the asylum's limits. The pressure to maintain autonomy vis-à-vis the welfare community actually contributed to the hardship of their working-class clients. By refusing to coordinate investigation with United Charities, the Half-Orphan Asylum condemned a family looking for help to search from asylum to asylum. This was a depressing and time-consuming task, roaming all over the city to find the "right" institution, then waiting for the investigation to take place. (Keep in mind this was before the telephone was common.) If one asylum did not work out, then the parent would have to begin the whole process again, canvassing the remaining institutions, undergoing still another investigation. All this took place right as the family (overwhelmingly with a single mother at its head) was literally disintegrating from loss of a parent, or loss of income, or, in many instances, the loss of both. Coordinating intake would have reduced dramatically the time it took for many families to get initial help.

The separate male and female boards, now being criticized by progressive reformers, was another traditional practice that caused problems.[70] Out of the blue, in the summer of 1899, the managers found themselves unable to pay several thousand dollars' worth of pressing bills. During July and August a crisis mentality reigned; a frantic search was made to find the money. The president of the Board of Directors, Azel Hatch, later wrote that he was "appalled" to learn that the debts were so great that women had to curtail new admissions for several months.[71] But the fact was that the male directors had no sense of the short-term financial needs of the institution. By the end of the year, loans from the endowment, some outright sale of endowment investments, and various gifts by leading board members solved the short-term problem. But the underlying difficulty remained. Dual boards made long-term financial planning very difficult, a problem that plagued the asylum into the 1970s.

If some of the asylum's traditionalism was misplaced, much of it was not. In fact, certain aspects of its traditionalism reveal holes in the progressive attack on the asylum. For example, progressives often asserted that keeping asylums in the city was simply due to the blind conservatism of philanthropy's old guard. In fact, it was not that the Half-Orphan managers wanted to stay in the congestion of North Halsted Street. Rather, there was no money to move. Reformers confused practical limitations with conservative resistance. The "failure" here reflected financial binds more than ideological blinders.

Reformers also portrayed asylums as places where children languished for years. In the progressive critique, impressionable young children entered asylums and left years later as misshapen young adults, a picture seriously misrepresenting what went on in the Half-Orphan Asylum. The Half-Orphan Asylum's managers ignored the anti-institutional message of the progressives because they knew the asylum provided relatively short-term services needed and wanted by the working-class community.

Up until 1910, the Half-Orphan Asylum's managers were not alone in ignoring the progressive message. Historians of progressive welfare too often focus on cutting-edge institutions to the detriment of discovering the norm. The actual delivery of children's services in Chicago led a far messier life.

Like the managers of the Half-Orphan Asylum, other defenders of asylums pointed out that they provided temporary care and that most of their children returned to a relative.[72] Because they provided short-term relief, these institutions typically claimed that they didn't have to worry so much about stunting children. Especially given the huge demand for services among the working class and the shortage of money, the managers of many institutions felt there were more pressing issues to confront.[73]

This in part explains the absence of interest in local foster care in Chicago. Catholic charities showed no interest at all in deinstitutionalization. Nor did most Protestant institutions. The Chicago Nursery and Half-Orphan Asylum was very typical in this regard. In 1910, the U.S. Census Bureau did an exhaustive study of children's institutions around the nation. Of the sixty-four Illinois orphanages responding, only twenty had developed a foster care program. Across the nation, only 26.9 percent of all dependent children were in a foster home.[74]

Nor were cottages vital necessities to many orphanage managers. The whole progressive rationalization for cottages assumed that children were in institutions for a number of years, something which was clearly not always the case. But regardless of whether an institution kept children for six months or six years, it is plain that there was no rush to the cottage plan in Chicago. There were scattered efforts to build cottages, but the overwhelming majority of Chicago homes for dependent children—orphanages and industrial schools—were like the Half-Orphan Asylum in not having any cottage plan by 1910. And this was true around the nation. In the 1910 Census Bureau survey, of 1,077 child-care institutions reporting on the subject, only 168, or 15.6 percent, had adopted the cottage system. Of the sixty-four Illinois orphanages responding, only sixteen had cottages.[75]

Even when a cottage plan was implemented, moreover, it was usually on a small scale, available only to the oldest children. The largest Catholic boys' orphanage, Angel Guardian, may have started building cottages in

1914, but its average daily population by 1919 was 989 children. Only a fraction of these boys ever lived in a cottage. Despite its cottages, Angel Guardian in the 1920s was one of the largest congregate orphanages in the city.

Large congregate institutions were still the norm until 1910. Of the five industrial schools with figures available in 1905, there were two Catholic institutions with more than 300 children each and two Protestant schools with 180 and 200 children respectively. The only home for dependent adolescents with fewer than 100 children was Allendale Farm, a nationally known progressive institution. Allendale had forty-eight boys attending. The important thing to note, however, is that Allendale was alone among the industrial schools. In 1910, Illinois orphanages and industrial schools averaged 144 residents each, a number very close to the population of the Chicago Nursery and Half-Orphan Asylum at that time.[76]

The same could be said of orphanages. In 1905, the Half-Orphan Asylum was one of ten orphanages in the city (out of twenty with available figures) that housed more than 100 children. Almost all of those children lived in congregate dormitories. And smaller orphanages did not necessarily mean progressive orphanages. Most of them were modest, neighborhood, ethnic institutions.[77]

Nor should one equate "new" orphanages with progressivism. That, too, is a mistake born of historians only looking at cutting-edge institutions like Allendale Farm. New institutions and new construction most often followed old lines. Marks Nathan Jewish Orphan Home, the Orthodox orphanage in Chicago, was chartered in 1904. By 1906 there were two to three children sleeping in each bed. This overcrowding in itself belies the picture-book image of progressive welfare. But to relieve the situation Marks Nathan built a new congregate orphanage for up to 200 children, a project completed in 1912. After a fire destroyed the main complex of St. Mary's Training School in 1899, a four-story building, with huge dormitories, was built to replace it. It had a capacity of more than three hundred. In 1919, St. Hedwig's Industrial School for Girls, a Polish institution, built a new dining room designed to serve 700 children at once, an absolute horror to those progressives who wanted more familial surroundings for dependent children. The size of the dining room only reflected the number of girls living at St. Hedwig's at the time.[78]

But what needs to be underlined most of all is how individual progressive ideas could be adopted at many of Chicago's children's institutions without embracing the whole progressive package. The pattern of selective adaption that the Half-Orphan Asylum displayed was very common, although the particular decisions were hugely varied. Turn-of-the-century Catholic child savers, for example, worried that institutionalized siblings were losing touch with each other. They also worried about the location of their orphanages in the most cramped, unhealthy neighborhoods of the city. The response in 1910 was to close down a number of Catholic orphanages in Chicago and bring institutionalized brothers and sisters together at St. Mary's in rural Des Plaines.[79] But despite the concern for family ties, a key progressive reform, the 1910 merger made St. Mary's one of the hugest congregate orphanages in the nation. Even though the merger entailed moving children to the country, another progressive goal, it was anathema to reformers from the beginning. At the center of the "progressive" years, much child welfare was proceeding as it had in the past.

Historians need to be more attuned to the resistance that progressives faced in the early years of the century, certainly in Chicago through 1910. Much welfare history portrays a progressive takeover after 1890. But that is misleading, implying that reformers had far more power over urban child welfare than they actually did. Asylums like the Chicago Nursery and Half-Orphan Asylum had the financial independence needed to ignore calls for reform. Most of Chicago's orphanages and industrial schools proceeded in the same way.

If historians have often attacked the progressive record, they have usually accepted the progressive critique of the late-nineteenth-century asylum. Yet, as we have seen, the conservatives at the Chicago Nursery and Half-Orphan Asylum did much to adapt to the new climate while still resisting wholesale acceptance of the progressive package. The managers knew that much of the progressive critique of the asylum simply did not apply to their institution.

Progressive reform swept into the new Juvenile Court but only haltingly made its way into Chicago's homes for dependent children. Reform also successfully ended the system of placing children out to western farms. The Home for the Friendless stopped this practice in the first decade of the century.[80] Fledgling foster care programs, with children staying in the city, were the replacements. But when looking at the institutions —orphanages and industrial schools—which were a growth industry at the turn of the century, there is far less sense of reform. Certainly until 1910, Chicago orphanages did little to conjure up a progressive image.

But around these institutions there was one key change. The informal consensus that had governed Protestant welfare in the late nineteenth century was gone. And if progressives could not coerce an orphanage like the Half-Orphan Asylum to change, they still had powerful long-term weapons. Progressives thought in terms of public opinion, citywide welfare organizations, and, indeed, national institutional and informational child welfare networks. The Half-Orphan Asylum managers, on the other hand, found their greatest source of strength in those informal neighborhood ties that were already beginning to fray. In the years after 1910, the Half-Orphan Asylum increasingly enmeshed itself in the institutional network created by the progressives.

∞ CHAPTER THREE ∞

Reforming the Orphanage, 1910–1930

I N THE TWO DECADES AFTER 1910, THE HALF-Orphan Asylum's defiance of progressive welfare weakened. The asylum managers became increasingly amenable to reform, their thinking more and more tinged with progressivism. Indeed, throughout the city's philanthropic community, the wary stand-off between conservatives and progressives was replaced by gentle give-and-take. By the 1920s, progressive reformers were becoming administrators of key new welfare bureaucracies such as the Chicago Council of Social Agencies. With the change, the reformers often became less insistent. They no longer demanded that charities like the Half-Orphan Asylum remake themselves immediately. Public criticism of conservative institutions became a rarity. The old–guard children's institutions, in turn, slowly adopted progressive suggestions. By 1930, the Half-Orphan Asylum was one of many such institutions that had accepted at least some of the progressive agenda for child care. And this was without being coerced. Half-Orphan Asylum managers, like so many other established charities doing the same thing, *wanted* to make the changes.

The "bonding" between the Half-Orphan Asylum and the progressives came about because of an institutional trajectory set in place during the Progressive Era. Progressive reformers created both state and private co-ordinating agencies, or "umbrella" agencies, to reform and manage child welfare in the city. By the 1920s, however, it was becoming apparent that the private managerial agencies—the Council of Social Agencies and its offshoots—were becoming far more important than the Cook County Juvenile Court in the effort to reshape private children's agencies such as the Half-Orphan Asylum. It was the Council of Social Agencies that convinced the Half-Orphan Asylum to keep detailed records on children and parents; the council that convinced the asylum to hire a social worker trained at the University of Chicago; and it was the council that got the orphanage to finally coordinate its intake through a central bureau.

Slowly, a private bureaucracy was emerging to manage child welfare in Chicago. A number of historians have noted the trend toward private bureaucratic management in the interwar years, most famously associating it with the ideas of Herbert Hoover. It was imagined by its proponents as an alternative to governmental regulation. It was the dream, put most concisely, of "a society managed by enlightened private groups."[1] The story of the Half-Orphan Asylum's contacts with "enlightened private groups" such as the Chicago Council of Social Agencies indicates an urban version of this vision. Private managerial agencies would bring order to the system, coordinating all those agencies actually providing services to dependent children in Chicago, agencies that had grown up chaotically in the previous half-century.

In the long run, the managerial agencies would triumph. But during the 1920s, the weight of power still resided in the very decentralized service-providing agencies. Organizations like the Council of Social Agencies were themselves strapped for money; nor did they control the finances of orphanages like the Half-Orphan Asylum. Without any financial clout, managerial agencies could not push service-providing agencies very hard. A new system had emerged by the end of the 1920s, but it was not firmly in place, nor were the "enlightened private groups" even in control. The rapprochement between institutions like the Council of Social Agencies and the Half-Orphan Asylum was due in very large part to the very weak bargaining position of the former.

One result of this was that Chicago's orphanages got a new lease on life. What progressives had attacked at the turn of the century was tolerated by welfare elites in the 1920s. At the end of that decade, there were still over forty orphanages and industrial schools in the city. Inside those institutions, moreover, the new attitudes only translated piecemeal into new programs. As David Rothman has put it, conscience had to stand aside for convenience.[2] The pace of change was slow, one reason why some historians have assumed that places like the Half-Orphan Asylum were intransigent during the 1920s.[3] In fact, the managers were quite ready to listen to new ideas. The absence of concerted outside pressure far more than any internal reluctance lulled the asylum to its pace. Still, after 1910 a new spirit reigned in the orphanage. And in the last years of the twenties, things moved quickly. By 1930, the Half-Orphan Asylum was a different institution.

CHAPIN HALL

Progressives had complained loudly about private charities located in urban slums. The criticism, of course, was directly applicable to the Half-Orphan Asylum. By 1900, Chicago's Near North was crowded, decrepit, and unhealthy. Children at the asylum had little room to play. "Bad influences" lived literally next door. As early as 1902, the managers expressed hope of building a new asylum outside the city. As Mrs. Florence Martin of the Board of Managers noted in a letter to Azel Hatch, the managers wanted a "modern and sanitary home further from town where the children can have more freedom in out-of-door life and work."[4]

This certainly reflected progressive thinking. Those new institutions considered "advanced" at the turn of the century—Allendale Farm, the Ridge Farm Preventorium, for example—were often far from any urban morass. This marked a changed sense of where homes for dependent children should lie in the landscape. The Half-Orphan Asylum was built in the late 1860s at 1931 North Halsted to be part of a suburban setting, on the edge of the city, removed from the dense center, but not removed from the urban landscape. This itself was a shift away from an earlier belief that the asylum should be in the center of Chicago so that the families served could have easy access. Early twentieth-century progressives favored neither the city nor its edges. They argued for the country.

Like many managers of Chicago children's institutions, the women running the Half-Orphan Asylum agreed. They regularly expressed distaste for the North Halsted site and spoke of the "long cherished dream of removing our young and impressionable wards from a neighborhood which is daily becoming more congested both by population and traffic." A country setting, Julia Thompson noted in her 1912 Secretary's Report, would provide a good physical environment and then some: "The outdoor life, so necessary for the best development and growth of the young, would surely be of incalculable benefit, while the removal from the harsher sights and sounds of a thickly settled city neighborhood must be infinitely desirable on moral grounds."[5] Whatever problems the new system might cause for parents trying to visit children far from home were offset by the many benefits that would accrue.

The urge for a country home reflected an accommodation to progressive thinking but it also reinforced other commitments. Managers might have wanted to remove children from the city, but until 1912 they saw this as a means of maintaining the asylum ideal. The managers suggested moving to the country but not giving up the congregate living arrangements so

disliked by progressives. Moving out of the city was simply one more way
to cut the children off from the physical and moral dangers of Chicago.

Finally, the interest in a country asylum also reflected the changing life-
styles of the managers themselves. In the 1890s, the managers began moving from the city to wealthy North Shore suburbs. By 1910, 30 percent of
the managers no longer lived in Chicago. In the ensuing years, even more
managers moved north. The women who founded the Chicago Nursery
and Half-Orphan Asylum in the nineteenth century were committed urbanites. Their asylum was a direct response to the problems around them,
in a very real sense to their own problems. In the early twentieth century,
that slowly changed. Julia Watson Thompson, who wrote so passionately
in the Secretary's Reports about the benefits of country living, was herself
a denizen of Lake Forest, miles away from the poverty of Chicago. At the
same time that the managers began expressing their distaste for the urban
asylum, they were also beginning to cut their own personal ties to the city.

The managers began talking of a new asylum as early as 1902. But to
dream of a country home was not to construct one. For years, funds proved
elusive. In 1904, when the managers first broached the issue of a new
building with the male Board of Directors, the latter told the women it was
financially impossible. The directors agreed to help raise $6,000 to con-
struct another addition on the grounds. Even this money never mate-
rialized.[6]

In 1909, the managers again tried to convince the directors that a new
asylum was needed. This time they were successful. A joint committee was
set up to explore the possibility and raise the money. By October 1911,
enough money had been collected to buy some land. The Half-Orphan
Asylum purchased a partially wooded, ten-acre tract on Foster Avenue and
California Street, in the far northwest corner of the city. Although within
city limits, the area was all farmland, if developed at all. Looking in three
directions from the asylum's new land, one saw nothing but fields dotted
with sturdy oaks. Turning east, there was a modern and spacious common
school about a quarter of a mile away, but little else than farmland. One-
half mile past the school was Lincoln Avenue, which cut a path through the
open fields. The trolley ran down Lincoln so access to the city was assured.
The new asylum could be in the country but the children's parents could
still visit from Chicago.[7]

Buying new land, however, did not mean building a new asylum. At
least $150,000 had to be secured to finance the construction. In the next
few years, inflation kept the directors focused on maintaining the current
asylum instead of building a new one. In 1913, a joint committee of men
and women tried to raise money for a new building, but with only scattered

success. Moreover, once the war in Europe started in 1914, it seemed that all philanthropy for local projects dried up. Less than one-half of the $150,000 needed to begin the project had materialized.[8]

In 1914, more than ten years after the managers first began exploring a move to the country, the Half-Orphan Asylum remained in its cramped quarters in Chicago's north side ghetto. The difficulty in raising money was a direct reflection of the increased size of Chicago's philanthropic world and the changing place of the Half-Orphan Asylum within that world. In the late nineteenth century, the Half-Orphan Asylum had relied on its contacts in the managers' "home" neighborhood of the Near North side and with the business community at large. By the 1910s, that was no longer effective. The managers were spreading out. To be sure, old friends of the asylum, like the Donnelleys and the Bentleys, still gave money. But with so many more charities around, and with other, newer charities appearing to be more "advanced" or "progressive," it was increasingly difficult to attract donors who did not already have established ties to the orphanage.

Downtown contacts no longer generated the money they did in the late nineteenth century. There were now more fashionable charities to give to. The Commercial Club, the Women's Club, and benefactors like Julius Rosenwald and Cyrus McCormick gave hundreds of thousands of dollars in the early years of the century to "child saving" agencies. The bulk of this money went to build cottages at institutions outside the city. A place like the Illinois Industrial School for Boys, situated in rural Glenwood and with eight cottages already in place by 1900 (and no congregate dormitories), could in 1901 get $125,000 from the Commercial Club of Chicago to build more cottages as part of an effort to provide alternatives to placing boys out in western states. Similarly, once the Illinois Industrial School for Girls moved to Park Ridge in 1907, Julius Rosenwald paid for the first cottage built there.[9] Up to the very end of the 1890s, the Half-Orphan Asylum was able to attract some money from downtown business sources. But not after 1900. With little public profile, no connections to welfare progressives, and no track record of progressive reform, the asylum was locked out of the considerable amount of money donated to children's institutions.[10]

If new sources of money proved elusive, the asylum could still call on old sources. In October 1914, Mrs. Charles Chapin gave $70,000 to finance the new building. The Chapin family had long-standing ties to the asylum. Mrs. Chapin's late husband had served on the Board of Directors. His mother had been a charter member of the asylum in 1865. Mrs. Chapin's mother had served on the Board of Managers. At a key moment, the key money came not from the larger community of Chicago's wealthy, nor from sources outside the city, nor from a government agency or a noted progressive donor, but from a family with long ties to the Nursery and Half-Orphan Asylum. What saved the campaign was the asylum's carefully nurtured traditionalism.

The gift changed everything. Overnight, pledged donations jumped from $55,000 to $125,000. While it was still not enough for construction to begin, the gloom that had surrounded the fundraising campaign evaporated. The goal was in sight. By September of 1915 the $150,000 was there and the Board of Directors voted to break ground.[11]

A year later the new building was ready. In honor of the donation, it was named Chapin Hall.[12] By the first days of September, employees and managers were frantically working out final details. The children were just as excited about the new quarters. On September 30, 1916, the move was made. All involved felt a deep sense of accomplishment. The "removal of our household from our out-grown, yet dear old asylum on Burling Street, to our new building on Foster Avenue, standing in its own ten acres of land, looking across open fields to a visible horizon, with air and light and space on every side, is an achievement of which we are proud." Years later, Julia Thompson would remember 1916 as the most exciting year in the history of the asylum.[13]

They immediately took advantage of the new setting. Vegetable gardens were started; the older children took over their own plots. A "farmerette" was hired to give advice. On summer evenings groups of children went out for campfire suppers. The managers regularly spoke of the pleasures of a "free outdoor life" for the children and how lucky the asylum was that the move was "not only to more commodious quarters but to country surroundings." The women saw other benefits as well: "The location of our building, far removed from the center of the city, with fresh air and the freedom of a large grounds no doubt contributes largely to the good health of the family."[14]

The orphanage was not isolated for long. By the end of 1917, the Swedish Covenant Hospital broke ground directly across the street. In the early twenties, the first subdivision went up in the vicinity. Still, the area grew modestly during the 1920s and once the Depression came all new construction stopped. In 1935, the Chicago Council of Social Agencies noted that Chapin Hall was located "in a neighborhood where very little building has been done and there are wide open spaces on three sides of the institution."[15]

This was the norm for the city's institutionalized dependent children. The Council of Social Agency's *Social Service Directory* of 1930 lists space for 5,258 dependent children outside the city limits and only 1,441 inside, a figure that underestimates by roughly 400 the number of dependent minors living outside the city.[16] This was a radical reversal from 1900. While the number of institutions remained rather evenly split between city and country, those in the city tended to be very small neighborhood orphanages, caring for twenty to forty children. Of the eleven children's homes able to house more than 300 children in 1930, only one, the Orthodox Jewish Marks Nathan Orphanage, remained in the center of the city. All the major Catholic, Protestant, and nonsectarian institutions were like Chapin Hall—sometime in the thirty years after 1900 they left the urban squalor. After 1945 many of these "rural" institutions would become suburban; the few subdivisions around Chapin Hall were symptoms of what was to come. In 1930, however, institutionalized dependent children in Chicago largely lived in the country.

In 1912, one year after the land was bought and three years before building began, Chapin Hall's managers made a decision as momentous as the move itself. The women decided to adopt the cottage system. The resolution was the work of Mrs. Carroll Sudler, who became president of the asylum in 1911. It was a dramatic indication of the increasingly progressive spirit among the managing board after 1910. In the new buildings, the managers decided, children would not be housed in large congregate barracks; there would be no dormitories. The nineteenth-century asylum system would be abandoned. Instead, the managers planned a large administration building surrounded by four separate homelike cottages where the children would live supervised by housemothers.[17]

Yet to commit to the cottage system was not to adopt it. Again, money was the problem. Even with Mrs. Chapin's gift, the funds were simply not there. In 1916, the money available only allowed the managers to build a single building—Chapin Hall. When the children moved to Foster Avenue, they moved into the same sort of large dormitories they had lived in on Halsted Street.

The managers hoped that the cottages would be built soon, and by 1917, "one step" had been taken "by grouping ten of the older girls in the lower floor of one detached building under the care of a Matron." The girls had most of the amenities of a private home. They shared their bedrooms with only one or two others. They had private baths. The ten had their own living room. Except for their meals (the girls continued to eat in the congregate cafeteria in Chapin Hall), they lived separately in their "cottage." The managers thought it a rousing success: "The plan has worked so well in teaching the girls the pleasures and responsibilities of a separate dwelling that we are more desirous than ever of trying the plan with other groups. This will be possible when we can complete our original plan for four detached cottages."[18]

But despite the early excitement, nothing else was done. The wartime economy was the first barrier. Through 1920, the managers and directors were preoccupied with rapidly escalating costs. Inflation kept the managers off-balance, constantly worrying about short-term problems like weekly food budgets instead of the grander issue of constructing new buildings. Just as the asylum had relied upon old friends to financially anchor the campaign for Chapin Hall, it also looked to traditional supporters to ease the burdens of inflation: "Many an old subscriber doubled his annual subscription and almost everyone responded in some way."[19]

By the early 1920s, the managers and directors had weathered almost fifteen years of debilitating inflation. When the prosperity of the 1920s arrived, the directors thought more about how to plan against future inflation than how to find money to build another cottage. They began a fundraising campaign to increase the endowment. Once again, the cottages were put on hold.

Into the mid-twenties the managers were not unduly worried about the slow pace. While they were in principle committed to the cottage ideal, they did not see the congregate asylum as dramatically inferior. The 1925 annual report asserted that the asylum did "most earnestly try to avoid what is called Institutionalism . . . by keeping the children in small groups" but the same report also conceded that only one cottage was in operation. Yet, the report continued, the cottage system was for children who would spend years in an institution while the Half-Orphan Asylum served "those parents who are temporarily unable to maintain a home for their children." Children in the Half-Orphan Asylum generally came for short-term care; most went home relatively quickly. For children only briefly institutionalized, the less expensive old asylum system was not a weighty burden. "The cottage system, though theoretically admirable, is not a necessity with our changing numbers and is too expensive for an Institution not richly endowed."[20]

It was not that agitation for the cottage system had ceased. The city (and the nation) was filled with calls for more foster care, more mothers' aid pensions, more cottages, and fewer asylums. And progressive reformers, by the 1920s often ensconced somewhere in some new welfare bureaucracy, knew that there was only so much progress.[21] But they bided their time about it. As we shall see below, partisans of "modern" philanthropy devoted their energies to solidifying the citywide welfare system they had begun to create before the war. And they did this with the carrot instead of the stick. No pressure was put on an agency like the Half-

Orphan Asylum to change its practices. Rather, the managers were gently told, over and over and over again, how they might improve the asylum.

Through much of the 1920s, then, the managers vaguely spoke of the superiority of the cottage system while they also contended that the cottage system was unnecessary. And they rather insistently pointed out that they provided temporary care.[22] In 1928, however, the tone changed. "We have urgent need of a cottage for the older boys and extra endowment for its support," the asylum's 1929 report read.[23] The women had decided to act. They wanted another cottage, one for the older boys.

This decision, like so many others, was part of a wave of cottage building in Chicago children's institutions. Angel Guardian, to take one example, decided in 1928 to add ten new cottages to its plant.[24] The managers of the Half-Orphan Asylum began fundraising in 1928. By May 1929, there was enough money pledged to call a joint meeting of the male and female boards to discuss a new cottage. Unlike the campaign for Chapin Hall, however, in 1929 the women took charge. Julia Thompson headed the fundraising committee. Mrs. Carroll Sudler, the president of the Board of Managers, worked with the architects and builders.

Both were shrewd choices. Thompson had been an officer of the Board of Managers since 1902; younger women respected her enormously. She was perfectly suited to motivate others during the fundraising drive. Like Thompson, Sudler had been on the Board of Managers since the beginning of the century. She had been president of the asylum since 1911. The decision to adopt the cottage system was made under her auspices, during the first year of her presidency. Sudler was also like Thompson in that she had the drive to get the job done. When the first architects suggested a price far above what she wanted to pay, Sudler quickly fired them and secured a cheaper bid.

Of course, circumstances aided the women. The drive was undertaken at the height of 1920s prosperity. Thompson, who had lived in Lake Forest since before 1900, was able to cultivate her neighbors. The Donnelley family gave several thousand dollars. The names of Cyrus McCormick, William Wrigley Jr., and other wealthy Lake Forest residents turned up as donors.[25] The whole process moved very smoothly and very quickly. On September 27, 1929, the Board of Directors voted to start construction. Work actually began in December. Dedication ceremonies were held on October 6, 1930. The building was complete and free of debt.

All the attention was not directed to the new cottage. The girls' cottage was soon repaired and painted to look as good as the boys'. In 1929, the older cottage was also remodeled so that the girls could cook and eat by themselves. (Such facilities were built into the boys' cottage.) None of the cottage children had to eat in Chapin Hall's cafeteria. To complete the homelike settings, husband and wife teams were hired to manage each cottage. They lived with the children and disciplined them. The men taught the boys baseball and carpentry; the women helped the girls learn to sew.[26]

The activity, at least for a short time, energized the institution. It seemed to be a good omen for the future of the whole asylum. The new cottage freed up space inside Chapin Hall for other uses. The managers were elated. "The sight of twenty boys, living a homelike life under one roof is a reward of great merit," Mrs. Thompson wrote in the 1931 annual report. At the 1930 joint meeting of directors and managers, Mrs. Sudler spoke of the hope that the institution could make a "new start" with the "Boys' Cottage to inspire us."[27]

The managers believed that the new cottage represented a significant step toward the elimination of the old asylum system. The dream of cottages instead of dormitories, a dream almost two decades old by 1930, suddenly seemed to be within reach. As we shall see later in this chapter, this activity was actually part of a larger effort by the managers to fundamentally change the way the orphanage handled children. By the end of the 1920s, the managers wanted the whole nineteenth-century asylum system dismantled.

The commitment to the "progressive" system even extended to the institution's name. The old keyword—asylum—by the end of the 1920s had strong negative connotations, invoking something old and out-of-date. As early as 1928, the managers were looking into the possibility of changing the institution's name. Their first efforts were not followed up on, but six months after the new cottage opened the managers reopened the question. A committee of managers and alumni suggested "Foster Hall" after the new location, but the full Board of Managers decided that "Chapin Hall" was more appropriate. The male directors, however, vetoed the idea, because of legal technicalities. Although the name never officially changed, after 1932 the managers and staff simply ignored the old name, even in most official correspondence. Within a few years, many who knew the institution only casually would not even be aware that it was legally "The Chicago Nursery and Half-Orphan Asylum." The whole complex was simply known as "Chapin Hall."[28]

This sense of renewal and change at Chapin Hall was part of a wave of reform going on around the city between 1927 and 1932. All sorts of children's agencies were in the throes of experimentation. Many were convinced that the old system was on its way out. Not only, as already mentioned, was the Catholic orphanage Angel Guardian building new cottages. The Chicago Home for the Friendless and the Chicago Orphan Asylum both decided to devote themselves entirely to foster home programs. By 1932 neither institution was any longer an orphanage. Jewish charities as well were expanding their foster care programs in these years, one of a number of reforms that would eventually put the Orthodox (and old-fashioned) Marks Nathan Orphanage out of business. Similarly, in 1929 Father William Cummings, the head of Catholic Charities, announced that a primary goal of the organization was to keep poor women and children out of institutions.[29]

If at first Chapin Hall's new cottage appeared a harbinger of changes going on all around the city, those changes were not to come. By the end of 1931, a year after the new building opened, the directors and managers were cutting salaries, dismissing staff, and slashing services. The full weight of the Depression had hit Chapin Hall. Throughout the city, economic hard times crushed the bud of reform growing in the late twenties. During the 1930s at Chapin Hall, no move to expand the cottage system was made. By the time prosperity returned and the Second World War was over, changes both in the needs of dependent children and in the strategies of child welfare professionals created a whole new agenda for reform. By that time, progressive proposals were out-of-date; further talk of cottages obsolete.

Very few of Chapin Hall's children ever lived in cottages. In 1930, only 40 of the orphanage's 130 children did so. That ratio did not change.[30] The new cottage, rather than standing for a new beginning, actually stood as the apotheosis of the progressive agenda.

It also marked the apotheosis of a whole generation of leadership. Mrs. Carroll Sudler, who engineered the initial moves away from the asylum system in 1912 and who supervised the construction of the new cottage in 1929, stepped down as president in 1931. Julia Thompson, secretary of the board from 1902, gave up that post in 1932. Cyrus Bentley, who had served on the board since the early years of the century, died in 1930, shortly after giving $1,000 to help build the boys' cottage. In many ways, the cottage marked an end rather than a new beginning. But that was unclear at the time. There were many other changes in the air.

JOINING THE SYSTEM

In the nineteenth century, the Half-Orphan Asylum, like many of Chicago's Protestant charities, was entirely free of any bureaucratic entanglement. The parents dealt directly with the asylum; the money was all from private sources; there was no governmental oversight. The Chicago Nursery and Half-Orphan Asylum was an autonomous entity.

Progressives had attempted to create an urban welfare system, largely but not entirely outside the public sector, to rationalize and upgrade the delivery of services to Chicago's needy. At first, the Chicago Nursery and Half-Orphan Asylum resisted. But beginning around 1910 the rancor disappeared; managers and directors were soon advertising the asylum's ties to other agencies. By 1913, the orphanage had established a working relationship with the Cook County Juvenile Court and actively pursued the endorsement of the Chicago Association of Commerce. Within a few years regular business was conducted with the Illinois Department of Welfare, the Juvenile Protection Association of Chicago, the Immigrants' Protective League, the Illinois Children's Home and Aid Society, the City of Chicago Department of Health, and the Chicago Council of Social Agencies—all progressive creations. By 1930, services were also provided to the orphanage by the Court of Domestic Relations, the Institute for Juvenile Research, Allendale Farm, the Joint Services Bureau, the University of Chicago School of Social Service Administration, and United Charities of Chicago—again, all outgrowths of the progressive movement. Between 1910 and 1930, the way the Half-Orphan Asylum did business changed significantly. The orphanage became enmeshed in the large organizational nexus first envisioned by the progressives at the turn of the century. The experience of the Half-Orphan Asylum reflected the experience of practically every children's institution in the city.

One key way that the Half-Orphan Asylum changed was by coordinating its intake with other agencies. In the nineteenth century, children came to the asylum from three sources. First, parents came who were told about the asylum by others in their own neighborhood. Second, employers who were neighbors of the managers sometimes directed employees with family problems to the institution. Third, another agency might suggest the Half-Orphan Asylum as the best place for a particular child. This system was uncoordinated and ad hoc. Nowhere in the city was there an effective central clearinghouse to direct troubled families to the appropriate agencies.

As late as 1910, all the Half-Orphan Asylum's referrals were private. The orphanage only used Juvenile Court to get rid of unwanted children. The managers had turned down several offers by the Bureau of Charities (and later United Charities) to do all case investigations and to route the appropriate children to the Half-Orphan Asylum. The Chicago Nursery and Half-Orphan Asylum remained independent.

By 1913, however, the orphanage's promotional literature touted the "spirit of cooperation" that existed between the asylum and Juvenile Court. "Children are admitted to the institution through the agency of the

Court and those losing their surviving parent are sent to the Court for home-placing or adoption."[31] By the late teens and through the twenties, the Half-Orphan Asylum regularly accepted children from Juvenile Court, although the court did not help pay for children's upkeep until the 1930s. By the 1920s, the managers' wariness about the progressive institution was forgotten.[32]

Even at the end of the 1920s the number of referrals from Juvenile Court remained small, not reaching above 10 percent of the orphanage's population.[33] By the middle of that decade, the Half-Orphan Asylum also relied on private agencies to refer needy children. Most important was the Joint Service Bureau, a centralized intake and referral service created by the Council of Social Agencies in 1922 to coordinate Protestant institutions caring for dependent children.[34] Protestant families throughout the Chicago area who were unable to care for their children would visit the bureau, which in turn would route the children to the appropriate agency.

By the 1920s, institutions such as Juvenile Court and the Joint Service Bureau institutionalized a key progressive goal. These were citywide clearinghouses (both public and private) that directed child placement throughout the metropolitan area. By the 1920s, no longer did ministers, aldermen, or other neighborhood notables tell needy parents to go to particular agencies such as the Half-Orphan Asylum. Instead, poor parents needing help were directed to the Joint Service Bureau, or the Social Service Exchange, or one of several other referral agencies. These clearinghouses, with information about all child-care institutions in the metropolitan area, directed the parents to the home best suited to fill their needs. In the nineteenth century, by contrast, parents often had to move from asylum to asylum looking for help. (The Half-Orphan Asylum, for example, accepted approximately one in three applications in the late nineteenth century. Those families turned down for help had to search out another asylum.) For families in crisis, the progressive clearinghouses reduced the burden of finding aid.[35]

While the new system certainly mitigated the difficulties of families in need, its impact on the Half-Orphan Asylum should not be overestimated. At no time during the twenties and thirties did a majority of children come to Chapin Hall from a referral agency. At least half the children continued to enter because their parents brought them to the orphanage. And most of these parents picked the asylum themselves. It appears that in place of advice from neighborhood notables, by the 1920s the phone book played a key role in directing families to the Half-Orphan Asylum.

By the middle of the twenties, reliance on outside agencies for intake referrals was one reason that the number of applications to the asylum fell, a decline being experienced at the same time by other agencies throughout the city.[36] The Joint Service Bureau only sent children it thought appropriate, radically reducing the workload of the asylum's investigation committee, which in the nineteenth century was one of the hardest-working committees of the Board of Managers.

Becoming part of a citywide intake system also allowed the asylum to continue caring for infants under the age of two—something dear to the managers' hearts. The baleful effects of institutional life on infants were central to the progressive attack on the asylum system. Nothing was more passionately denounced. Progressives knew how many infants died in asylums; of all who might conceivably be institutionalized, progressives put infants last on the list.

Yet there were special cases. In particular, facilities were needed for short-term emergency care. There had to be a place equipped to handle infants if a parent unexpectedly died or suddenly became ill and no other relatives or friends could take the baby. The Half-Orphan Asylum by the late twenties was known throughout the city as one of the few orphanages that would care for children under two. In 1929, the Illinois Children's Home and Aid Society, the Joint Service Bureau, and the Visiting Nurse Association approached the Half-Orphan Asylum to expand their facilities to take care of the bulk of short-term emergency infant care for the whole city. The managers had mixed emotions. It was a service they cared about deeply yet it was the most expensive kind of care there was.

A year of negotiations followed before the managers agreed. In 1931 Chapin Hall became the central Chicago institution for emergency care of infants. Facilities were expanded and all the major clearinghouses of the city—the Children's Home and Aid Society, United Charities, Social Service Exchange, the Joint Service Bureau, as well as Catholic and Jewish placing agencies—looked to the Half-Orphan Asylum for this special service.[37]

The arrangement was under strain from the beginning. Within a year, the Depression forced the Half-Orphan Asylum to temporarily close down the infant nursery. Still, the negotiations of the late twenties are perfect examples of what progressives meant when they spoke of rationalizing the system, a good example of the spirit of reform in the air at the time. Referral agencies thoughout the city knew which agency could take infants for emergency care. Moreover, this rather specialized service was not duplicated. It was agreed that Chapin Hall and only Chapin Hall would do this work. Intake was made predictable; the system efficient.

Apart from coordinating intake, the umbrella agencies also induced the Half-Orphan Asylum to follow-up on children who had left the asylum.

Progressives had criticized asylums for failing to make sure that institutionalized children were discharged to a supportive home. In the early years of the century, Half-Orphan Asylum managers defended the absence of follow-up work on the basis of the institution's special mission—the orphanage only kept children for short periods of time, only accepted children from "worthy" families, and returned children to a parent. With intake so carefully guarded, the managers contended, there was no reason for systematic follow-up. Because "each child has a parent to whom he will eventually return," they argued in 1913, the orphanage was "not a home-finding society" and did not have "to deal with many of the more serious problems concerning the care and placing of dependent children."[38]

In November 1914, the Chicago Association of Commerce attacked the Half-Orphan Asylum's practice of dismissing children without investigating what kind of home was to be provided outside the asylum. The association had been rating Chicago charities since 1910. Unlike any earlier progressive attacks, the Half-Orphan Asylum's managers took the 1914 broadside very seriously. First, they placated the association by sending Henry Sweet (read: businessman, director, and male) to discuss the situation. More important, the women began to change the way children were discharged. In 1917, the Board of Managers created a Social Services Committee to monitor children after they left the asylum. This committee wound up being one of the most active committees of the mid-1920s, having the kind of work load that the Investigation Committee had in the nineteenth century.[39]

By the mid-twenties, Half-Orphan Asylum managers also used numerous outside agencies to either look after children who had left the orphanage or else to help find other institutional homes for those children no longer suited for the asylum. The Home Finding Society, Juvenile Court, the Juvenile Protective Association, the Children's Aid Society, and the Dependent Court, all creations of the Progressive Era, were among the agencies that performed such services for the Half-Orphan Asylum.[40] An alumni organization was started in 1925 to do the same. Children, girls in particular, who reached the asylum's age limit but who did not have satisfactory homes to return to were sometimes allowed to stay until suitable arrangements could be made.[41]

By 1930, children coming to the Half-Orphan Asylum no longer entered a single institution; they entered an urban welfare system. For the great bulk of dependent families, it made the task of finding initial help less time-consuming and emotionally taxing than it had been before. Other parents, on the other hand, found the new system a convenient way to neglect their children. Such children found themselves being passed from one agency to another by a "caring" but bureaucratic system. And finally, those few parents who got on the wrong side of the authorities found themselves battling with what seemed to them an administrative behemoth to free their children. The Half-Orphan Asylum had prided itself on not taking legal charge of children. By the end of the 1920s, however, the managers were very willing to use Juvenile Court to get custody when they were suspicious of parents.[42]

Joining the system not only meant coordinating the intake and outgo of children with other agencies, it also meant listening to the new experts. Before the war, this had meant listening to progressive reformers. By the 1920s, however, "expertise" was associated with those welfare professionals staffing organizations like the Chicago Council of Social Agencies (founded 1914) or the University of Chicago's School of Social Service Administration (founded 1920). One early example of how the institution began to rely upon the advice of reformers has already been cited—in 1912 the managers voted to adopt the cottage system. This was done, it was noted the next year, "in deference to the unanimous judgment of advisors trained in the solving of problems of dependent children."[43]

Another early sign of the new dependence on outside expertise was the decision to join the Chicago Council of Social Agencies in 1919. The council was created five years earlier to be a clearinghouse for the most advanced information on social work in Chicago. Some of the city's leading social workers were involved. Soon after its inception, such notables as Jane Addams, Louise de Koven Bowen, and Julius Rosenwald lent their names or gave their money to the group. The council also sponsored research on Chicago poverty and welfare by people like University of Chicago sociologist Ernest W. Burgess. It was not council policy to censure any particular institution; it simply provided the most "up-to-date" information on poverty, welfare, and social work. It functioned as a subtle propaganda machine for the progressive cause.[44]

By the 1920s, the Chicago Nursery and Half-Orphan Asylum was listening. After the asylum became a dues-paying member several managers regularly attended meetings. In 1922, two managers from the orphanage were designated permanent delegates to the council. When the council created the Joint Service Bureau in 1922 to help coordinate intake around the city, the Half-Orphan Asylum immediately began using it. In 1928, at the urging of the council, the Half-Orphan Asylum began keeping detailed case histories of all children who entered the orphanage. This information was available to other agencies and, conversely, the Half-Orphan Asylum made use of similar files compiled elsewhere, thus creating a coordinated information system on dependent children and their families. The

Half-Orphan Asylum even adopted the standardized forms recommended by the Council of Social Agencies.[45]

In 1928, after years of prompting by the council, the managers made a decision that ensured that the standardized forms would really include standardized information, the kind of information that council professionals wanted. The Half-Orphan Asylum hired its first professional social worker. This innovation, as like so much else in these years, was part of a massive change in institutions around the city. Social workers were being hired at all sorts of children's institutions—Protestant, Jewish, and Catholic—in the 1920s and early 1930s.[46]

The events involved in the Half-Orphan Asylum's decision to bring a social worker on staff illustrate very well what had replaced the informal neighborhood network of nineteenth-century Chicago social work, not only for the Half-Orphan Asylum but for dozens of other Protestant and Jewish organizations as well. In October 1927, the asylum agreed to hire Helen Hardy, a graduate of the University of Chicago School of Social Service Administration. Hardy was recommended to the managers by the Joint Service Bureau, an arm of the Council of Social Agencies. She had been recommended to the bureau, in turn, by her teacher, Edith Abbott of the university. Her salary, moreover, was initially paid by the university. The Half-Orphan Asylum had the advantage of a professional social worker without having the cost.[47]

From the beginning, the managers were very happy with Hardy's work. In January 1928, they hired her part-time, began paying her salary, and bought her a car to use for case investigations around the city. By April of that year, Hardy was hired full-time. Her responsibilities quickly grew; the managers had great trust in her judgment. By August, the managers let Hardy handle parents who were behind on payments. In December, she began investigating applications for admission without the board examining them first. While the managers retained final judgment about who would be in the Half-Orphan Asylum, the social worker had a large range of discretionary authority.[48]

There were other ways that outside judgment was relied upon. Even before 1910, the asylum had begun to make use of medical expertise offered by outside agencies.[49] In the ensuing years the asylum also came to rely on public agencies for psychiatric evaluations of children. By 1920, the Illinois Department of Public Welfare (founded 1905) routinely did such work for the asylum. So did the Juvenile Protective Association of Chicago (founded 1904). Both agencies (one public, the other private) were products of the high tide of progressivism. Both were staffed by partisan progressives. Into the 1920s, the president of the Juvenile Protective

Association was Louise de Koven Bowen, one of the city's key progressives working in the field of dependent children. Also serving on the board were Jane Addams and University of Chicago psychology professor James Angell, another prominent reformer. But by 1920, more staid men, usually from Chicago's business community, were also on the board, one sign that the tensions between progressives and other philanthropists had abated. Cyrus Bentley was one of the conservatives who served. Bentley was also on the Board of Directors of the Half-Orphan Asylum; his wife for a time was president of the orphanage.[50]

In retrospect, the advice was only as good as the expertise. Letters from the late teens reflect the rather haughty biological determinism of that era's psychology. Racist themes run through the letters, as in one evaluation from the Department of Public Welfare's Juvenile Psychopathic Institute: "The family history indicates that he comes of poor stock. The physical examination reveals evidence . . . of defective mental development [such as] smaller head circumference than is normal for a child of his age."[51] Still, when the theory changed in the late twenties, so did the Half-Orphan's assessments of their own children.

Relying on outside expertise put the orphanage under the experts' tutelage. And there lies the crux of the matter. The changes that made the Half-Orphan Asylum part of a complex urban welfare system also undermined the orphanage's carefully wrought autonomy. Becoming up-to-date and progressive subtly bred dependence. The asylum found itself enmeshed in a large bureaucratic web. Moreover, it developed the need for expert guidance in negotiating the system.

Chicago by the late twenties had developed two distinct kinds of welfare institutions—those providing care and those coordinating the system. The latter devised policy, did research, trained social workers, and managed the care-providing agencies. Rarely, however, did they deliver any direct services to the needy. Examples of these coordinating or umbrella agencies include the Chicago Council of Social Agencies (founded 1914), United Charities (1909), the Joint Service Bureau (1922), and the University of Chicago School of Social Service Administration (1920). By the 1920s, these institutions were all run by women and men who had been a part of the progressive movement. Care-providing institutions, on the other hand, were like Chapin Hall. They provided services to clients. Their job was to help children and families one at a time.

Chapin Hall became involved with public agencies as well, but they provided services for the children instead of guidance for the program. As a result, the nascent regulatory system that emerged in the 1920s was dominated by private agencies, not public, a phenomenon that would shape child welfare in Chicago for the next half-century. Institutions without any ongoing accountability to the public would wind up regulating agencies like Chapin Hall.

When Chapin Hall and like-minded service agencies became involved with the new coordinating institutions, there was little sense that dependency would result. Yet, by agreeing to let central agencies define intake, or train staff, or set agendas, that is what eventually happened. By the end of the 1920s, the women serving on Chapin Hall's Board of Managers no longer trusted their instincts in the same way that the women who ran the asylum in the nineteenth century had. The earlier managers had both set policy and managed the orphanage. Now those tasks began to split. The modern Board of Managers did not discuss among themselves in their neighborhood the best ways to run the asylum. They increasingly relied upon outside judgment. Divorcing policy making from care providing was still another change that had enormous consequences for the whole urban welfare system into the 1980s.

Why did the managers agree to undermine the autonomy they had so carefully worked to preserve? Various reasons. The country's general fascination with expertise during the 1920s should not be overlooked. The women, like many Americans, were fascinated by the image of the technical expert.

Beyond that there were local considerations. Most important was the fact that the umbrella agencies did not seem so very threatening. Through the 1920s, the Half-Orphan Asylum gave up no legal prerogatives. It was not forced to do anything. Reform was to proceed at the asylum's pace. No longer did Juvenile Court ask that the orphanage take whatever child was sent. Now the court gratefully accepted Chapin Hall's help but left the orphanage free to refuse those children the managers thought did not belong. Similarly, the Council of Social Agencies did not publicly criticize any agency, unlike the practice of the Bureau of Charities at the turn of the century.[52] None of the coordinating agencies that Chapin Hall dealt with—not Juvenile Court, United Charities, or the Council of Social Agencies—tried to twist the arm of the orphanage to change its practice. Rather, they encouraged the orphanage to become part of an urban welfare system. The managers did not mind joining this system because it seemed so benign.

In the 1920s, the child welfare committee of the Council of Social Agencies (CSA) worked on a number of worthwhile projects, but forcing change in institutions was not one of them.[53] A 1923 suggestion to have the council sponsor a public debate on the relative merits of foster care versus institutionalization was quickly and firmly squashed. It was thought that such a debate would antagonize local agencies like Chapin Hall. The next year when the director of the Child Welfare League of America came to talk at the council, he spoke of a new sense of responsibility in the country's orphanages. In 1929, Ethel Verry, a CSA staff person, spoke of the "marked change" in Chicago's children's institutions. The widespread hiring of social workers meant increasing individual treatment and better understanding of community needs. During the 1920s, the council was quite supportive of children's agencies.[54]

At the turn of the century, progressive reformers had tried to do two things—rationalize the system and reform the nature of care. The first entailed creating effective citywide bureaucracies and the second, changing what happened to each dependent child. In the 1920s, the umbrella agencies, led by the Council of Social Agencies and the University of Chicago School of Social Service Administration, focused on building the urban welfare network. As a consequence, they readily accepted piecemeal reform of services. While the welfare reform continued in the 1920s, affecting institutions like the Half-Orphan Asylum, the movement was altered in tone, becoming more subdued and given to bureaucratic imperatives.

The umbrella agencies were very reluctant to criticize serviceproviding agencies because they were in no position to force change. All were still on shaky financial footing. The Council of Social Agencies came to Chapin Hall (and other agencies) in 1925 to keep the Joint Service Bureau from going broke. From that year on, member agencies donated annually to the council. Yet these were not dues paid for vital services. Each year the council had to come back to the agencies (including Chapin Hall), hat in hand, to beg the money needed to survive. Such an agency was not in the position to force the Half-Orphan Asylum to do anything. Attacking agencies like Chapin Hall could very well have spelled the death of any citywide coordination of intake, something which had demonstrably helped working-class families in need.

The one pressure point left by the progressives was well chosen. The decision to systematically follow-up on children leaving the Half-Orphan Asylum came in 1914 after the orphanage was criticized by Chicago's Association of Commerce, a group that had been rating charities since 1910. Prior to that, the Chicago Bureau of Charities had rated institutions since 1899. The bureau (renamed United Charities in 1909) was the single most important private progressive organization devoted to welfare reform. Yet in 1907, the bureau itself was strongly criticized for its ratings, as it depended on the same philanthropic sources for its income as did the charities it rated. Conflict of interest was charged. Bureau leaders began looking for someone else to do the job, and in 1910 they turned it over to the Association of Commerce, then dominated by businessmen progressives.

Since most private agencies were dependent upon money from the business community, a poor rating from the association could have disastrous results. The business group's ratings proved to be far more potent than those of United Charities. In 1914, the Half-Orphan Asylum stood up and noticed when the chamber criticized it. Fear of the chamber's displeasure edged the Half-Orphan Asylum into the urban welfare system.

An interlocking network of private agencies—the Association of Commerce, the Council of Social Agencies, the University of Chicago School of Social Service Administration—emerged in the 1910s and 1920s to manage the dozens of private children's orphanages and industrial schools scattered around the city. Here was the start of a system of "enlightened private groups" managing child welfare in Chicago. But without any grip on the finances of the private agencies, what could be done was limited. The success of the Association of Commerce in 1914 was due to its perceived ability to affect purse strings. The weakness of the Council of Social Agencies in the next decade was just as much due to its inability to affect the finances of the private agencies.

It would be wrong to say a "regulatory" system emerged in the 1920s. The umbrella agencies had to depend upon cultivating good relations with the Chapin Halls of the city, of gently prodding them to make change. Even at the close of the 1920s, institutions created a generation earlier by progressive reformers still did not have the clout to impose their will on agencies like Chapin Hall. It is not at all surprising that the Council of Social Agencies and the School of Social Service Administration primarily tried to build a coordinated child welfare system in the 1920s instead of trying to force changes in the actual services provided to children. You can't manage agencies that don't belong to your system.

But as a consequence, the orphanage continued to thrive. In 1930, there were still forty-five orphanages and industrial schools in the Chicago area. (The practical distinction between these institutional types effectively broke down after 1910. Almost all, regardless of what they were called, were like Chapin Hall in accepting children from two to sixteen years of age. Almost all had some training programs.) Eleven orphanages still housed more than 300 children. Another eleven (including Chapin Hall) accommodated between one and two hundred. While there was some decline in the number of children institutionalized, the orphanage still lived on.[55]

FROM PRAYING TO PLAYING—THE
SOFTENING OF CARE

Yet it was, increasingly, a new sort of orphanage. One of the most dramatic ways that the progressive ethos affected Chapin Hall was through the adoption of a distinctly "modern" attitude toward the children. The tough-mindedness of the early twentieth century disappeared. Indeed, the whole nineteenth-century tradition of child care was swept away. How to get children to enjoy themselves became a pressing issue for managers and staff. The deep-felt religiosity of the asylum sank from view. Children were encouraged to play with others in the neighborhood; by the end of the twenties the asylum ideal was dead. Managers and staff, relying on social-work theories of "individualization," tried to bury all vestiges of Victorianism. New theory gave birth to new tenderness.

Here too Chapin Hall was reflective of changes happening in a number of Chicago's orphanages. The exact moment of change varied enormously from institution to institution, and clearly the Catholic and Jewish Orthodox orphanages lagged behind the Protestant and Reformed Jewish institutions.[56] It is very difficult to say exactly how many institutions had made the sorts of changes found at Chapin Hall, but it is clear that it was a trend. Whatever the pace of change, between 1910 and the 1930s, various (but certainly not all) Chicago orphanages began relating to their children quite differently. The sterner moralism was waning.

As with the other changes at Chapin Hall, the new approach toward children sometimes seemed to make only glacial headway. The diminishing influence of religion provides one example. As late as 1900, manager meetings regularly began with a prayer. Children said prayers when they got up, at all meals, and when they went to sleep. There was a Sunday service, Sunday school, and a religious service in the middle of the week. Matrons and schoolteachers were hired only if they had the requisite Protestant zeal.

In the next few decades, however, the heavy religiosity diminished. Managers' prayers were the first to go. After 1905, they are no longer mentioned in the minutes. Over the years, the staff and managers put less and less emphasis on the religious convictions of parents or children. By the 1920s, religion played no significant role in the day-to-day management of children, a major change from the nineteenth century. Still, many of the formalities remained. As late as 1923, young women from the Moody Bible Institute came to teach Sunday school and conduct a midweek prayer service. Each Sunday, children and staff attended Bowmanville Congregational Church. By the end of the decade, however, only one Sunday service was required and the midweek prayer service was gone. By 1929, the managers pointed proudly to the parties the children attended at Bowmanville Congregational.[57] When the Illinois Department of Public Welfare inspected Chapin Hall in 1932, it found only a nominal commitment to Protestantism. Three years later the Chicago Council of Social Agencies said of the institution: "No religious services except grace at meals." Children were not even required to attend church on Sunday.[58]

In the place of religion was play. By the early twenties, managers and staff gave increased attention to the children's recreation. This was, in fact, a reflection of contemporary child welfare theory. Play, from the progressive period on, increasingly became central to social psychologists, reformers, and others who thought about child development. In the early years of the century, the interest was often tied to a stern moralism. As Jane Addams argued in *The Spirit of Youth and the City Streets,* children must be taught the right kinds of recreation to keep them from turning to that morally debilitating leisure found in dance halls, taverns, or movie theaters. Urban playgrounds were one result of the early interest in children's play.

In the 1920s, theorists continued to contrast healthy children who enjoyed socially sanctioned play with juvenile delinquents. And while some of the moralizing about activities like movie-going or dancing softened, it did not disappear entirely. Play was considered central to developing a rounded personality. Through play children could both indulge their individual interests and learn to interact with others. By the middle of the decade, a whole literature on play had been spawned. Books with titles like *Play in Education, The Play Movement and Its Significance,* and *Wholesome Citizens and Spare Time* all attested to the social import of play. The movement, indeed, reached beyond educators, psychologists, and child welfare professionals. Henry Ford introduced the forty-hour work week in the twenties, stressing the importance of leisure to a productive and happy workforce.[59]

Within the Half-Orphan Asylum, a host of changes reflected the new sensibility. By 1922, the children were being taken on outings to Ravinia Park each summer. By 1923, an arrangement had been worked out with the local movie theaters to get the children in free. In 1924, the older boys and girls began to be sent to summer camp in Michigan.[60]

From 1926, the pace of change quickened. In February, the managers brought in a "recreation specialist" from Hull House to evaluate their program. On her suggestion, a baseball instructor was hired the next month for the boys. In April, a choral group was formed among the children. That November, a singing instructor was hired to lead the group. The choral group became one of the most beloved institutions at the asylum. For nearly four decades it was thoroughly enjoyed by managers, staff, and children. By the 1930s a high point of each Christmas season would be a downtown performance by the choral group that was usually broadcast on radio. The Hull House consultant also suggested in 1926 that a full-time play director be hired to manage recreation. While this was not done, a credentialed expert was hired during July and August of that year, while the children were out of school.[61]

Other innovations appeared in the next few years. In 1928, the managers hired a summertime play director for the boys.[62] Although this was supposed to be an annual practice, the Depression soon put an end to it. Also in the late twenties, some of the older girls joined a neighborhood Girl Scout troop. By that time the children were being encouraged to develop friendships outside the asylum. In 1929, the children began receiving a weekly allowance and the girls' cottage was given a radio. (When the boys' cottage opened in 1930 it also had a radio.) In May of 1929 a baseball diamond was built on the grounds. The next winter, the younger boys were taught carpentry.[63]

In December 1927, a Winnetka educator attended the Board of Managers meeting to sing the praises of the newest form of organized recreation for younger children—the nursery school. The nursery school movement of the 1920s was an extension of the kindergarten movement of the progressive years. Both were meant to provide structured support for young children, socializing and developing skills at the same time. The managers were convinced. "We are expecting to install very soon in the house a Nursery School with the newest and most approved methods of teaching and amusing very young children," they reported the next month. By March 1928, a temporary teacher had been hired and the needed equipment ordered. The school opened in April; all the asylum's two- to four-year-olds attended. In October a full-time teacher was hired. "This comparatively new system of training the very young is of undeniable value," the Secretary's Report of 1929 asserted.[64]

In those same years, the strictest policies left from the nineteenth century disappeared. In 1929, vacation policy was liberalized. Parents no longer needed clearance from the Board of Managers to take their children on a vacation. By 1930, mandatory short haircuts for both boys and girls were a thing of the past. So too were uniforms. Children brought clothes from home and when new clothes had to be bought the older children picked out their own. These changes reflect diminished fear of disease as much as the new attitude toward children. The policies on haircuts and clothes also reflect the desire of the managers and staff to integrate the children into the community. The children in Chapin Hall were being encouraged to play with neighborhood children; now they would look like them as well. The child's identity ideally would be bound to his or her peer group instead of the orphanage.

Another change of the late twenties, however, was a pure sign of a softened attitude toward children. In 1928, the managers voted to allow children to talk at meals. The enforced silence, which must have been one of the hardest things about living in the asylum for children three to ten years old, was eliminated.[65]

Coupled with all the changes of the late twenties was a new self-consciousness about the importance of recreation. Although children attended movies since 1923, it was only in the 1927 annual report that the practice was noted, with Julia Thompson stating that children need to enjoy the "leading diversion of modern youth." The next year the annual report observed that "the evidences that recreation and healthful play are not omitted from life in the Institution are too abundant to be completely designated in a brief report." Among the activities mentioned were singing and dancing lessons, picnics, hikes, holidays, summer camps, movies, and plays.[66]

The recreation, of course, was not for its own sake. It was designed to do a number of things. In the theory of the day, it was supposed to foster individuality. When social-work theorists of the 1920s contrasted the oppressive congregate living of nineteenth-century asylums with more relaxed, progressive institutions, they did so to contrast the rigid conformity of the former with the individuality nurtured by the latter. Play was key to the new approach, a way of allowing children to creatively develop a sense of self.[67]

The play, however, would have to be *structured* play. Play directors were important because undisciplined play led to disastrous results. Well-directed play would socialize children as well as foster individuality. George Mangold argued in *Problems of Child Welfare* (1924) that play was "a most important school of citizenship, and the social results which follow are expressed in such ethical values as order, obedience, self-denial, and discipline." But this did not mean that individuality would suffocate. Mangold suggested that organized play encouraged "self-repression" (which was good), not "self-effacement" (which was bad).[68] Structured recreation would nurture both the sense of self and social responsibility that Protestant moralism did before 1900.

Chapin Hall's recreational smorgasbord clearly reflected contemporary assumptions. Play was not simply frivolous release (although there needed to be an element of that); it rather contributed to individualization and socialization. As for developing individuality, it was important that the children choose their own activities and that their play allow them to develop talents they could take pride in. At the same time, play socialized children by teaching them to interact with peers both from the orphanage and the neighborhood.

The specifics reflect the ends. Baseball, Girl Scouts, the nursery school—each allowed children to enjoy themselves, cultivate personal interests, and learn to get along with others. Even going to the movies contributed, the staff thought, by giving the half-orphans the same cultural baggage that "normal" children had. Indeed, the recreational movement was designed to nurture "normal" children—kids who did not "feel" different.

By 1932, the recreational emphasis was reflected in hiring policy. For the first time, expertise was more important than religiosity. The managers hired a new superintendent that year, Mabel Morrow.[69] Morrow was the first person with some training in social work to hold that post. While she did not have a degree (something which became an issue in the 1940s), she had taken classes in recreation therapy. The 1932 state evaluation of the orphanage indicates Morrow's distrust of the old refuge ideal and her commitment to modern theory: "It is the feeling of the superintendent, who is a trained recreational worker, that the children have in the past been welded too much into one group. She has attempted to break this up and to get the children identified with groups in the neighborhood, which will give them opportunity to express their primary individual interest." Three years later, the Council of Social Agencies noted the same: "The underlying philosophy [of Chapin Hall] is to integrate the children's recreational activities into the community as a whole, rather than to set up an isolated program within the institution itself."[70]

The principal of Budlong School, the public school that Chapin Hall children attended, also testified to the benevolence of the new approach. In the early 1930s, she spoke at length to an investigator from the Chicago Council of Social Agencies who later reported that the principal "believes that there must have been a change in the institution from a rather strict regime for the children to that of greater understanding and freedom for expression of individual personalities." The principal noted that "in former years Chapin Hall children . . . always appeared to be well cared for and well dressed, [but] they presented difficulties because of an apparent lack of emotional stability; they were timid, shy and easily frightened." All this reflects the effects of the "tough-minded" discipline of the early twentieth century.

At present, however, the principal thought, "Chapin Hall children not only appear well dressed and cared for, but do not stand out in the group and . . . present no difficulties other than found in an average group of children, from average houses." The principal worked closely with Chapin Hall's superintendent and social worker when any half-orphan caused trouble in school. Because of this, she felt she knew how Chapin Hall was managed. She believed that "the increased ease with which the institution's children are assimilated in the total group as being due to the extention [sic] of the play spirit within the institution."[71]

THE NEW INSTITUTION AND SENSE OF FAMILY

The changes at Chapin Hall in the teens and twenties tell one version of a story going on in a number of Chicago children's homes. A wide array of piecemeal changes were bringing the city's orphanages into an integrated urban system. Social workers, coordinated intake, the cottage system—all these were happening throughout the city.

Yet if the general direction was clear, it is very hazardous to generalize about how far the collective move was. Chapin Hall developed an extensive recreation program in the late twenties; other orphanages did nothing. On the other hand, Angel Guardian built five new cottages in the late 1920s; Chapin Hall built one. What was "progressive" to Chapin Hall, a social worker and new cottage, was irrelevant elsewhere. The Home for the Friendless and the Chicago Orphan Asylum closed their orphanages and refounded themselves as foster home placing organizations. Such a radically deinstitutionalizing idea was never contemplated at Chapin Hall. What should be stressed about children's institutions in the city at large is the general story of Chapin Hall as opposed to any of its particulars: Change was slow, much of the old remained, but there was a new ethos emerging.

This new ethos was very real. The key goals of the nineteenth-century Half-Orphan Asylum were refuge, religion, and relief. By 1930 those goals were no more. No longer was the orphanage supposed to be an asylum from the world outside. Now children were encouraged to integrate themselves into the neighborhood. Recreation replaced religion as the key means of socialization. The play policy was also a sign that the managers no longer saw Chapin Hall as a custodial institution, one that simply provided temporary relief. Now the orphanage would help mold the personalities of the children under care.

The nineteenth-century orphanage thought in terms of saving families. It was not simply serving dependent children; it served needy families. By the late 1920s the managers of the asylum saw the children as individuals separate from their parents. Managers felt a direct responsibility for the larger nurturance of the children under their care and were willing to move to take legal custody of children if they thought the parents were not fit.

The nineteenth-century managers, on the other hand, saw themselves as running a place where the working poor facing a crisis could leave their children for a short period of time. "Family" was an absolutely key value to the nineteenth-century managers, but "family" was something that happened elsewhere—in a home, not an asylum. By the 1920s and 1930s, however, the managers increasingly saw Chapin Hall as providing a substitute home. The commitment to cottages, the "hiding" of the old name, breaking the children up into smaller groups, the new recreational activities, the hope that children would find friends in the neighborhood —all this reflected the new sense that it was the job of an orphanage to simulate a "normal," family-like environment. Quite simply, a children's institution should now be a "home," not an "asylum."

Harriet Kemper, the orphanage's superintendent between 1916 and 1921, articulated the new viewpoint well. "The dormitory you have charge of is your home," she wrote to her matrons while recouping from an illness. "You are here to show these children how a home should be kept." Children had to learn "home duties" at the orphanage, she added later in the letter. "We are working with the melting pot"; it was their job to make "American citizens." As we shall see in the next chapter, the notion of children as individuals and the sense of the institution as "family" were connected to new fears about what sort of parents were bringing their children to Chapin Hall.[72]

The changes at the institution were large. The new social worker, the reliance on the outside agencies, even the change of name to Chapin Hall were all signs of the effort to do away with the asylum ideal. The managers by the late twenties were keenly interested in adopting all "progressive" methods. Yet the Depression would interfere. Very soon Chapin Hall would find itself tested. And the implications of the new dependency would become painfully obvious.

The Chicago Nursery and Half-Orphan Asylum presented itself to the public in very different ways over the years. The history of its visual representations are one guide to its changing sense of purpose. The above is an unpublished photo taken in the 1890s showing three girls in their orphanage uniform. Chapin Hall Center for Children at the University of Chicago.

CHICAGO

Nursery Half-Orphan

ASYLUM.

INCORPORATED 1860.

TWENTY-THIRD ANNUAL REPORT.

CHICAGO:
THE J. M. W. JONES STATIONERY AND PRINTING COMPANY.
1884.

In the late nineteenth century, the orphanage was unhesitatingly portrayed as an institution. It was an asylum, not a home. This drawing of the building put up in 1871 appeared on the cover of the annual report for about twenty years. The right side of the building is the addition of 1884. When using photos became feasible in the 1890s, this same picture, right down to the angle, was reproduced in the annual reports as a photograph. The picture was last printed in 1906, a time when progressive reformers were sharply attacking congregate institutions. It was now counterproductive to advertise the building. Chicago Historical Society.

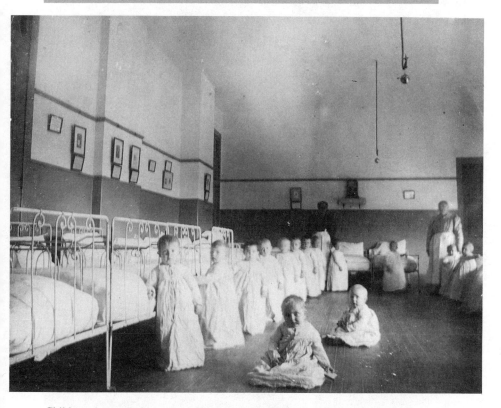

Children also were pictured as being in an institution. That these babies were in a congregate nursery was no source of shame to the Half-Orphan Asylum. This picture ran in the annual reports between 1895 and 1904, one sign of the distance of the asylum's managers from the ethos of progressive reformers. Chapin Hall Center for Children at the University of Chicago.

Older children, too, were portrayed as living in a group. These pictures also ran in the annual reports between 1899 and 1904. It was a portrait of collective, Protestant living. Chapin Hall Center for Children at the University of Chicago.

The edifice at Foster and California, completed in 1916, put a different face on the Half-Orphan Asylum. The building was a large, integrated structure, but the staggered front suggested (and was meant to suggest) a series of "cottages" rather than a single institution. The long grassy foreground, moreover, hinted at the country setting, a real concern to the philanthropic community. The 1920s shift in visual representation parallels the 1930 name change from the Chicago Nursery and Half-Orphan Asylum to Chapin Hall. This picture was published in the annual reports of the orphanage during the 1920s and 1930s. Chicago Historical Society.

By the 1930s, the children were also being portrayed differently. Group shots disappeared, as did any representation of congregate living quarters. Instead, apropos of the new emphasis on recreation, Chapin Hall literature was filled with staged shots of children having fun, of "average" kids living a "normal" life. No longer an asylum separate from the community, the new institution tried to replicate the community norm. Chicago Historical Society

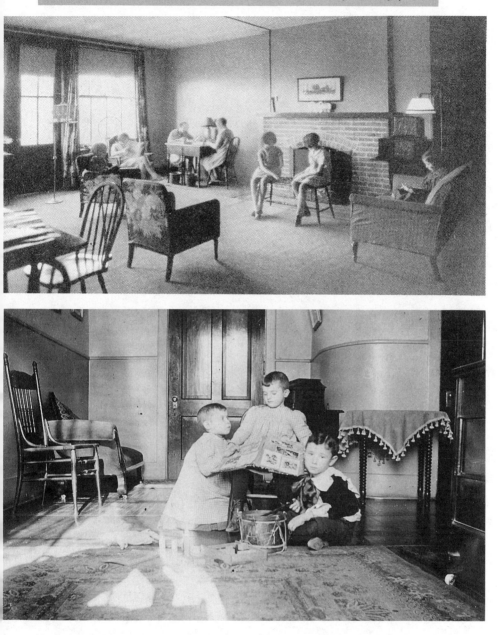

That these pictures represented a new sense of the children is given more weight by the fact that the same sorts of shots—staged pictures of small groups of kids playing—were taken in the 1890s. The bottom picture is one example. At that time, however, such pictures were never published. Only when congregate living was no longer the ideal did this sort of picture get printed in promotional literature. The top picture is an example, published in the 1930s annual reports. (Top) Chicago Historical Society. (Bottom) Chapin Hall Center for Children at the University of Chicago.

The shattered child. As the professional staff took over the preparation of promotional literature after World War II, the representation of children at Chapin Hall shifted once again. The tones of this eight-page, 1973 fund-raising pamphlet are all dark; a sense of menace surrounds the children. Not Protestant kids living in a group, not average kids playing—these were children at risk. Chapin Hall Center for Children at the University of Chicago.

Volunteerism. This ink drawing, from a 1960s fund-raising pamphlet, is actually part of a style developed by managers in the late forties, at the moment the professionals were moving to the center of the asylum. While the professionals portrayed children in trouble, the volunteer managers continued to picture the children in warm ways, far closer to the "normalcy" motifs important in the 1930s. The almost self-conscious amateurism of these drawings, especially when contrasted with the professionals' portrayal, hints at the growing gap between the professionals and the managers after the war. Chapin Hall Center for Children at the University of Chicago.

The invisible managers—Victorian and modern. Despite their critical importance over the years, the managers resolutely avoided presenting themselves in any Chapin Hall literature. *Above*, a president and vice-president of the Board of Managers in the 1890s. They cannot be identified. *Left*, is of Clarissa Haffner, one of the more important post–World War II managers. Chapin Hall Center for Children at the University of Chicago.

∽ *CHAPTER FOUR* ∾

The End of the Nineteenth Century, 1920–1945

I N THE 1920s AND 1930s, THE NINETEENTH-CENTURY system broke down irretrievably. Subtle, hidden changes were underway at Chapin Hall, changes not fully recognized or understood at the time. Yet they would have as profound an effect on the institution as the new policies described in the last chapter. By the end of the 1940s, the whole configuration of problems that led to the creation of the Chicago Nursery and Half-Orphan Asylum in the mid-nineteenth century was gone. The number of orphans had dropped to almost zero. Rank poverty no longer brought children to the door. Wealthy women were losing the interest and confidence to do volunteer work. The Depression began altering funding patterns. Distantly conceived welfare policy changed the kind of family needing Chapin Hall's help. On every point—the managers, the money, the children—the old system was disappearing. Large demographic, political, and economic forces laid it to ruin.

Such changes, obviously, affected orphanages throughout the city, indeed, across the nation.[1] It was not only that structural changes were making the nineteenth-century orphanage obsolete. The progressive vision of how dependent children should be cared for that was imagined at the turn of the century was itself meant to address nineteenth-century problems. The new regime introduced at orphanages like Chapin Hall in the early decades of the century collided with the changing needs of children. Upon adoption of the progressive agenda, intake was not monitored as it was before. No one distinguished between "worthy" and "unworthy" parents. At Chapin Hall, children began staying for years, something very rare in the nineteenth century. Less and less was the agency providing temporary care. Welfare professionals by the 1940s were noting this as a fact for orphanages in general.[2] Chapin Hall provides a good example of how or-

93

phanages, with progressive programs actually in place, brought children into a warm but unstructured environment.

Coupled with the increasing mismatch between child and program was the continued inability of the forces of managerial rationality to bring the private, service-providing agencies into line. The various orphanages scattered across the city stubbornly defied takeover, although the Depression gave the welfare managers a wedge that they would use very effectively after World War II. In the mid-thirties, however, Chapin Hall and other children's agencies deflected the efforts of the Council of Social Agencies and the newly created Community Fund to take over management of Chicago child welfare.

By the time of the Second World War, then, the progressive program was seemingly out-of-date while progressive management by private bureaucracies was not yet effectively in place. The result was drift.

THE NEW DEPENDENTS

During the 1920s and early 1930s, the number of children in Chapin Hall gently declined. Even the Depression did not occasion any increase. In 1918, some 165 children lived at Chapin Hall. By 1934, the average number was 132, the number hovering there through the 1940s.[3] What needs to be explained is why the decline occurred, why it was so small, and what it did to Chapin Hall.

The decrease in the 1920s was indicative of similar trends throughout the city and state. Between 1923 and 1933 the number of institutionalized dependent children in Illinois fell by 8.5 percent. While comparative statistics are not available for later years, it is clear that the number of children in institutions continued to decline until the outbreak of World War II.[4]

One important change was the increasing number of children living in foster homes. Illinois, as late as 1923, had fewer children in foster homes than any other major industrial state. The ratio was 5:1 in favor of institutions. By 1933, Illinois' institution / foster care ratio was 2:1.[5] Through the 1930s, the number of children in foster homes continued to grow while the number of children in institutions continued to drop.

Even with the advances of the 1920s, however, Illinois foster care lagged behind that of other industrial states.[6] Nor did the city seem particularly advanced. In 1936, about 50 percent of Chicago's dependent children were still in institutions, while only 37.9 percent were in Los Angeles, 19.3 percent in Cleveland, and 14.5 percent in Detroit.[7] The differences can be attributed to one overriding factor—the relative stinginess of state officials in paying foster parents.[8] While the increase in foster care helps explain why the number of children in institutions like Chapin Hall declined after 1920, the slowness of the expansion of foster care also helps explain why Chapin Hall's population did not decrease more dramatically.

Foster care did not radically reduce the population of institutions for another reason. The increase in foster parenting largely served to expand the number of children formally involved with the welfare system rather than shift population from institutions to homes. In other words, the slow rise of foster care offered more dependent children some assistance; it did not, except marginally, decrease the number of children in places like Chapin Hall.

The same is true of mothers' aid. Illinois passed mothers' aid legislation in 1911, the first state in the nation to do so. Over the next three decades the numbers of dependent children receiving this help steadily rose. By 1933, an estimated 15,452 children were receiving benefits. By 1940, an estimated 17,000 Illinois children were getting aid.[9] Yet here too, the increase did not lead to deinstitutionalization. Between 1910 and 1933, the number of dependent children receiving some kind of help in Illinois more than doubled, with mothers' aid accounting for almost all of the increase. Yet in those same years, the number of children in institutions did not decline at all.[10]

State policy that pre-war progressives had imagined would empty institutions was implemented after World War I to expand the welfare system as a whole. The private coordinating agencies like the Council of Social Agencies, still another progressive invention, were a party to this. While the rhetoric about the benefits of foster care never stopped during the 1920s and early 1930s, it floated far above any real dealings with local officials or institutions like Chapin Hall. In practical day-in, day-out interaction, Chapin Hall was never pressured to move any of its children to foster homes until the last half of the 1930s, and at that point all the Council on Social Agencies wanted was the removal of infants under the age of two. The council did not suggest that the population of children should be drastically reduced until the late forties. They did not stop the dozens of children being sent to Chapin Hall from the Joint Service Bureau or the Juvenile Court.

In still one more way the new social work helped maintain the population of Chapin Hall during the 1930s. The softer attitude toward children was extended to their parents. In the 1950s, social workers would encourage, indeed force parents to either reunite their family or else find a foster home. But in the 1930s this was not the case. Huge deference was paid to the parents' wishes. In a number of cases the social worker suggested foster care, but the parent vetoed it. Parents often distrusted foster care because they feared it could draw the affection of their children to other adults. They sent their children to institutions because they did not fear them as rivals for their children's affections.

Yet even more striking is the large number of case histories that are silent about any effort to convince parents that foster care was an option.[11] The willingness of the Chapin Hall staff to casually accept parental desires was common in the thirties and forties. The attitude arrived with the coming of trained social workers and the new tenderness associated with advanced styles of child care.[12] It disappeared after 1948 when foster care had become a top priority in the professional welfare community and Chapin Hall was forced to change its behavior. In the meantime, the new professionalism contributed significantly to the continued high population at Chapin Hall.

Finally, Chapin Hall's good standing in the professional social service community contributed to its stable population during the 1930s. The transformation of Chapin Hall's approach described in the last chapter— the boys' cottage, social worker, recreational emphasis, coordinated intake, and so on—was favorably looked upon by the Council of Social Agencies and the Community Fund in the 1920s and first half of the 1930s. Apart from the more progressive policies, Chapin Hall was attractive to outsiders because it was a clean, healthy institution. The children's diet was excellent. They were well clothed. The buildings were brightly lit. There were other, more nefarious institutions that the professional community wanted to go after. All homes for dependent children did not fare equally during the 1930s.[13] Those that folded in the 1930s were very small and marginal Protestant or nonsectarian institutions, housing twenty to fifty children. (No Catholic institutions closed during this period.) Orphanages like the Chicago Junior School, the Ruth Club, or the Dorcas House had very shaky financial grounding and no real visible presence in the city. Both in Chicago and downstate, these were the orphanages that did not survive the Depression. No children's home as substantial as Chapin Hall collapsed.

A second change accounting for the decline in the number of orphanages was the shift of some major Protestant and Jewish agencies from residential institutions to foster home placement agencies. Three major Lutheran industrial schools closed in this way; other major Protestant-born (and now nonsectarian) institutions such as the Chicago Orphan Asylum, the Chicago Home for the Friendless, and the Illinois Children's Home and Aid Society did so also. And two Jewish orphanages followed suit in the early 1940s, thanks to pressure from Jewish social workers committed to foster care. These institutions were truly fulfilling the progressive dream of deinstitutionalization.

But at the end of World War II there were still thirty-three orphanages and industrial schools in the city, many of them huge. Angel Guardian's population during the 1930s swelled to a record high 1,200. St. Mary's Training School in Des Plaines in 1946 still accepted 700; the Illinois Masonic Orphan's Home, 243; the state's Soldiers' and Sailors' Children's School, 635. In all, there were seventeen orphanages serving the city still willing to accept more than 100 children. Over 5,000 dependent children continued to live in institutions in Cook County at the end of the 1930s.[14]

While the Community Fund and the Council of Social Agencies were pleased with many of the innovations at Chapin Hall, this should not be taken to mean they were happy with everything about the agency. Far from it. In the late thirties, Chapin Hall was again under pressure to change. The good working relationship during the twenties and first half of the thirties reflects, once again, the weakness of the professional welfare community. With change coming at so slow a pace, and with no way to coerce change, the managerial social workers were thankful for those institutions moving in the right direction. Until the very end of the interwar years, Chapin Hall seemed to be one of them.

While the number of children in Chapin Hall only fell slightly after 1920, and not at all after the early 1930s, the children in the institution were very different from those of the nineteenth century. They were older. They stayed in Chapin Hall a longer time. While still predominantly working class, there were more instances of lower-middle-class and middle-class children. There were fewer half-orphans, and probably fewer children whose parents were physically ill. Conversely, there were far more children from divorced or separated parents. Illegitimate children were accepted for the first time.[15] At the heart of the change was one major difference—fewer children came to Chapin Hall because their families were destitute. More arrived because their parents had troubles of their own.

There had never been a lot of full orphans in nineteenth-century orphanages. But their absence was being discovered in the 1920s, and it was interpreted as a sign that the orphanage had to change with the times.[16] A 1928 City of Chicago study noted that "surprising as it may appear," only 8.2 percent of the residents of Chicago's child-care institutions were actually orphans.[17]

While there was no real decline in full orphans, there certainly was a decline in half-orphans. Fewer and fewer of the children arrived at Chapin Hall because one of their parents had died, a fact the managers were commenting on by the 1920s. Scattered evidence suggests that in the 1890s about one of every two children was in the asylum because of a parent's death. By the mid-thirties, only about 30 percent were. World War II interrupted the trend but did not end it. By the late forties, less than two out of every ten residents of Chapin Hall were there because of the death of a parent.[18]

Behind the change were simple demographics—the number of orphans and half-orphans dropped dramatically after 1920. In that year, it is estimated, one of every six children in the United States under the age of eighteen had lost at least one parent. By the mid-fifties, only one in twenty had. The drop in full orphans alone was even more dramatic. They had become a small statistical blip by mid-century.[19]

Public policy reinforced the demographics. Mothers' aid legislation did not empty out Chapin Hall, but it did help change the kind of child that came to the institution. During the interwar years, as Theda Skocpol has observed, mothers' aid did not affect all dependent children uniformly. The new policy overwhelmingly favored half-orphans. Most states refused benefits to mothers whose husbands had deserted, were imprisoned, or were physically or mentally impaired. As a result, children with dead fathers benefited more than anyone else. A 1931 study by the U.S. Children's Bureau showed that 82 percent of the nation's mothers' aid recipients were receiving help because a father had died; this at a time when only some 38 percent of broken homes were the result of the male spouse's death.[20]

Even where legislative policy did not explicitly favor orphans, financial pressures worked to the same end. The mothers' aid programs were all woefully underfunded. In Illinois during the 1920s and 1930s, there was *always* a waiting list of eligible mothers for whom there was simply no money. As late as 1940, eligible families in Chicago had a two-year wait from the time of the application to the granting of the pension, despite a five-year concerted effort to speed the process.[21] In 1939, 673 eligible families were turned down in Cook County, primarily families whose father had deserted or was ill but not confined in a mental hospital. As the Council of Social Agencies reported, "the policy of granting pensions on a selective basis is still in effect."[22] Mothers' aid gave anti-institutional options not to all dependent children, but primarily to those who had lost a father through death. The result, however, was that the pool of half-orphans needing institutional care shrank.

Divorce, separation, and desertion became the leading causes for entry into Chapin Hall. Yet there is more to it than that. In the nineteenth-century asylum, children came because their family had collapsed financially. Death, serious illness, or desertion was combined with a complete inability to keep the home together. Crushing poverty, especially for women, was the rule rather than the exception for nineteenth-century clients of the Half-Orphan Asylum. That was often tied to the suddenness of the catastrophe (a father running out without warning, or a mother dying in childbirth) as well as the absence of extended family who could help.

By the 1920s, it was very different. For one thing, dire poverty had become relatively unimportant. While the clientele of the institution remained overwhelmingly working class, the managers regularly commented that poverty no longer brought many children to the home.[23] During the 1920s, the amount of board money that parents could pay for their children jumped significantly.[24] A turn-of-the-century rule that no child be accepted if her or his parent earned too much money was also set aside. While crushing poverty reemerged during the Depression, even before the end of the thirties the new pattern had again triumphed. Basic lack of money—a poverty so complete that even a grubby, small apartment for parent and children was not possible—ceased to be a major factor in Chapin Hall's intake.

More subtle, psychological difficulties replaced the destitution of previous years. Parents looked for help because they just could not get on. Increasingly, the children came from very unsettled homes, where love and nurturance had largely been missing. The most basic change in who came to Chapin Hall was from families in trouble to troubled families.

The male/female ratio of the parents was not different. At any moment mothers were approaching the orphanage over fathers by a three-to-one ratio.[25] The obvious reason is the correct one. In cases of family break-up, it was assumed that the mother would keep the children. She usually did. Moreover, as Linda Gordon has argued, single mothers faced a variety of forms of discrimination from welfare institutions in the early twentieth century. Coming to an orphanage happened after other agencies refused help.[26]

Most of these mothers were just beaten down by life. Fathers who had run out were common, leaving the wife to support and raise two, three, or more small children. The lot of divorced women was not much different. Desertion and divorce, remember, did not make one eligible for mothers' aid. Many of Chapin Hall's case files indicate mothers who were physically exhausted, working long hours for modest wages, simply without the energy to care for their children. Many women had the help of extended families for a time after the dissolution of their marriage. The aging of a mother or illness of an aunt could be the occasion for bringing children to Chapin Hall.

But there were also more tangled stories. The depression of having a marriage not work and having to cope with youngsters could itself be debilitating, physically sapping some parents. The inability to let go of the relationship at times generated unbearable stress, with stories of very destructive relationships with former in-laws turning up from time to time. What is perhaps most important about these problems is that in many cases they were disabling for years. More and more, parents came to Chapin Hall because they were just unable or unwilling to cope. And children suffered the consequences.

There were, for example, the three children of a mother who had committed suicide in 1939. Her suicide was apparently related to depression over long dealings with the father, who himself had been under psychiatric care since 1918, when he was shell-shocked in France. The case worker interviewed neighbors and relatives. The father, all agreed, was a kind person, who deeply cared about his children, but was just without the emotional maturity to direct a household. The children were admitted to Chapin Hall.[27]

Another instance was a woman who brought her one-year-old daughter to Chapin Hall in 1926. The woman was middle-class Austrian by birth, but hit hard times during World War I. She was forced to do domestic work until she married a man of the "laboring class" who, in turn, died in the mid-1920s. The woman originally hoped to train as a nurse and then reunite her family, "after a year or two." Yet her daughter stayed at Chapin Hall for fifteen years—from age two until age seventeen. And she brought in a second daughter in 1932 (age eight) who remained until 1941. While Depression economics explain some of the stay, by 1934 the mother was steadily employed in various blue-collar jobs. To the social workers involved, the mother's "rejection of the children was obvious." Indeed, the mother had few friends in this country, felt she had been dealt cruel blows by life, and clearly believed she was of a "better" sort than her circumstances indicated. She quarreled with all around her. The mother, a Juvenile Court caseworker indicated in 1940, "was emotionally deprived and would have very little to give in a family set-up." Yet the mother resisted foster care for years, always saying that she soon planned on reuniting her family.[28]

With the men, emotional immaturity merged quickly with gender assumptions. Males were not expected to shoulder the responsibility of raising children. Chapin Hall's social workers (all women) were entirely complicit on this point, as were the social workers at the Council of Social Agencies. In 1935, a widower brought his three children to Chapin Hall. There was a girl, seven years old, and two boys, six and four. The father was a laborer with regular employment. In the five months since his wife had died, his children had been going to day nurseries, but, the case worker reported, the father "feels now it is too hard for him after working all day to come home and do the washing, ironing and cooking in the evening." He wanted his children put into an institution. Authorities at Juvenile Court referred him to Chapin Hall. Chapin Hall took the children in.

There was no particularly stunning character defect in the father's make-up. The caseworker's initial observation was not contradicted in the ensuing years: "From [the father's] conversation he seemed to be a very fine man, very sensible in his efforts . . . for the children." (Caseworkers, it might be pointed out, did not hesitate to state failings of other parents.) Later investigation indicated the same. The father was a man of temperate habits and steady employment. In his own way he certainly cared for his children. He was scrupulous about visiting them, bringing them gifts, and buying them clothes. Yet he also allowed his three children to live in Chapin Hall for ten years.

The father, a Greek immigrant, never felt he actually had to bring up his children. While he worried about them, and visited them, he just did not want to accept the day-to-day responsibility of raising them. In the end, as the children reached the upper age limit for Chapin Hall residents, he began looking for excuses. When his daughter approached sixteen, she had lived nine years at Chapin Hall. Yet the father, clearly fearing the change in routine a teenage daughter would bring, argued that she should stay one more year because the local high school was better than the one in his neighborhood. The caseworker reported that the daughter "begged and pled with Father to take her home." He finally did so.

In the first months after these children came to Chapin Hall, their health improved significantly. But the long-term consequences were destructive. When the girl got home she refused to help around the house and badgered her father for spending money. In general, relations were strained. The father blamed the orphanage for not teaching the girl the value of money, not even beginning to see that the years of neglect might have engendered hostility.

For the boys the outcome was even worse. They slowly evolved into delinquents, ringleaders inside Chapin Hall whenever any trouble was afoot. They ran away numerous times. The last entry in the case file for the younger son is a letter to military authorities during the Korean War. The young man was under arrest, facing court martial for "offenses committed against military law." The social worker in 1952 summed up his stay in Chapin Hall: "John was only four years old when he came to live here and there is no record of any serious difficulties in this early period. However, as his nine years passed here, the staff members saw signs of what they considered growing unhappiness. The many years here without any close dependable family ties for a young child can be very depressing. John became a rather careless boy who was not too reliable."[29]

While the above indicate evasion and emotional immaturity, there could be even worse. Outright child-dumping reappeared for the first time since the 1870s. In one such case dating from 1928, a widowed father brought in his eight-year-old son. He was to pay $8.00 a week for upkeep. Within a month, however, he disappeared. Later it was determined that he had lost his job and went to Cleveland to look for work. But he never came back for his child, who waited for a year for the father's return before Chapin Hall's caseworker sent the boy to Juvenile Court as a charity case.[30]

While fathers clearly abandoned their children more than mothers, there were a few cases of the opposite. And while the caseworker reports were clearly more censorious about women who neglected their children, again reflecting deeply held gender assumptions, for the children involved that made little practical difference. If a mother dismissed her children from her life, the social workers might have complained about it, but they did not concretely challenge it. There was support for the children at the orphanage, but there were few efforts to work with parents to remake the home. Again, it is the passivity toward parents that is most striking about the records of the 1930s and early 1940s.[31]

In many cases, it was both parents who either could not or would not deal with their children. In one case a divorced father brought in two children in 1934. He was a field manager for General Motors. He was also an alcoholic with little sense of responsibility for his children. The mother, in turn, came from a family of small-time criminals, slept with numerous men while married, and finally abandoned the family by running away to Hollywood. When the children came to Chapin Hall, she was back in Chicago, divorcing her second husband, who was another alcoholic, but a wife-beater as well. After the children were in Chapin Hall for three years, it was discovered that the mother had remarried in 1935, but had not told orphanage officials because she didn't want the girls. As she was in the process of a third divorce when this was discovered, the Chapin Hall staff made no effort to force the family to reunite. The father, for his part, remained at the edges of his daughters' lives, always proclaiming that their welfare was important, but going for months without contacting them and never taking any concrete steps to bring them home. This family's file is page after page of small-time crime, violence against women, alcoholism, varied sexual liaisons in and outside of marriage complete with private detectives breaking down doors to gather evidence for divorces, and, in general, a basic inability of all the adults involved to handle responsibility in any area of their lives. Through it all the girls were ignored, going for weeks, sometimes months at a time without hearing from either parent. The girls stayed at Chapin Hall for seven years.[32]

As the above stories indicate, not only did a different kind of family come to Chapin Hall in the decades after World War I. More and more, the children stayed a long time. The managers did not realize this at first. In the 1920s they mistakenly continued to talk about providing temporary care even as it ceased to be the norm. By the late 1940s, however, the trends were clear. Less than 30 percent of the children stayed under a year (as opposed to 74 percent in the 1870s). A full 50 percent spent over two years in Chapin Hall. During the nineteenth century, on the other hand, only 14 percent of the children had a two-year stay. By the forties, it was not uncommon for children to spend six, seven, or eight years in Chapin Hall.[33]

The coming of troubled families, the deference of social workers to parents, and the lengthening stay of children in Chapin Hall can all be related to the new conception of family and welfare developed in the early twentieth century. After 1910, I argued in the last chapter, officials at Chapin Hall began seeing children as individuals instead of as inseparable parts of a family unit. Children were no longer refused admission because their parents exhibited the wrong behavior. At the same time, Chapin Hall managers and social workers began thinking of the orphanage as a surrogate home instead of as a custodial institution. The new warmth toward the children was a part of this ethos.

These attitudes were, in fact, the flip side of the implied notions of family responsibility implicit in mothers' aid legislation. Mothers' aid was designed to deinstitutionalize dependent children, to make it possible for children to live with their mother, who was presumed to be the natural child raiser. Mothers' aid would keep families together by paying single mothers so they did not have to work so much outside the home. But in the first half of the century, only women of "good character" were eligible for these pensions. The intrusive investigations into the applicants' lives, the search by welfare officials for unmarried cohabitation, excessive drinking, or the squandering of money on needless frivolities were essential to mothers' aid programs, a new version of nineteenth-century "friendly visiting." This monitoring made operative Theodore Roosevelt's 1909 assertion that help should be given to a poor mother if she was "a good woman."[34]

If mothers' aid was for "good" women, progressive orphanages turned into the place where "bad" parents would send their children, especially in those cities where foster care was not extensively available. And, in turn, orphanages would increasingly think of their task as providing surrogate homes; becoming warm, nurturing environments for neglected children. They would provide the stability and support the children did not get elsewhere. These ideas about welfare and family ties not only explain the new

ways of handling children, discussed in the last chapter, but also the orphanage's remarkable disinterest in parents during these years. Children
could be saved in two different ways. Those with "good" mothers would
stay at home, thanks to mothers' aid. Those with "irresponsible" parents
would go to institutions, now supposedly attempting to approximate a familial setting.

We are so accustomed to viewing the orphanage negatively that it is
hard to see that some children might have seen their years at Chapin Hall
positively. But that was certainly the case. Not all children, of course.
There were just as many casualties, kids who saw themselves as deposited
in a cold institution by their parents. These should absolutely not be forgotten. But scattered through the case records are reminiscences of children who remembered their years at Chapin Hall fondly. The orphanage
provided a continuity and support that many of these children had never
experienced in their short lives.

One report, from 1940, will suffice. Anthony lived at Chapin Hall from
1930 to 1934. His mother had disappeared some time before that. By the
age of seven Anthony had been passed around to a friend of the father, to
the father, then to a cousin, to an aunt, back to the cousin, followed by a
short stint with both his parents while they attempted a reconciliation.
When the mother disappeared again after just two weeks the boy lived with
his landlady before coming to Chapin Hall.[35]

Anthony came back to visit one evening in 1940, six years after living in
the orphanage. He was eighteen years old. He stopped to talk to some of
the boys while they were getting ready for bed. "You fellows stay here as
long as you can," he told them. "When I was here I thought it would be
nice to leave. Well, I left and I hadn't been gone two weeks when I wanted
to come back. You'll never be any place else where you will have so much
fun or so much to eat or learn how to behave so well."[36]

The mid-century orphanage had very mixed results. Different children
responded very differently to Chapin Hall's efforts to nurture youngsters
without functioning parents. On some the warmth of the staff was not
enough. Such children saw themselves as locked in a warehouse, abandoned by their biological parents. Others, however, viewed the orphanage
as providing more continuity and support than they had ever had in their
lives. It is impossible to make any generalization about which sort of child
was more common at Chapin Hall. It is possible to note that in the last half
of the 1930s, welfare professionals became increasingly distrustful of
Chapin Hall, indeed, of all of Chicago's surviving orphanages. The professionals, at any rate, came to see the orphanage as a warehouse, an out-
moded relic of the nineteenth century. By the mid-1940s, this would lead

to a concerted attack on Chapin Hall by the Council of Social Agencies, the Community Fund, the Illinois Department of Welfare, and Chicago's Association of Commerce. The length of stay and lack of services was at the heart of the attack. To these reformers, Chapin Hall was all too typical of Chicago orphanages. It was not a stabilizing force for children from disorganized families. It was, according to the professionals, a backward-looking, untherapeutic holding pen. The attack would lead to the biggest single transformation in the orphanage's history.

THE MONEY

The Depression staggered all of Chicago's social service agencies. The problems faced were severe, but only in a very few cases did they prove to be overwhelming. How Chapin Hall dealt with money problems gives a bit of insight into how the whole system of financing child welfare was affected by the massive economic downturn of the 1930s. The old money sources—parental payment, endowment income, and yearly donations— were no longer enough. But new sources of income appeared to fill the gap. Public money came to Chapin Hall for the first time, as well as private federated charity through the Community Fund. The amounts were small, but with large effects. The Community Fund money was enough to challenge the managerial autonomy of the boards. When the outside money came, so too came outside pressure.

The expansion of welfare services during the Progressive Era undermined one of Chapin Hall's key sources of support, the downtown business community. At the same time, neighborhood connections were also fraying. The male and female boards of the Half-Orphan Asylum were in transition, gradually moving from the Near North side of Chicago to the wealthy North Shore suburbs. The persistent inflation of the early twentieth century added to the problems. The asylum became more expensive to run, and new money became earmarked for operating expenses instead of new buildings.

If new sources of money were not easily forthcoming during the Progressive Era, there was some relief during the 1920s. The managers gradually re-created neighborhood ties, although the relevant neighborhood became the wealthy suburb of Lake Forest instead of the Near North side of Chicago. One sign of this was the successful drive to raise the endowment in the mid-twenties. Separate fundraising committees were created in 1923—one for the Near North of the city and the other for lakefront suburbs. The "new friends" reported by Julia Thompson were all from the North Shore suburbs.[37] By the end of the decade, the transformation was complete. Wealthy Lake Foresters such as Cyrus McCormick and Philip Wrigley Jr. were key contributors to the drive to build the boys' cottage. Their names stood alongside those families of Lake Forest that had long been connected to the asylum—families such as the Bentleys, the Thompsons, and the Clarks.

The prosperity of the 1920s allowed Chapin Hall to reconstitute its old financial base—the combination of endowment, donations, and parental board payment. But there were changes within that framework. Instead of downtown businessmen, fundraisers looked to traditional friends of Chapin Hall. Families with long (and at times not so long) ties to the Half-Orphan Asylum were pursued with the same relish with which the women in the 1880s had gone and asked businessmen in the center of the city for money. At the same time, the community base of donations had shifted. Instead of the Near North side, funds came, by the 1920s, from the wealthy North Shore suburbs.[38]

Another modification of the 1920s was the increasing reliance on yearly donations and parental board payments. Between 1900 and 1914, yearly donations were not a major factor, accounting for only 14 percent of the yearly operating budget. Interest from the endowment, on the other hand, accounted for 53 percent of the yearly budget. Board from parents covered 25 percent of costs.[39]

During the 1920s, however, yearly donations made up almost 22 percent of costs (instead of 14 percent) and the amount of the budget dependent upon parental payment crept up to 31 percent (from 25 percent). Interest from the endowment, on the other hand, covered only 34 percent of costs during the 1920s (as opposed to 53 percent before).[40]

These changes made Chapin Hall far more dependent upon what we might call "transitory income," money that could not be guaranteed from year to year, that each season had to be earned from scratch. Whereas in the years before World War I, only 39 percent of income depended upon such yearly renewal, in the 1920s, 56 percent of operating costs did so.[41] This would have important consequences during the 1930s. As the asylum got back on its feet during the 1920s, it set itself up for a fall.

The first money problems surfaced in 1930, but the managers and directors were unsure of the cause. In this they were no different from the rest of the nation—it took some time to realize that the crash of 1929 was actually setting off something that we have now come to call the Great Depression. Moreover, the effects of the Depression first hit Chapin Hall right as the boys' cottage was being built. Some of the directors initially attributed the money problems to this. By early 1931, however, all confusion was erased. Money—or rather the lack of it—was the primary topic of conversation among the managers. The larger source of the problem was depressingly clear—the downturn in the nation's economy was severely straining the asylum's resources.

For the next five years, money problems never let the directors or managers alone. Several times they found themselves unable to pay the bills. In February 1931 the managers borrowed $3,000 from the endowment to cover current expenses. Three months later they needed another $5,000. In April 1933 the managers asked the directors for $1,000 from the endowment to spend "if it became necessary." It did. In October of 1935, the directors made still another loan, this time for $4,000, so the managers could pay bills. None of these debts was ever repaid.[42]

Money "borrowed" from the endowment, however, did not cover all expenses. Budget reductions of all kinds were resorted to again and again. Between April 1931 and August 1932, salaries were cut three times. In February 1932, sick leave benefits were drastically reduced. In August, paid vacations were eliminated. Some employees lost as much as 25 percent of their income in a little over a year. But at least they had jobs. In February 1932, the office secretary was let go in an effort to save more money.[43]

There were other cuts. When the social worker quit in March 1931, three months passed without any discussion of a replacement. Then the managers decided to do without a caseworker altogether. The managers' motives, no doubt, were complicated—the last social worker, Dorothy Puttee, had been quarrelsome, insufficiently deferential to the managers, enamored of her own professional credentials. Yet if the professional/volunteer split was mixed up in the managers' decision, money problems were at the core. Puttee had quit one month after the managers had borrowed $3,000 to pay current debts and two weeks after they had voted a 10 percent across-the-board budget reduction.[44]

On the same day the managers decided to do without a social worker, they also voted to close the nursery school and dismiss the teacher.[45] The temporary emergency shelter for infants was another service cut in 1931, just a few months after Chapin Hall had worked out the arrangement with the Social Service Exchange of the Council of Social Agencies to be the city's primary caretaker for infants needing short-term emergency care.[46]

All cuts in the services proved to be temporary. The managers turned to the State of Illinois and the local Community Fund to support the infant nursery. In November 1931, the managers hired a social worker who worked three days a week, at no salary, but for free room and board. A nursery school teacher was hired under a similar arrangement. She got room and board for herself and her two-year-old but no other income.

House parents for the boys' and girls' cottages were hired in the same way.[47]

By the middle of the next year, salaries were reinstated. In June 1932, when still another new caseworker was hired, Mrs. Thompson personally donated the salary for the first three months. At about the same time, the nursery school teacher began receiving a salary again.[48]

This did not mean the crisis was over. The reduced staff, slashed salaries, foregone vacations, diminished endowment, as well as countless additional budget cuts were all too real. The asylum's aggregate income fell by a third between 1928 and 1934, from $75,000 to $50,000.[49] Chapin Hall's 1934 income was its lowest since 1916. Never since the asylum had moved to Foster and California was there so little money.

Central to the financial crisis was the asylum's deep dependence on income that had to be reearned from ground zero each year. This most fluid source of money was also the most vulnerable. Once the Depression hit, it began drying up immediately.

Yearly donations had come to account for 16.5 percent of the budget by the end of the twenties. But that income dropped steadily during the 1930s.[50] The drop in another sort of transitory income, however, did the most damage. "The principle cause for financial concern and consequent reduction of running expenses in 1931," Julia Thompson noted, "has come from the inability of parents who are unemployed to pay the board of their children." While the number of children in the institution remained constant between 1928 and 1932, the amount of money that parents paid for their children's upkeep fell by 54.8 percent.[51] The managers, in keeping with a policy dating back to the 1860s, would not refuse children because their parents were indigent. Consequently, the number of free cases jumped dramatically. In 1935, the worst year, on average 91 out of 134 children in the institution paid no board. Since during the 1920s Chapin Hall had come to rely on parental board for 30 percent of its yearly income, the loss was devastating.[52]

While income from the endowment did not rise between 1928 and 1940, neither did it fall.[53] The explicitly conservative investment policies of the twenties worked to Chapin Hall's advantage during the Depression.[54]

How was the crisis weathered? Budget cuts, service cuts, "loans" from the endowment, and staff layoffs have all been mentioned. All this, however, was not enough. During the 1930s, Chapin Hall began to reconstitute its financial base. Under the weight of the Depression, the philanthropic system that had emerged in the last decade of the nineteenth century—a system relying on a combination of private philanthropy, a healthy endowment, and parental payment—began to change. Federated funding and public money became a part of Chapin Hall's revenues. The old system began a slow fade.

Of course, Chapin Hall was not the only Chicago institution to feel the Depression. The new sources of funding were related to major structural changes in Chicago's whole system of welfare, and not only child welfare. Even during the 1920s, Chicago lagged behind other cities in the reformation of welfare financing. Community Trusts were established in numerous cities throughout the nation after 1914. They were generally organized by people in the financial community, one of the various umbrella organizations created to reform the welfare system. Federated charity was meant to organize welfare financing in the same way that the United Charities was supposed to reform welfare services. It would centrally organize fundraising drives and parcel out the money to the appropriate agencies.

Chicago's Community Trust was organized at the Harris Trust and Savings Bank in May 1915, but for the next fifteen years it was a marginal and ineffective institution. Opposition was deep-seated. Even many institutions amenable to progressive ideas about reforming welfare services were skeptical about reforming welfare finances. They accurately sensed that controlling money was central to controlling the system.[55] Jews and Catholics, in fact, had coordinated their own social service financing. Confederated Jewish charity had existed since the first years of the century, a result of the war between Orthodox and Reformed charities.[56] Catholic Charities of Chicago was organized in 1918 in part to stave off any citywide schemes for confederated charity.

Both Catholics and Jews had federated their finances not to reform the system but to help their own. Protestant charities were even more decentralized, but with their own reasons for resistance. Many Protestant institutions, like Chapin Hall, had a handful of traditional donors who could be counted on for support. Coordinated charity threatened to redistribute that income. Institutions like Chapin Hall wanted an uncoordinated system for the same reasons that Jewish and Catholic groups had organized internally—to protect established interests. Despite another exploratory effort in 1924, Chicago's Community Trust made no headway in coordinating welfare financing through the 1920s.

The Depression opened up new possibilities. By the early 1930s literally hundreds of social service agencies in the Chicago area had money problems similar to those of Chapin Hall. The agencies, formerly the biggest opponents of welfare financing reform, were themselves crying out for action. Both private federated charity and the public sector firmly established themselves as philanthropists to private agencies like Chapin Hall.

With so many agencies in chaos by 1931, the Community Fund eyed its chance. Philip Clarke, fundraising chairman of Community Trust and president of the City National Bank, raised $5.5 million that was distributed to agencies during the summer. Another campaign, organized by Samuel Insull Jr., raised $10.5 million, money distributed in four short months.[57] Two other campaigns followed, and in 1934, Chicago's Community Fund was organized to put the campaigns on a permanent basis. The response could not have been more different from that of the failed 1924 campaign: "Agency acceptance of the plan was overwhelming. All the major agencies came in. All the federations came in—Catholic, Jewish, Lutheran, the YMCA, the YWCA; even the Chicago Red Cross."[58]

The managers and directors of Chapin Hall were also enthusiastic, although they clung to the stubborn faith that they could go it alone as late as 1931.[59] In October 1932, the managers and directors agreed to accept Community Trust money to help keep open the infant nursery. In March 1934, when the Community Fund was organized, Mrs. McDougal, the president of Chapin Hall's Board of Managers, eagerly attended the initial meeting. By the end of that year, the Community Fund had arranged monthly payments to Chapin Hall. Total support that year reached 4.2 percent of the orphanage's revenue. By 1936, Community Fund money accounted for 7.7 percent of Chapin Hall's budget, helping to fill the gap left by lost parental board payment.[60]

But there was a price for the money, and Chapin Hall officials soon grew wary. Community Fund, from the beginning, used the financial aid to try to regulate Chapin Hall. By the late thirties, both male and female boards were looking for ways to rid themselves of the Community Fund obligations. In 1941, they cut their ties with the Community Fund.

The severance was friendly.[61] The boards (male and female) sensed that federated charity would be around for a long time, and they were chastened enough by the Depression to want to remain on good terms with fund officials. The contact with federated charity inaugurated an on-again-off-again relationship that continued into the 1980s. At the heart of this was Chapin Hall's need for money versus Community Fund's desire to shape the city's welfare system. The former kept drawing Chapin Hall to the fund; the latter kept pushing it away.

One reason that the orphanage could dismiss Community Fund in the early forties was the steadily increasing amount of public money available. It first came as emergency aid in 1932 and 1933.[62] In 1935, Illinois massively revamped its welfare law, expanding the public presence in dozens of ways.[63] One change directly affecting Chapin Hall was that the Cook County Juvenile Court was now able to pay Chapin Hall to house wards of the court. By 1941, payments from Juvenile Court accounted for 8.8 percent of Chapin Hall's income. Other public money became available to Chapin Hall during World War II. By 1948, public funds accounted for 13.2 percent of the institution's operating expenses.[64] After 1935, public money became a permanent part of Chapin Hall's budget.

It might be argued that not much had changed by the 1940s. While federated money was accepted for awhile, Chapin Hall withdrew in 1941. And public money came in significant but not huge amounts. The public money Chapin Hall received during the thirties and forties was less than that received by similar institutions in Chicago and by most child-care institutions in the nation. Even as late as 1945, over 80 percent of Chapin Hall's income came from its traditional sources—donations, the endowment, and parental payment.[65]

While the changes were not dramatic in immediate empirical terms, they were portentous in other ways. The initial experience with Community Fund and State of Illinois funding made Chapin Hall officials very skeptical about federated charity but quite placid about the public money. Community Fund money was accompanied by unwanted pressure to change Chapin Hall's program. State money was not.

The reasons for this are rooted in the ways that Chicago, and indeed the whole nation, tried to create a managerial system in the early twentieth century. In the United States, far more than Europe, state bureaucracies remained relatively weak. Private bureaucracies were seen as an alternative. For decades after its creation in 1905, Illinois' Department of Public Welfare had lacked the legal mandate to regulate private institutions. After it got the authority, it lacked the resources. As a consequence, into the 1940s, the state did no effective regulation of any private welfare agency.[66] Any control over an agency like Chapin Hall came from coordinating agencies such as the Council of Social Agencies, the Chicago Association of Commerce, or the Community Fund. These institutions were examples of a type—quasi-private organizations created in the early twentieth century as alternatives to state control. They saw themselves, to borrow Ellen Lagemann's very useful phrase, as using "private power for the public good."[67] While ostensibly in the private sector, and therefore accountable to no public, they actually made much early-twentieth-century public policy. The major foundations are good examples of such institutions. So are the Community Trust and the Council of Social Agencies. To the extent that Chapin Hall was regulated, it was by these private organizations and not by any governmental body.

Chapin Hall's directors were not liberal Democrats. Indeed, by the mid-thirties, they were overwhelmingly Republican and opposed to the New Deal.[68] We know little about the managers' political sympathies, but there is certainly no evidence that they were dramatically different from their husbands'. Still, in the thirties and forties, the women had no qualms about public money and the men raised no objections. At that time, it was a way out of the financial crisis. Moreover, given the ineffectiveness of public regulation, any confrontations they had with "New Deal types" took place at the offices of the Council of Social Agencies, not at the State of Illinois' Department of Welfare. Chapin Hall became rather serenely addicted to public money. It was only in the 1970s that the full implications of this would become apparent.

WHO'S IN CHARGE?

Hidden changes at Chapin Hall during the 1920s and 1930s led to movement on still another front—that of control within the institution. Slowly, the professional staff took on more responsibility while the managers did less. Part was the managers' own doing, part the result of a giant push from the Council of Social Agencies. Whatever the cause, by the end of World War II, the women volunteers were doing less. The hired professional help, guided by the welfare elite of the CSA, the Community Fund and, more indirectly, by the University of Chicago School of Social Service Administration, did more and more.

Yet the transformation was by no means total. Like the other underlying changes going on at the same time—the new kind of family served, the lengthier stay for children, the new sources of philanthropy—the move from volunteer to professional was still incomplete as late as 1945. The managers might have given up some, but they still did a lot and were still in ultimate control, despite a concerted effort in the mid-1930s to push them aside.

Yet more fundamental changes were only a matter of time. By the 1930s, the managers themselves were a diminished band. They could no longer count on finding enough volunteers to adequately run the institution. By the late 1920s, attendance at managers' bimonthly meetings had declined to the point where it was a source of concern.[69] After that, not a year went by without someone asking what could be done to boost attendance. By the 1940s only about one in three managers were coming to monthly meetings. The best-attended sessions were always those attached to the summer luncheon in Lake Geneva, Wisconsin, and the winter fash-ion show at a downtown Chicago department store.[70]

It also became more difficult to find women who would do committee work. The committee system, developed in the 1870s, had been the ad-ministrative backbone of the Half-Orphan Asylum. Women divided the labor to effectively watch over the institution. By the thirties, interest was lagging. In 1939, a questionnaire was sent to the managers asking them which committee they would be willing to chair. The results, as one board member put it, were "amazing and very disconcerting." Only nine women agreed to chair a committee, and one of them would be out of town for much of the year. "That left us," the Policy Committee chairwoman dryly noted, "with eight chairmen and twenty-one committees."[71]

Why did the women's interest sag? Since the 1890s, there had been a slow but steady exodus of the managing board (and Board of Directors) from the Near North side of Chicago to wealthy North Shore suburbs, notably Lake Forest. During the 1920s, the slow exodus turned into a mad rush. By the 1930s, well over half the managing board lived in the North Shore, and almost all of the officers did so.

The move to the suburbs reflected nationwide trends. Suburbs like Brookline, Massachusetts, Scarsdale, New York, and Lake Forest, Illinois, were increasingly catering to wealthy physicians, industrialists, and law-yers who wanted to live away from the city.[72] By the 1920s, Lake Forest was home to such famous "Chicago" families as the McCormicks, Palmers, Swifts, Donnelleys, Ryersons, and Armours. Lake Forest during the 1920s grew faster than at any other time in its history, nearly doubling its popula-tion. The rapid movement of Chapin Hall's managers and directors from the city to Lake Forest after 1920 reflected the larger change.[73]

The shift to the North Shore distanced the women from the or-phanage's physical plant. During the nineteenth century, the asylum on 1931 North Halsted was eight to twelve blocks from the homes of most of the managers. The move to California and Foster, in 1916, roughly coin-cided with the managing board's move to the suburbs. The asylum became harder to get to.

Differences between Chapin Hall and the Chicago Orphan Asylum (COA) are instructive here. The board of the COA also underwent an ex-odus in the early twentieth century, from the wealthy neighborhood around South Prairie Avenue to the Hyde Park–Kenwood area about four miles south. Yet when COA officials decided to move the orphanage from downtown, just as the Half-Orphan managers wanted to leave the near North Side, they took the institution to Hyde Park. As a result, in 1930 the COA board of managers lived minutes from their orphanage while Chapin

Hall managers lived miles. And just as important, the COA managers lived in the same neighborhood as professors at the University of Chicago's School of Social Service Administration.[74]

The shift to the North Shore distanced Chapin Hall's managers from city problems in a more general way. Historian Kenneth Jackson has pointed out: "Places like Lake Forest, Bronxville, and Brookline enabled the select few—and their supporting minions—to enjoy the benefits of American production and resources without bearing the burden of living near the noxious fumes, deafening noises, and poor people who made the prosperity possible in the first place."[75] The nineteenth-century managers of the Half-Orphan Asylum were committed urbanites. Even with the residential segregation that occurred in Chicago after the fire of 1871, managers like Helen Goudy or Elizabeth Chesbrough were never more than a mile or two away from poorer neighborhoods. These were women who saw themselves as attacking the problems of their own environment, in short, attacking their own problems as city dwellers.

But by the 1930s, this was no longer the case. Less and less did the women managers think what they were doing was coming to grips with the problems of contemporary urban life. (That sense passed to the Council of Social Agencies, the schools of social work, and Community Fund.) And even less did the managers talk about doing the Lord's work. Instead, they increasingly saw themselves as maintaining family traditions. Doing work for Chapin Hall was something that the family had always done, the women thought, and the younger generation should do its bit. By the close of the 1930s, the Board of Managers was motivated by a honed sense of tradition combined with North Shore noblesse oblige.

Traditionalism could produce its gems. Some very powerful women appeared at this time who managed the institution as well as any had before. In the late 1930s, for example, Kay Milliken and Clarissa Haffner joined the board, two women who would ably guide the institution through a major transformation in the late 1940s. But the system also brought too many young women onto the board who had little talent or inclination to work at Chapin Hall. Living in Lake Forest, far from the problems of urban life, these women just lived off the capital of their mothers. They did little except contribute to the declining attendance figures at the bimonthly managers' meetings.

In the nineteenth century, a small group of women, centered in the Executive Committee, ran the institution. This had not really changed by the 1930s. Yet in the nineteenth century, the Executive Committee could count on thirty to forty other volunteers to do the committee work. By the middle of the twentieth century, that support was gone. A Clarissa Haffner in the 1940s could do as much as Helen Goudy did in the 1870s, but she lacked the volunteer support that Goudy took for granted. The core of active volunteers increasingly had to turn to the staff for help.

If movement away from the city contributed to the decline of the Board of Managers, so too did their own dependence upon expertise. Late into the 1920s, Julia Thompson had agonized over the new professionalism of the Half-Orphan Asylum.[76] But the next generation unabashedly praised the scientific spirit and readily looked to the Council of Social Agencies for guidance. Mrs. David McDougal and Mrs. Clarissa Haffner, two of the most engaged members of the managing board, lacked that sense of assurance that Helen Goudy had in the late nineteenth century and which Julia Thompson mourned in the 1920s. The new generation's faith in expertise also translated into a form of dependency. This, too, contributed to the increased importance of the staff.

The basic trend toward giving more authority to the professional staff gathered steam in the decades after the First World War. The superintendent did more and more of the hiring. After 1928, social workers did much of the admissions work. By the mid-1930s, the superintendent and social worker were giving monthly reports to the managing board. In the nineteenth century, the managers had been deeply involved in the details of the institution. Now, increasingly, the staff had to tell them what was going on.

Yet it would be quite misleading to say that the managers handed over the institution to the staff. The volunteer managers directly asserted their control when they wanted to. The managing board continued to think of the staff during the 1930s and 1940s as subordinate. When a forceful employee was hired, there were sparks. Dorothy Puttee, a social worker who worked at Chapin Hall in 1930, provides a good example. Puttee had recently received her master's degree in social work from the University of Chicago. Within weeks after she came to Chapin Hall, she locked horns with the managers. She inaugurated an acrimonious argument over whether a troublesome girl should be kept, inveighed against a set of houseparents she thought inept, and informed the board that certain houseparents were hitting children. The board was not hostile to all of Puttee's charges, especially the last. The board quickly fired the offending houseparents. Yet the managers were largely impatient with Puttee, and the feeling was indeed mutual. After less than a year's employment, Puttee angrily quit, demanding that her reasons be read into the record. She complained of the "ambiguous position of the social worker, her duties not being defined." She objected to the board admitting children "without her sanction and knowledge." And she protested that the "full text" of a report on the children's diet was not made available to her.[77]

Puttee's complaints all reveal her belief that the volunteer managers should abdicate certain decision-making powers to the professional social worker. Puttee wanted more authority, and more explicitly defined authority. The managers refused, happy to be rid of unruly staff. A replacement was not hired for six months.[78]

Such disputes were rare, however, because the managers generally avoided hiring assertive employees. Temperament was the primary tool used to quash professional hubris and salve the volunteers' egos. The women who held the superintendent post between 1932 and 1964 were temperamentally disposed not to antagonize the managers. Mabel Morrow in the thirties and forties and Adrianna Bouterse in the fifties and early sixties were not forceful personalities.[79] They took over many of the supervisory and even policy-setting tasks inside Chapin Hall precisely because they remained deferential to their "boss," the Board of Managers. It is certainly not accidental that no men were hired to be in positions of authority until the 1960s.

Despite the slow drift to staff control, into the 1940s the volunteer managers still made the major decisions. They still controlled the money. The staff remained without the managerial skills, educational expertise, and personal disposition to adequately run the institution. But the patterns of control were shifting. And to complicate the picture further, a third force appeared on the scene. Beginning in the 1930s, the coordinating agencies downtown, the Council of Social Agencies and the Community Fund, began to inject themselves into the management of Chapin Hall.

During the 1920s, the Council of Social Agencies, intent upon system building and mindful of its weak financial position, had not pressured the Half-Orphan Asylum (or any Chicago children's institution) to change policy. The agency's new aggressiveness dated from 1931 and became more intense as the Depression continued.[80]

It was, however, the creation of the Community Fund in March 1934 that led to sustained and explicit efforts to establish regulatory control. Money, in other words, was the key to control. As a condition of membership in the Community Fund, Chapin Hall agreed to let the Council of Social Agencies conduct an in-depth analysis of the agency and make hard recommendations about changes. The 1935 study of Chapin Hall was part of a larger analysis of private child-care institutions in the city. Twenty-one other agencies underwent the same microscopic scrutiny the Half-Orphan Asylum suffered, all the work paid for by the Community Fund and done by CSA staffers. The project was overseen by a blue-chip advisory committee made up of civic-minded businessmen, leading Chicago welfare professionals, and professors from the School of Social Service Administration at the University of Chicago.

In November 1935, a detailed report of over 100 pages on the workings of the Chicago Nursery and Half-Orphan Asylum was completed. By October 1936 all the agency studies were finished. After careful analysis of the individual reports, the council in the summer of 1937 privately printed the most exhaustive study of private Protestant care for dependent children in Chicago that had ever been done. The reports all led to the same conclusions. The old agency system was inadequate. The volunteer managers should hand over the institutions to the staff.[81]

The study of Chapin Hall was done by Isabel Devine of the CSA. She praised certain aspects of the orphanage's program—the physical plant, the children's diet, and the emphasis on recreation—but her remarks were essentially critical. Her suggestions for reform were specific—hire more professional staff, give the staff more responsibility, have the managers do less, combine the managers and directors into one board, do more psychological analysis of the children, and close down the temporary infant care nursery. All these ideas reflected state-of-the-art opinion in the field of professional social work. Nor is that surprising, considering her own background—she was the recent recipient of an M.A. in social work— and her employer, the Council of Social Agencies. (The report, of course, was cleared by her supervisors. Three days before discussing her results with Chapin Hall executives, Devine took part in a strategy session at the offices of the CSA to explore how best to present the findings to Chapin Hall so that the managers would be amenable to reform.) Devine, and her employers, wanted Chapin Hall to adopt a system that the professional social welfare community would be comfortable with.

The key theme of the report was professionalism. The superintendent should be in absolute control of the institution. Devine noted the busyness of the managers' committees but suggested that it was all very atavistic, "the probable continuance of work begun in the early days when the personal efforts of board members were necessary in order to provide care for children."[82]

What did she want the volunteer women to do? The report waffled and double-talked on this issue, with vague gestures to continuing education and substantial leadership in the field, but practical suggestions moved in a different direction. Devine wanted the managers marginalized. She envisioned far fewer committees, because she thought there would be far less work for the managers. She thought volunteer women could do publicity work, raise small amounts of money through bazaars, and help maintain the beauty of the physical plant.

Devine's suggestion ignored what the women managers *wanted* to do. Volunteerism, at the Half-Orphan Asylum, had always been a managerial ethos. Yet it also allowed a close relationship to a particular institution that provided specific services to children. The managerial "distance" in Chapin Hall had never been very great, certainly far, far less than that of the downtown umbrella agencies or those schools of social work whose business was what Devine called "the broader program of community planning for child-care."[83] For decades, the managers had watched over their institution carefully. They saw dependent children all the time, they knew their names, their families, and their problems. The women could legitimately say they were involved in the business of helping children one at a time. Downtown architects of the welfare system did not, in the managers' eyes, work this way. To the volunteer women, the professionals of the Council of Social Agencies or the Community Fund thought in terms of "system" instead of individual children. They were bureaucrats.

The managers' distrust of downtown was never complete. By the 1930s, it was always offset by the managers' gnawing sense that they just did not know what to do without the experts. Still, the managers would have agreed with Devine's musing as to whether the same "spirit of enthusiasm" was possible if the managing board shifted its role.[84]

From the 1860s into the 1920s, volunteer women had almost single-handedly managed the Half-Orphan Asylum. From the 1860s into the 1930s they had done almost all of the fundraising. The Council of Social Agencies in their 1935 report suggested a dramatic restructuring of this system. They advocated an intensification of the trend toward professionalism begun in the 1920s. Chapin Hall would be run by staff trained by elite professionals at a school of social work. Fund-raising patterns were also to change. The money would be raised largely by the male directors in tandem with the Community Fund and the Council of Social Agencies. The women, the report implied, were to do marginal busywork.

The council was not successful. One problem was that the men did not want change. CSA officials wanted to work with the businessmen directors instead of the women managers. This was because they thought the men—all sophisticated businessmen—would better understand the professionals' idiom—statistical talk about Chicago's needs, aggregate discussion of financing, and the like. The effort to push aside the volunteer women was clearly related to the larger shift in the 1920s and 1930s where policy-planning agencies began leading separate lives from service-providing agencies. The men, CSA staffers figured, were more cosmopolitan than the women. They would understand discussion of the child-care "system." The women volunteers, however, remained mired in their personal connection to the particular institution, more committed to seeing particular children helped than to figuring out how best to organize the city's welfare system.

This proved a strategic error. The men were unwilling to take on the burden, something that only became apparent to council professionals at the close of the decade. When Devine's report was presented to the Board of Managers in December 1935, the president of the Board of Managers, Mrs. David McDougal, tried to get all the directors to read it, but not one did, all citing the pressure of their own businesses as an excuse. The men dragged their feet on integrating the two boards. They refused to serve on committees to explore other changes. The Board of Directors, one of the men had told Mrs. McDougal in 1938, was "dead on its feet," an assessment she and the CSA officials soon concurred with.[85] The same traditionalism that dissipated the collective energies of the Board of Managers was affecting the Board of Directors, which was never very active in the first place.[86]

Still another reason that no significant change took place was the weak bargaining position of Community Fund. The new philanthropy in 1935 made the coordinating agencies more aggressive, but they could not yet coerce change. They learned that their "private power for the public good" had limits. Chapin Hall got less than 10 percent of its income from the fund. And with the increasing amounts of public money becoming available in the late 1930s, a private agency had other options.

But that was not yet apparent in 1935. At that point, downtown welfare professionals were very optimistic that the creation of the Community Fund would allow them to revamp Chicago charities. Devine's 1935 report on Chapin Hall was actually meant to be a prelude to much bigger reforms. When the CSA report on all Chicago Protestant child-care institutions was completed in 1937, a number of mergers were suggested to reduce the number of Protestant agencies in the city. The rationale was greater efficiency. Chapin Hall, it was urged, should merge with the Chicago Orphan Asylum, the Chicago Home for the Friendless, and the Protestant Child Haven.[87]

This was a serious attempt to break the decentralization of the Protestant charity. Merging most of the independent agencies would break traditional ties to particular institutions. At the same time, staff educated in allegiance to the professional community would be put in charge of the agencies. With one bold stroke, the nineteenth-century residues would be swept away.

The Realignment Committee that drew up the proposals represented a cross-section of interests, including the care-giving agencies. Mrs. David McDougal, the president of Chapin Hall, was a member. Still, the proposals themselves came from the welfare professionals.[88] Moreover, CSA officials had the mergers in mind at least since 1935. In the private meetings held before Isabel Devine's analysis of Chapin Hall was delivered in December 1935, CSA officials spoke among themselves about having Chapin Hall merge with exactly the same agencies named in the 1937 report, a full two years before the idea was officially a "proposal." One reason that the council staff did not try to force more reform in 1935 was because they thought there would be no such thing as Chapin Hall in a few years.

The merger movement failed. The individualism of the Protestant system proved too strong; their dependence on Community Fund too weak. While Chapin Hall women took part in the discussion for merger, following it until it "died a natural death," the institutions would not give up their traditional prerogatives. The Chicago Orphan Asylum and the Home for the Friendless were just as adamant about their autonomy as was Chapin Hall.[89]

The failed merger movement marked a substantial defeat for the CSA. Instead of centrally controlling the whole welfare system, the decentralized Protestant agencies remained intact. Moreover, the effort had antagonized the orphanage. Chapin Hall's 1941 decision to step away from the Community Fund was largely a response to the pressure CSA officials had tried to exert.

Once World War II started, hope for reform disappeared. The war burst Chicago's child-care system at its seams. New pressure would come only after the war, in 1948. And then it would be more intense, more pointed, and more successful. But just as in the Depression decade, the postwar pressure would be directly related to new sources of funding. Money once again would be the wedge for welfare reform.

CHILD WELFARE ADRIFT

Three things came together in the twenties and thirties to set Chapin Hall adrift. First, the number of volunteer women capable or willing to take on managerial duties shrank significantly. Second, public policy and demographics redesigned the nature of dependency so that a more prosperous but more troubled family came to Chapin Hall. Finally, the internal checks over intake that had been prominent during the nineteenth century disappeared as staff and managers turned to softer, more progressive ways of dealing with their clients.

While mentally troubled, overwhelmed, or just plain incapable parents increasingly wanted Chapin Hall to take their children, the procedures designed in the nineteenth century to keep out "unworthy" families were declared oppressive. And at the same time, the managers were losing the confidence to shape the institution themselves. Children wound up staying for years. Some found solace in a staff willing to share real affection; others felt crushed by circumstances. From the outside, however, the orphanage looked more like a warehouse than it ever did in the nineteenth century. The irony, of course, is that this happened not because the orphanage was hidebound and conservative, but because it had adopted progressive ways.

The drift at Chapin Hall can be seen as a symbol for the whole city. Forces hoping to reshape child welfare did not yet have the power to do so. Portents of the future were there to be seen—new sources of philanthropy would be central to restructuring child welfare—but the critical mass was not yet evident. The downtown professionals at the Council of Social Agencies could not assert their dominance. The real changes in Chicago child welfare in the 1930s—gradual increase in foster home care and the much more dramatic increase of mothers' aid—did not challenge the orphanages and industrial schools. Only the smallest and most marginal orphanages closed their doors in these years. A few other homes for dependent children did "modernize" their program in a directly anti-institutional way. The Chicago Orphan Asylum, the Chicago Home for the Friendless, and the Marks Nathan Jewish Orphans Home all went out of the business of housing dependent children and into the business of finding foster homes for them. Yet in each case, this came about because managers and staff of these institutions decided for themselves (with the advice of the downtown professionals) to make the change. Yet most institutions certainly did not make any such shift. They rather drifted like Chapin Hall, where wealthy volunteers in the Protestant homes, or priests and nuns in Catholic institutions, tried to create a warm, caring environment for the children who came under their care. In the middle of the 1940s, there were still over thirty orphanages and industrial homes in Chicago, with the capacity to house more than 5,000 children. In 1940, as noted above, there were still more children in institutions than in foster care. Chapin Hall's wealthy volunteer women represent what was happening in a lot of Protestant and nonsectarian agencies in Chicago: Although unable to provide direction of their own, they were not yet ready to hand over the institution to the staff. That left a profound hole at the center. By the 1940s, authority was shifting but no one could yet confidently take command.

∞ CHAPTER FIVE ∞

Group Living for Children

T HE IMPASSE OF THE 1940s WAS EVENTUALLY SOLVED by a new generation of women managers. A number of women were involved, among the most important Clarissa Haffner and Kay Milliken. These women were the last generation of female volunteers to really make significant decisions about the institution. It is not too extreme to say that in the late forties their guidance saved Chapin Hall from closing.

Haffner and Milliken joined the board in the late 1930s, recruited in the traditional manner, via friends and family in the North Shore suburbs. After World War II, however, they became key figures in Chapin Hall's management. By that time, the institution was confronting a new challenge from the professional welfare community. The Council of Social Agencies (now renamed the Welfare Council of Metropolitan Chicago) was once again pressing for change. Moreover, financing Chapin Hall continued to be a problem. Throughout the 1940s, managers and directors constantly bantered about schemes for new revenue.

What went on at Chapin Hall was happening at children's institutions all over the city. Postwar ideas about the importance of family life helped push welfare elites to finally destroy the nineteenth-century orphanage. "Normal" children should be in a home, the argument ran, and if the "natural" home was unavailable, a foster home should be provided. Orphanages, in turn, should be reconstituted as specialized institutions for emotionally disturbed children. Between 1945 and 1960, this thinking, which we will see at work in Chapin Hall, massively restructured urban child welfare throughout the whole city of Chicago.

This restructuring was evidence that managerial ideas first emerging in the 1920s had finally come of age. Private coordinating agencies with their roots in the Progressive Era took de facto control of the bulk of Chicago child welfare. The Welfare Council of Metropolitan Chicago, the Community Fund, the Association of Commerce, and the University of Chicago's School of Social Service Administration constituted an informal network that worked to rearrange and watch over the private orphanages and industrial schools scattered through the city. These "enlightened private groups" were finally defining the kinds of programs that would be available to dependent children in the city. Their power came via the money they controlled at the Community Fund.

At Chapin Hall, the restructuring began in earnest in 1947. In the next few years, the new generation of managers patiently instructed the male directors, soothed the egos of truculent staff, gently prodded the older and more skeptical female managers, and continually negotiated with downtown welfare professionals—all in an effort to remake Chapin Hall. (It is no surprise that Clarissa Haffner was affectionately called "The General" by some of the other managers, a reference to her considerable organizational skills.) By 1949 Chapin Hall would be in the middle of the largest transformation in its history, changes so extensive that the institution would no longer be an "orphanage" in any meaningful sense of the word.

THE CHANGE

In the mid-1940s the professional welfare community began a new round of criticism aimed at Chapin Hall, part of another large-scale effort to alter the system of child welfare in the Chicago area. But unlike in the 1930s, this time the efforts would work. Chapin Hall was not the only institution to bend; by the late 1950s, the whole landscape of Chicago child welfare would be different. The number of dependent children in institutions fell significantly. The urban orphanage, while not dead, would be seriously wounded. And there would be an increasing number of institutions devoting themselves to the psychotherapeutic treatment of emotionally disturbed or psychotic children. The "homey" progressive orphanage was increasingly displaced by foster home care and by institutions defining themselves via a medical model. Chapin Hall provides a good example of the latter.

The Second World War was not a good time for reform. War pressures overloaded all of Chicago's children's agencies. No one had enough space. No one had enough staff. Mabel Morrow, Chapin Hall's superintendent, told the managers in 1942 that "foster homes are becoming scarce and institutions have moved from their former low state to a place in the sun."[1] The staff and board of Chapin Hall took pride in providing desperately needed services. This crisis atmosphere, however, also helped staff and older managers avoid thinking about the institution's basic orientation. Lackadaisical attitudes about parents and length of stay persisted.

New and well-articulated ideas about the specific place of children's institutions were behind the assault. Since the turn of the century, social welfare theory generally pictured institutions as the second-best alternative for dependent children, where one went when home options weren't available. The task of the orphanage, then, was to try and replicate the home. During the forties, however, welfare professionals began talking about the limited but positive functions of *institutional* living. There were certain children who should not be in a home, it was argued. Children who were disruptive, unable to get along with others, and who were not developing an appropriately socialized personality would benefit from institutional life. Adolescents especially needed peer support, and if certain adolescents were too hard for either their own or foster parents to handle, a group home could help. These notions were so new in the 1940s that there was no agreed-on name for such institutions. They were variously called "study homes" or "group homes." In the early fifties, the name "residential treatment center" became widely used for those homes working with the most troubled children.[2]

No longer should the children's institution try to replicate a private home, as the progressive era "cottage ideal" did. The group home was a therapeutic institution for troubled youth. This was a widely held view in the 1950s, the stated opinion of the executive director of the Child Welfare League of America, to take but one example.[3] Nowhere, however, were the ideas more forcefully presented than by Susanne Schulze of the University of Chicago School of Social Service Administration. The so-called cottage system was a mirage, Schulze argued in 1942. Groups of twenty to thirty were not "families." The "true character of institutions then is *group living* and not family living." But this, to Schulze, did not mean that institutions were useless. For small groups of troubled adolescents this was exactly what was called for. Group living, Schulze reasoned, could make happier lives and better citizens. Schulze is especially important as she proved to be a regular consultant to Chapin Hall between the late 1940s and early 1960s.[4]

If the "good" institution was being reconceptualized as something other than a home, this was a solution meant for only a small number of emotionally disturbed children. And Schulze was only articulating what was rapidly becoming the accepted wisdom in professional welfare circles. As Andrew Polsky has recently pointed out, the Social Security Act threw therapeutic-minded welfare experts on the defensive. Since the Progressive Era, such experts had argued that great expanses of the working class were maladjusted and needed help from professional caseworkers. New Deal programs, aimed at people who were "no different from you or me," undermined that assumption. But by the 1940s, Polsky notes, social workers had refigured their role as providing far more intense services for a small minority of the population.[5] This was exactly the sort of thinking that led Chicago welfare managers to attack orphanages and argue that they should be turned into smaller, more intensely therapeutic environments for emotionally disturbed children.

As the overwhelming majority of dependent children were now assumed to be "normal," it was argued that they belonged at home. The new thinking about institutions was the reverse side of a deep hostility to the mid-twentieth-century urban orphanage. Too many children were in institutions, welfare reformers argued. Almost every child in a place like Chapin Hall shouldn't be there.

Elaine Tyler May has suggested that a deeply conservative notion of the nuclear family served as a central ideological bulwark of the Cold War. By the late 1940s, it was commonly argued that traditional family roles had to be maintained in the face of the communist threat.[6] While too much might be made of this point, especially in the realm of welfare policy,[7] it is nonetheless true that the will to force the closing of many Chicago orphanages was finally mustered at a moment of intense pressure to maintain the nuclear family. Moreover, these closings were done in the name of reuniting families.

If new welfare thinking contributed to the assault on orphanages in Chicago, demographic shifts were another factor. The general decline of orphans in the twentieth century has already been remarked on. By 1949, only 23 of the 149 children who resided in Chapin Hall had either parent dead.[8] The problem that had led to the creation of the asylum in the nineteenth-century had, for all practical purposes, disappeared.

The new social welfare theory, in fact, in part reflected the realization that children with altogether different problems were the new clients of children's institutions. As early as the 1920s, staffers at the Council of Social Agencies were arguing that "children who present behavior problems" were increasingly difficult to place. That theme became a rallying cry in the years after the war, all over the nation. Wilfred Reynolds, director of the Welfare Council of Metropolitan Chicago, noted in 1949 that increasing numbers of children "with scars in the form of serious behavior and emotional problems" were coming for help, the result of "broken homes and parental irresponsibility." By the 1940s the U.S. Children's Bureau was estimating that "72 percent of the requests for placement of children involved deep emotional problems of family relationships," indicating that "other members of the family, as well as the children, needed help." By the late 1940s, as welfare theorists asserted that "normal" children belonged at home, the troubled child became the "new" dependent needing institutionalization.[9]

Black migration from the South created demographic problems of a very different sort. A large new population needing social services had almost no institutions to provide them. Julius Rosenwald had funded an African-American orphanage in the 1920s, so there was always at least one home for this population in the next decade. But these were small, underfunded institutions. In 1930 the Martha Washington Home for Dependent Crippled Children (capacity: fifty children) served the African-American population, although it was not, strictly speaking, an orphanage. The only other institution for dependent black children was a small home with a capacity of fourteen. This was at a time when white institutions in the city could accommodate over 5,600 children.[10]

The Welfare Council had tried to ignore the issue until the mid-thirties, when it began pressing Protestant placing agencies to develop more extensive foster care programs and tried to force the city of Chicago to take more responsibility for dependent black children. These efforts were unsuccessful, meaning that into the 1940s dependent African-American children had, for practical purposes, no access to either institutional or foster home care. The council changed its strategy in 1943, creating the Committee on Facilities for Negro Children. This committee turned away from the earlier strategy of expanding the foster care system for African-Americans and began looking at ways of supporting institutional services for dependent black youngsters—either by creating a new home for dependent black youth or by integrating existing institutions. The last led them to Chapin Hall.[11]

Chapin Hall had regularly accepted African-Americans in the nineteenth century. As late as 1914, black children were being admitted. But by the middle of the 1920s, the orphanage excluded blacks. White hostility had risen after the race riots of the First World War. And migration from the South during 1917 and 1918 changed the racial composition of the city, hugely increasing the number of black children needing assistance. It was in this climate that Chapin Hall stopped serving African-Americans. In retrospect, the integration of the nineteenth century was largely dependent on the small numbers of blacks in Chicago.

From the middle of the Second World War on, downtown welfare agencies steadily called on Chicago orphanages to reconsider their white-only policy.[12] Chapin Hall steadfastly resisted, citing the prejudice of the neighborhood and children as insuperable obstacles. It "would take too long to break down prejudices," Mabel Morrow argued at one point. Chapin Hall, she told the managers, "had troubles of our own without that being added."[13]

There was nothing unique about Chapin Hall's resistance to integration, something that continued for over another decade. In the mid-forties all sorts of Chicago's non-profit institutions were variously complicit in different sorts of explicit segregation. The University of Chicago, to take one example, supported restrictive covenants until they were outlawed by the Supreme Court in 1949. Such covenants, written into real estate contracts, legally forbade white professors from selling their homes to blacks. And up to 1953 *no* private Protestant children's home in the city accepted black children. The walls remained high. And as a consequence, there were next to no social services in Chicago for African-American youth into the middle of the 1950s.[14]

The downtown agencies were also pushing Chapin Hall to change the ways it dealt with its children. Social work professionals from the University of Chicago and the Council of Social Agencies let the managers know they thought the orphanage's services were dreadfully inadequate. Chapin Hall was told that children with "marked behavior problems" were the single group most neglected by the city's private agencies. In 1944, Ethel Verry of the Council of Social Agencies asked Chapin Hall to admit more "problem cases." But here too the managers threw up their hands, arguing that resources were stretched thin, the orphanage already bursting at the seams.[15]

The failure to bend Chapin Hall reveals how inopportune wartime was for change. The immensity of the problems created by the war left everyone—downtown professionals as well as the private agencies—just struggling to keep up. The large numbers of African-Americans who came to Chicago for work added to an already viciously inadequate system.

After the war, the welfare professionals came back at Chapin Hall and the other children's institutions. But by this time there were key managers at Chapin Hall more amenable to reform and who started to raise their voices. Kay Milliken, president of the Board of Managers by 1947, and Clarissa Haffner, who would serve as president later, were two very important catalysts of change. These women began hunting around for ways that the institution could adapt to the new needs of child welfare in the mid-twentieth century, a search which led to an alliance with the downtown professionals. Together they would push everyone else connected with

Chapin Hall in a new direction. What went on at Chapin Hall in the late 1940s and early 1950s was being repeated at dozens of children's homes in the city.

Behind the change in heart at Chapin Hall were money woes. There was an ongoing financial crisis at the orphanage during the 1940s. In 1943 the directors and managers began to reapply for membership in Community Fund, but when the agency raised the specter of integration, the orphanage withdrew its application.[16] By 1948, however, the managers were feeling desperate. In 1947 and 1948, there was a deficit of $30,000, money taken from the general endowment. It was this, the financial problem, that led Milliken, Haffner, and a few other key managers to begin to look for ways to reorient Chapin Hall. In 1948, these women organized an Easter season fundraising drive that became an annual effort for Chapin Hall. But even that was not enough. The managers decided to rejoin Community Fund.

This set in motion huge changes. By the middle of 1948, Haffner and Milliken were working with downtown professionals like Connie Fish of the Welfare Council to maneuver Chapin Hall in a new direction. As a condition of membership in the Community Fund, Chapin Hall had to be intensively studied. The report was done by Elizabeth Goddard, a Welfare Council staffer. Her suggestions were all in keeping with newly evolved notions of what a child-care institution should be. Psychiatric counseling, more extensive casework services, and more professionalization were recommended along with a "richer and more creative" program for the children. All of this implied, but did not state, that emotionally disturbed children would be the norm. The whole drift of the report was to edge Chapin Hall toward becoming a residential group home.[17]

The evaluation was critical but mild. And in June 1948 the Welfare Council formally approved Chapin Hall's program.[18] Yet what was expressed privately was far more blistering. Elizabeth Goddard told Kay Milliken, the president of the Board of Managers, that "things were very much worse than they had put in the report." Chapin Hall was hopelessly out-of-date, Goddard said. Her superiors concurred. Many of the smallest children regularly wet their beds, something "which had never been reported to the Board." This, Goddard noted, was "a sure sign of disturbed children." The caseworker had too big a load, and Mabel Morrow had been totally uncooperative with the investigators. The whole place looked "like an old ladies home instead of a children's institution."[19]

The report reflected the larger desire of the professional community to challenge the urban orphanage. At the same time, Chapin Hall felt pressure from other sources. The state's Department of Public Welfare, for the first time ever, gave a basically negative evaluation of Chapin Hall in 1948. The specific suggestions made by the state were almost identical to those Goddard had made in the Welfare Council report finished just four months before. In January of 1949, the state ominously requested information about "policy and facilities for caring for negro children." But far more shocking to the managers and directors, in the autumn of 1948 Chicago's Association of Commerce threatened to withhold accreditation from Chapin Hall. Since Chapin Hall was not a member of the Community Fund, about 15 percent of its yearly income came from donations from wealthy North Shore families. Without the Association's imprimatur such support would have been almost impossible. While the orphanage was endorsed for 1949, Clarissa Haffner warned the male directors that "they may come back at us again."[20]

The Welfare Council held a series of informational meetings for Chapin Hall's managers. Things were so bad, the managers were told, that if any children were actually helped it was just "accidental."[21] For those sympathetic to change, like Haffner and Milliken, such meetings were informational, giving guidance on what had to be done. For the older and less receptive managers, the meetings were warnings—the agency was in such bad shape that no one should expect that it could go on this way indefinitely.

If managers like Haffner actually initiated the change, they had to contend with others who resisted. The male directors remained largely passive, some of the older managers skeptical. Key staff was also opposed. To Mabel Morrow, the superintendent, and Blanche Robertson, the caseworker, any new policy was a threat. Morrow in particular was obstructionist, uncooperative with Welfare Council investigators, and strongly hostile to suggestions for any substantial shift in the institution's direction.[22]

Neither Milliken nor Haffner wanted to treat Morrow shabbily. Morrow had served the agency well and was, moreover, sixty-six years old, in poor health, and without a pension. (Chapin Hall had no pension system at the time.) Still, by the end of 1948, Elizabeth Goddard had told the managers that nothing was more important than getting rid of Morrow. She suggested ways of doing this gently but if that didn't work, she added, Morrow would have to be told to leave. And while a new caseworker was not an immediate necessity, that department would soon have to be strengthened.[23]

The situation dragged on for several months. Finally, the staff, who probably saw the writing on the wall, took the initiative. In April 1949 caseworker Blanche Robertson resigned to pursue her master's at the University of Chicago. One month later Mabel Morrow submitted her resignation. A farewell luncheon was held and board members worked out a private pension.

These were the final impediments to change. By the summer of 1949 there was a emphatic effort to modernize Chapin Hall. By the middle of 1952, countless changes had occurred, changes in personnel, intake, program, financing, and in the role of the Board of Managers. It was the largest change in the institution's history up until that time.

The story of Chapin Hall in these years is just one piece of a huge change in Chicago child welfare in the postwar years. Between 1945 and 1960, a whole range of orphanages and industrial schools moved on to other sorts of services. A number, like Chapin Hall, became homes for emotionally disturbed children. Ridge Farm in 1946 advertised itself as caring for "undernourished, pre-tuberculous girls." By 1961 it touted itself as providing "residential treatment for emotionally disturbed girls." Lawrence Hall for Boys in 1961 would advertise its "psychiatric consultation and casework service," both absent in 1946. In 1946 the Ridge Park School for Girls claimed it offered "an academic course from sixth through twelfth grade." In 1961 it offered "casework oriented psychotherapy under the supervision of a psychiatric consultant."[24]

There were also new institutions created to serve emotionally disturbed or developmentally disabled children, the children who would need intensive therapy. The Orthogenic School at the University of Chicago, run by Bruno Bettelheim, opened in the late 1940s. So too did the Joseph P. Kennedy School for Exceptional Children, a Catholic institution funded by the Kennedy family. Lutheran social welfare, still as self-contained as the Catholic system, opened the Lutherbrook Children's Center in Addison. In all, six new institutions appeared in Chicago between 1946 and 1961 to provide specialized services for emotionally disturbed and developmentally disabled youth.[25]

Other orphanages turned in different directions in those years. A couple revamped their facilities to become homes for seniors instead of children. Another choice was to turn into a foster-home finding agency. Still others just shut their doors. Most of these agencies closed in the early 1950s. In all, the number of orphanages in Chicago dropped from thirty-one in 1946 to fourteen in 1961.[26] Central to this change was the new power of Community Fund and the Welfare Council.

To be sure, not every institution changed. Particularly recalcitrant were the huge Catholic orphanages which managed to resist Community Fund pressure and continued to amble on as before. There were also scattered nonsectarian agencies outside the fold. But, nevertheless, the aggregate change was striking. The urban orphanage was dealt a real blow. And the number of children's institutions providing some sort of therapeutic program for emotionally disturbed or disabled children went from zero to at least eleven.[27] If one takes into account every sort of children's institution, including hospitals, temporary institutions for children on their way to foster care, and homes for unwed mothers and their children, the number of institutions in Chicago a child might live in dropped from sixty-three to forty-six.[28] As we shall see below, all these changes were tied to a very successful effort by welfare managers to reduce the number of institutionalized dependent children.

At Chapin Hall, the program change solved the institution's money woes. But it also subjected the agency to the de facto regulation of the downtown welfare agencies. After 1949, budgets had to be submitted each year to Community Fund for approval. All fundraising, key hiring, and new building had to be approved in advance. Chapin Hall did not just join the Community Fund. It joined an urban welfare system managed by the fund, the Welfare Council of Metropolitan Chicago, Chicago's Association of Commerce, and key professors at the University of Chicago's School of Social Service Administration.

The State of Illinois, it should be emphasized, was not a major factor. Significantly, in 1948 Haffner thought the bad report from the Association of Commerce was "the crowning blow."[29] The important players were the private institutions created in the Progressive Era to monitor Chicago welfare. The changes at Chapin Hall had nothing to do with any New Deal legislation. They rather reflected Chapin Hall's integration into the system of "private power for the public good" dreamt of by turn-of-the-century welfare reformers. In the late forties, at long last, the system appeared to be in place and working.

But there were a few differences. Unlike at the turn of the century, there was now no desire to force change through publicity. The Welfare Council negotiated with agencies like Chapin Hall in paneled offices and not in the newspapers, an approach soothing to the reputations (and egos) of those well-established Chicago commercial families on Chapin Hall's boards. At the worst, only the threat of publicity was dangled in front of the managers.

Moreover, the dream of managing the system as a piece disappeared. There was no repeat of the 1937 effort to alter all Chicago area child welfare in one fell swoop. Instead, each agency was dealt with individually through subtle combinations of pressure and negotiation. While more cumbersome, it also proved more effective, as witnessed by the sea change in Chicago's children's agencies during the late forties and fifties.

What had evolved was a private bureaucracy with the capacity to manage Chicago's Protestant and Jewish welfare system. Commercial elites who served on the boards of agencies like Community Fund were at the center, supported (or perhaps controlled) by welfare professionals like Connie Fish, Ethel Verry, or Susanne Schulze. Central to the regulatory power was the control of small but critical sources of funding, combined with quiet, behind-the-scenes pressure.

A HOME FOR TROUBLED CHILDREN

Between the spring of 1949 and the middle of 1952 managers like Haffner and Milliken shepherded Chapin Hall through its biggest change ever. There were new written policies on intake and personnel. A consulting psychiatrist was hired. New caseworkers were brought in. Numerous housemothers were replaced. The responsibilities of the Board of Managers changed significantly. Even the physical plant was altered, as children were split into groups of ten to fifteen. All these changes, as well as others, revolved around creating a more "advanced," "modern" program for the children.

As noted above, one of the major changes in child care after the war was the rise of therapeutically oriented institutions throughout the city. Chapin Hall's program was one of a range developed by downtown professionals at mid-century to treat those children categorized as "emotionally disturbed." It was the mildest option imagined. Other agencies in these years took in far more troubled youth, those labeled "psychotic," or those developmentally disabled. In the 1960s, as we shall see, federal law and the State of Illinois would be critical catalysts for turning all Chicago children's institutions, including Chapin Hall, in a far more intensely therapeutic direction. In terms of later developments, the 1950s Chapin Hall was a sort of way station between the orphanage of the earlier years and the more involved therapeutic environment of the 1960s through 1980s.

Perhaps the most important move made by the managers was to hire a new head administrator, Adrianna Bouterse. Bouterse, who had an M.A. in social work from the University of Chicago, took over in September 1949 and threw herself into the remaking of Chapin Hall.[30]

The first task was to reduce the population. A month before Bouterse was hired, Haffner convinced the managing board to temporarily halt new admissions and begin telling selected parents they had to take their children home. Bouterse heartily endorsed the policy and implemented it vigorously. Between 1949 and 1951, the number of children living in Chapin

Hall fell from 121 to sixty-nine. Further cuts were made until the middle of the decade when somewhere around fifty to fifty-five children would live in Chapin Hall at any given time. This contrasts with the 120 to 130 living there in the twenties, thirties, and forties.

In 1948 and 1949, the downtown professionals firmly told the managers that too many children who belonged at home were languishing in Chapin Hall. This was one of Elizabeth Goddard's main criticisms. In June 1949, the managers fell into line with the professionals' wishes, radically altering their ideas about the institutionalization of children.

Welfare professionals had long argued that very young children should never be in institutions, that foster care was always better. The Board of Managers closed the nursery for children two to six years old. All these children were sent to either natural or foster parents. In April 1950 the managers formally decided that Chapin Hall no longer accepted any children not yet in grade school.[31]

The managers also changed their attitude toward parents. Many mothers and fathers were told in no uncertain terms that their children had to go home, something unheard of in the thirties and forties. Relaxed attitudes toward the parents abruptly ended. The focus on the nuclear family, which became so important during the Cold War, was certainly a driving force behind the changes at Chapin Hall. The present focus, the Case Committee observed, was "the re-education of the parents and the rehabilitation of the home." They continued:

> An example of the respect our new policies have created in the minds of parents is a Father who has had two daughters here for six years. He has promised to remove them but never did. He was finally told firmly to remove them by the end of the school year. This scared him so that he immediately placed them with an aunt where they had been spending their weekends and could have been living all along.[32]

Caseworkers in 1950 routinely threatened recalcitrant parents with court action. If the children were not removed, Chapin Hall would attempt to take legal custody. The board also decided that "free" cases would no longer be accepted, ending a policy that dated back to the 1860s. There was simply no longer any logic to the policy, Bouterse told the managers. In an age when the state paid for those without resources, solvent parents "must not be allowed to neglect their responsibilities."[33]

Most of the children leaving Chapin Hall did return home. Of the fifty-two children who left in 1949, thirty-five returned to their parents, six were placed with relatives, and another six went to foster homes. Only five found their way to other institutions. In 1950, a few more children went to foster homes, but the general drift was the same—many children who had been in an institution were now at home.[34]

By becoming a much smaller place, Chapin Hall reflected larger trends. Throughout the city, the staffs at service-providing agencies were forcing parents to remove their children from the institutions. While a number of orphanages in Chicago closed in the 1950s, many more changed policy so as to house far fewer children. As happened at Chapin Hall, the same physical plant would be reconverted to maintain as many as 100 fewer children. Between 1948 and 1953, at least ten other children's institutions in the city made such a change, accounting for much of the fall in the number of institutionalized dependent children.[35]

After 1948 the number of dependent children living in institutions fell swiftly, a change due to the administrative pressures exerted by the Community Fund, the Welfare Council of Metropolitan Chicago, and by academics like Susanne Schulze. As late as 1945, Chicago's ratio of children in institutions to children in foster homes was still about 1:1. There were still almost 5,000 children in orphanages and industrial schools. By 1960, however, 6,538 Chicago area children were in foster homes with only 2,904 in institutions. In those years, the number of available beds in children's institutions dropped by over two thousand. By every yardstick, the fifteen years after World War II marked a huge change in attitudes about the institutionalization of dependent children.[36]

What happened in Chicago was going on all over the country. Industrial schools were closing. Orphanages were turning into much smaller homes for emotionally disturbed children. In the 1950s, the number of institutionalized dependent minors (under the age of eighteen) dropped by 25 percent. Still, we should interpret this cautiously, for the overall number of institutionalized minors actually rose 18 percent in those years.[37] It appears that a number of children who might have been put in an orphanage in the 1930s were in the 1950s eventually finding their way into reformatories for juvenile delinquents. It is at least worth speculating that the rising interest in juvenile delinquency after 1945 might be connected to the fact that far fewer children from marginal families were being allowed into homes for dependent children. It is quite likely that one major side effect of the decline in orphanages after World War II was to redefine large groups of children from dependent to delinquent.

What sort of child was supposed to live at the new Chapin Hall? The phrase "emotionally disturbed" is a notoriously vague one, something social workers realized at the time. According to Susanne Schulze, it included those children who "need protection from unstable parents," who have suffered "a succession of failures in foster homes," who are "being used as a pawn" by separated parents. If these children became troubled, if they needed "regular habit training," then a group home was a good solution. "Emotionally disturbed," for Schulze, quite explicitly did not mean "psychotic." There was a "consensus of opinion," she argued, that institutions could handle only a "limited number of seriously disturbed children" before the other children would suffer.[38]

It was exactly this kind of child who was being thought of in 1945 when the Council on Social Agencies began asking Chapin Hall to take more "problem children."[39] And in 1949, Chapin Hall formally acceded to the professionals' wishes. When Chapin Hall redesigned intake policy in 1951, it listed guidelines that almost exactly echoed Schulze's 1947 article. Indeed, at some points the correspondence was word for word.[40]

In the late 1940s, emotionally disturbed meant "troubled"—no more, no less. The children who came to Chapin Hall in the early 1950s were not very different from those of previous decades. They came almost exclusively from working-class families. They were evenly split between boys and girls. Although all denominations were accepted by the 1950s, the children were overwhelmingly from Protestant backgrounds. Until the early 1960s, the children were all white. By the 1950s, almost all children were from broken homes; it was overwhelmingly the mother who had previous custody.

Moreover, the case records do not indicate any markedly different behavioral traits. Certainly until the late 1950s, children who came to Chapin Hall were essentially functional, able to get on in some fashion at home, school, and with peers. In fact, through the middle of the decade, most children came to Chapin Hall for the same reasons they had in the 1930s, because their parents were having difficulties coping. Caseworkers often spent page after page discussing the parent's maladjustments or immaturity. Mothers who were overtly psychotic, who lacked any sense of self-worth, who smothered their children, who were incapable of organizing a household, were all common. Fathers, when they entered the picture at all, were overwhelmingly alcoholics.[41]

Not surprisingly, children from such families did have problems. Yet, when compared with later years, the difficulties the children presented were quite minor. Boys were often aggressive, girls depressed. Both sexes could be unusually immature or insecure. Yet rarely do we find these problems being profoundly debilitating. In one typical case from the early 1950s, the oldest of three siblings dominated other children, the middle child often wanted adults to hug him, and the six-year-old girl would break into tears when thinking about her parents. Sometimes after weekend visits home she would not eat.[42] All three had friends, could generally relate to adult authority, and did tolerably well in school. In another case, a boy was described as "difficult," although the word meant that he "wants to do things his own way," not doing chores, bullying others, and on occasion picking fights. At other times, however, he could be "a loving child."[43] In still a third case, one brother was a "bully" who dominated peers by "fighting with other boys" and who used "bad language." His sibling was quiet and shy, "immature and unable to maintain himself in the group."[44] Such children had problems to be sure, but by 1980s standards such children would never even be considered for placement in a residential treatment center. Up to the mid-fifties, such children were the norm at Chapin Hall.

Children who were admitted because of their own behavioral problems instead of their parents' were extremely rare before 1955. After that, however, they came with more frequency. In 1956 Adrianna Bouterse reported that "we are getting an increased number of children who can be classified as potentially delinquent." In 1963, George Headley, Bouterse's successor, noted that many Chapin Hall children had "a difficult time" in the regular public school: "Many unadjusted, disturbed children . . . are being referred to us." Children who couldn't cope in public school were not the sort of children that the Policy Committee had in mind when it developed intake regulations in 1951. In fact, such children had been explicitly excluded as too disturbed.[45]

Through the 1950s, welfare policy professionals remained very concerned that both African-American and the most emotionally disturbed adolescents could not find placements in Chicago children's institutions. Moreover, officials were convinced that the number of children in need was rising faster than the population. In 1954, county officials proposed setting up a child-placing office of their own. On June 1, 1955, the Cook County Division of Child Welfare was chartered as a part of the Illinois Department of Welfare. Public authorities immediately began using the division to press private agencies into taking "tougher" children.[46] What Adrianna Bouterse was commenting on in 1956 was the first of what would be many efforts by state officials in the next three decades to push back the meaning of "emotionally disturbed." For Chapin Hall and other children's institutions, this would mean persistent calls to take harder cases, more disturbed children.

By the early 1960s, it was common to have in Chapin Hall children who exposed themselves, had sex with each other (as early as age twelve), or who habitually stole and lied. Boys, especially, could be frequent brawlers.

An increasing number did not respond well to adult authority of any kind. A small but growing number were not welcome in Chicago public schools.

These children came from more thoroughly disorganized households. Between the 1920s and mid-1950s, children came to Chapin Hall mostly because divorce, separation, and desertion left one parent who could not (or would not) cope. But beginning in the late 1950s, there are more cases of more disturbingly fractured parents. As before, many fathers had disappeared so it was the mother who dealt with the agency. There was, for example, the mother who couldn't seem to ever stop crying and desperately tried to keep her son from growing up. She had married a policeman who beat her and lived openly with other women. She feared that when her son matured, he would, like all men, become a "sex maniac."[47] Or there was the mother who moved in with another man and took care of his children while leaving her natural son, age two, in the hands of the state. The mother hated her son's father, who had vanished by the time the social worker became involved; she wanted nothing to do with her boy. The boy arrived at Chapin Hall at age six, an emotional cripple.[48]

About one out of three children were most recently in the custody of a father. These parents, too, were increasingly unstable. The father of a boy and girl admitted in 1961 was a Serbian Orthodox concentration camp survivor with no emotional stamina at all. He was overwhelmed by his past and inability to prosper in the United States. He was alcoholic, with poor English, and had trouble holding a job. He fought constantly with his wife, who was Catholic and wanted the children raised in her faith. The father, for his part, violently opposed Catholic foster parents. After his wife left, the father and the two children (ages eleven and nine) lived in a horribly dirty basement apartment. He gave no direction to their lives, alternately beating and ignoring them. They were malnourished and dirty. After neighbors complained, the state brought them to Chapin Hall.[49]

The evolution of the program reflected the changing problems of the children. At first, in the early 1950s, the case records show a preoccupation with parents. Their disorders were uppermost in the minds of the staff, their incapacities worked on. Since social work was only for "troubled" children, only a handful of the children living in Chapin Hall had a caseworker assigned to them. Most kids, who were not as troublesome as their parents, had regular contact only with the houseparents. When a psychiatrist was hired in 1952, he only consulted with a handful of children.

But as the decade wore on and more troubled children came in, the professional staff grew. A second caseworker was hired in 1955, a third in

1960. Added funds were found to extend the coverage the psychiatrist could give. By 1962, all children were regularly visiting with caseworkers, and more than half were being seen by the psychoanalyst.

After 1957, the shift toward more psychiatric care was especially pronounced. In that year, "staffings" were introduced. These were biannual sessions where everyone involved with the child—caseworker, houseparents, psychiatrist, and executive director—would come together and discuss the case. The focus was psychoanalytic. Where it was thought possible, the staff was willing to work with the whole family. But in that increasing number of cases where the staff decided the parents were hopeless, the focus shifted to building the ego resources of the children.

The staff was trained to not present themselves as "family," one sign of the new professional ethos. Throughout the case records are reports of Chapin Hall social workers telling children that "they are caseworkers, not mommies." Yet children with little in their lives often clung to caseworkers; the departure of a caseworker could be as traumatic as the change of a foster parent. The whole system too easily tipped into cruelty. One particularly poignant report is of a caseworker asking a neglected eight-year-old boy how it felt not having a family. As the boy fell apart, descending into rage, the caseworker would not back off, trying to force the boy to answer, reporting that she gradually faced "a pervasive, persistent, snarling, pettish, destructive kind of anger."[50]

The whole system encouraged children to think they were "sick." The professional distance of the staff, the psychoanalytic jargon, the psychologist's visits, the pervasive talk of "emotional disturbance"—it all added up. For the less troubled children, the presence of more disturbed peers reflected back on them. Were they as "sick" as the others? At the same time, while the system taught children they were "disturbed," there is evidence in the case records that at least some children, even young children, resisted the label, disagreeing with the professionals' assessment.

While children with their own personality problems appeared increasingly after 1955, they still did not exhibit the extreme personality disorders that later children would. Until 1963, those who could not function in public school were not admitted. Nor were overtly psychotic or extremely violent children admitted.[51] One boy who would drift into trances for hours, who could not connect with children, and who was simply unable to function in school was deemed unsuited for Chapin Hall. A girl, admitted in 1952, was dismissed in 1953 as too tough a case. She provides a good example of the kind of child that even in the early 1960s was not wanted:

Sheila must be continuously watched to see that she does not have any sharp objects or else she would jab these into the children. Also, her strength is greater than any of her peers and she will lock her hands and hammer them down on an unsuspecting victims head. Her cruelty to animals is extreme. When she finds beetles, butterflies, etc., or is given a bird, she will system-matically tear them to pieces. Her trance-like behavior has continued and she can sit for the better part of an hour staring vacantly into space when she should be getting dressed or doing other things.

Diagnosed as schizophrenic, she was sent to a more restrictive institu-tion.[52]

Scholars have often interpreted the professional social work commu-nity's growing interest in psychiatry as an effort to win professional re-spectability.[53] Yet by the time psychiatric social work came to Chicago social service agencies such as Chapin Hall, it had nothing to do with that. At the agency level, at least, interest in psychiatry was linked to the chang-ing character of the clientele rather than to any quest for status. The belief that the "new" dependent child was the emotionally troubled youth was what made psychotherapy important. This is not to defend all the mis-taken prejudices of mid-century psychoanalysis—the tendency to overin-terpret small events, to blame mothers for their family problems, to blur the line between normal and sick behavior. All this has been aptly re-ported; I am not disputing it.[54] But I do want to add a point not mentioned in the secondary literature: The push for psychoanalytic analysis came from the sense that a more emotionally fractured child was entering the system. Despite its being severely myopic in many ways, the introduction of psychoanalysis marks the first time in Chapin Hall's history that there is a record of someone seriously listening to the children. With the shift to psychoanalytic case records in 1957, the child's voice appears.

It may be the case that by the 1990s the children coming into contact with the social welfare system are so disturbed that psychiatric social work is inappropriate and that continued usage represents "a turn away from the profession's historical roots."[55] That, however, was not so in the middle decades of the century. In Chicago children's agencies, that is at the point where services were actually delivered to children, psychoanalysis repre-sented an attempt to come to terms with a clientele that suffered more emotional disorganization than previously.

After World War II, children whose parents were receiving Aid to Fam-ilies with Dependent Children no longer were classified as "dependent." Poverty itself, in other words, did not equal "dependence." This reflects changing attitudes about the relevant population needing casework intervention. Only those children who were emotionally troubled themselves or whose parents could not cope continued to be thought of as dependents. And even here, most children were moved to a foster home and away from an institution. By 1961, as noted above, only twelve orphanages and two industrial schools were left in the city. This was down from thirty-one such institutions in 1946. At the same time, there were five homes for emotionally disturbed children such as Chapin Hall and six residential treatment centers offering more extensive psychotherapy for more troubled children. The trend toward the medical model would continue in the next decade. And the state's entrance into the child-placing business would prove crucial. Public authorities would continue to search for those institutions that could house and "treat" the most troubled of the city's youth.

REARRANGING CONTROL

The arrival of Adrianna Bouterse in the fall of 1949 signaled more than a change in attitude toward the children. It also marked a massive shift in the respective roles of staff and managers in Chapin Hall, and in the relationship among staff, managers, and the professional welfare community. In the 1950s Chapin Hall's professional staff took control of the day-to-day running of the institution. And, indirectly, downtown welfare professionals set the grand course of the institution. During the 1950s, the managers were marginalized. Ironically, in their effort to save Chapin Hall and reset its course, Clarissa Haffner and Kay Milliken implemented policies that would make them the last volunteer managers to have a major say in how the institution was run.

While the particulars of the story are Chapin Hall's own, some variation was going on at almost all of the non-Catholic children's institutions in the city. Between the end of the 1940s and the early 1960s, the volunteer descendants of the nineteenth-century founders stepped aside at agency after agency, all through the prodding of the downtown welfare professionals. It was in those years that a significant number of agencies first had executive directors with master's degrees in social work. This was the moment, at least outside the Catholic welfare system, where the professionals took over the agencies for good.

It was the culmination of a long process. At Chapin Hall, for example, the staff had been taking over certain tasks previously done by the managers as early as the 1920s. But by the early 1960s it was clear that the workload had been essentially redefined. And from the moment Adrianna Bouterse arrived in the autumn of 1949, there was a new tone in the relationship between staff and managers.

It was Bouterse and not the managers who shaped written policy on intake and personnel, something downtown agencies had long wanted. (In general, formal and written policies were ways for downtown professionals to exert control. They defined intake, volunteer board duties, and staff requirements in ways that bound the caring agencies to the professional agenda.) Chapin Hall's managers had actually tried their hand at a written personnel policy in 1949, but Bouterse privately told Welfare Council staffers that the guidelines were "so poor" that "they should not be thought of as official practices." She redid them in 1951. In a general way Bouterse's version was more sympathetic to the support staff. There were better salaries and more relaxed rules about reprimands and dismissal. Bouterse also placed far more emphasis on having houseparents understand what a group home was. Rather than simply the warm and tender care that the managers had stressed, Bouterse demanded that houseparents keep abreast of developments in social work theory.[56]

Bouterse had come to Chapin Hall with clear ideas about what the institution should be. Mabel Morrow never had such an independent vision. Bouterse also came with the self-confidence that went along with her professional credentials. She knew what a "group home" should look like and she knew she was hired to create one. Very quickly, by the mid-1950s, Bouterse had control over all hiring except for that of the consulting psychiatrist.

Similarly, by the early 1960s control over the daily finances of Chapin Hall also passed from the managers to the staff. New accounting procedures were brought in by Bouterse in 1950. Kay Milliken was the last effective treasurer from the Board of Managers, and when she resigned in the late fifties, there was no one to replace her. The situation dragged along for some years until, under the presidency of Julia McNulty, a professional was hired to do the work.

Intake decisions also passed from the managing board to the professional staff. While a caseworker had been doing much of the work since the late 1920s, the Board of Managers still made the final decisions. In the 1930s, the professional welfare community failed to convince the managers to hand intake decisions to the staff. After World War II, they tried again.

Not all the managers were willing. In the discussions that took place in the winter of 1948–49 at the Welfare Council of Metropolitan Chicago, Connie Fish told the managers that it was "not their function to decide admission." Susanne Schulze, who was also at the meeting, agreed. Some of the Chapin Hall women, however, protested that the board must "take responsibility for formulating general intake policy and for giving help to the staff when cases arose that fell outside policy." Handing intake decisions to the staff "might cause board members to lose interest," they argued.[57]

By ending the managers' involvement with intake and finances, the professionals also effectively ended the managers' knowledge of the day-to-
day workings of Chapin Hall. For working on admissions, even with only
troublesome cases, kept the active board members in the 1940s abreast of
the basic details of the orphanage's workings. It also gave them some contact with parents. Keeping track of daily finances did the same. By the end
of the 1950s such knowledge was gone; the staff had to regularly brief the
Board of Managers about what was going on inside Chapin Hall.

Staff briefings originated in the 1930s, so they were not entirely new.
Still, in the years after World War II, especially after the loss of control
over money and intake, even the Executive Committee of the Board had to
be told who the children were, how they were being treated, and how much
it was all costing. Knowledge of the day-to-day workings of the institution
had largely disappeared.

Exactly how removed the managers had become can be gleaned from
the Building Committee's May 1955 report to the whole board on the need
for remodeling. The report was given by Nancy Rich, one of the more
active managers of the decade. Still, her report shows how little the chair of
the Building Committee actually knew about the building. She noted that
despite having "come to Chapin Hall for many years," it "was with quite a
shock" that the committee toured the whole complex. Managers' knowledge of the plant was restricted to their meeting rooms and a few showplaces. We "have all seen and admired our new wing, the living and dining
rooms at the Girls' Cottage, the revamped offices and maybe even the
boiler room—but when you look at the rest of the building you begin to
wonder where you are and what you are doing." Rich noted a desperate
need for new plumbing, cramped quarters for some of the girls, cavernous
and impersonal space for some of the boys (fifteen being housed in a room
that formerly slept forty). She reported on the atrocious living quarters of
Adrianna Bouterse. And as for the housemothers: "You cannot visualize
how small their rooms are until you see them, nor do you believe there
really isn't [a] closet for them." Rich noted that the committee "grew more
and more appalled" at what they found and she urged all of the managers
to "take time today or soon to go through the rooms and look particularly
at our housemothers' rooms, the bathrooms and the closets, if you can find
them."[58]

Despite the monthly meetings at the institution, the Building Committee was woefully ignorant of the building. In the nineteenth century, the

Building Committee had combed the asylum on a regular basis. The kind of shock that Rich expressed would have been absolutely unthinkable during the 1880s. Yet by the 1950s, the volunteer managers, encouraged by the downtown professionals, had lost touch with the daily workings of Chapin Hall.

If day-to-day management was increasingly handled by the staff, more and more of the larger direction of Chapin Hall passed to the downtown umbrella agencies. After Chapin Hall rejoined the Community Fund in 1949, it found all its actions scrutinized each year. Program policy, fundraising, remodeling decisions, hiring, salaries—all were reviewed annually by Community Fund officials. Moreover, major decisions had to be approved by the Community Fund ahead of time. Chapin Hall needed fund approval before it could hire a third caseworker in the mid-1950s. In 1956, the managers and directors had to ask Community Fund if it could launch a fundraising campaign to pay for remodeling. Community Fund restricted who the money could be raised from (no corporate donations) and when the money could be raised (not from September 1 to November 15, the time of the annual Community Fund drive). Community Fund became a de facto regulatory body in a way that the State of Illinois had never been.[59]

The Community Fund was not alone in directing Chapin Hall. The Welfare Council of Metropolitan Chicago was also consulted regularly. And while the State of Illinois Department of Welfare was of little importance, Professor Susanne Schulze of the University of Chicago often contributed. At any pivotal point she was a presence, often brought to the agency by the Metropolitan Council or the Community Fund. In 1948 and 1949 she was very active in the discussions about the new course of the institution. She offered a carrot to the managers during the negotiations, saying that she wanted to have Chapin Hall become a "model" for other agencies, promising a free graduate student to help with the casework. She made critical suggestions about the hiring of an executive director. A few years later she was brought in to explain to the board the connection between remodeling Chapin Hall and the most advanced ideas about social work. She was engaged in the negotiations over the integration of Chapin Hall. Again in 1963 she was consulted on the hiring of an executive director. Julia McNulty, president of the Board of Managers, called Schulze (and Connie Fish of the Welfare Council) a "great assistance" in finding George Headley.[60]

The new system presumed shared interests between two sorts of professionals—the downtown managers and the agency staffers. The downtown agencies would make basic policy and develop the broader

vision while women with master's degrees could be counted on to run institutions in a "professional" manner. The gap between the planning agencies and the caring agencies that had existed in some form or another since
the Progressive Era would be ended by marginalizing the volunteers.

This was the way it worked in Chapin Hall. In 1948, downtown hostility
to Mabel Morrow was due to all sorts of things, but Morrow's dependency
upon the Board of Managers was certainly one factor. She had no degree in
social work and, to the professionals at the Metropolitan Council, her
1920s classes in recreation therapy were no longer even worth mentioning.
Morrow's defenders were on the Board of Managers and she knew it.
Adrianna Bouterse, on the other hand, was part of a completely different
network, with correspondingly different loyalties. She had a master's degree in social work from the University of Chicago but there was far more
to it than simple credentials. Her career depended upon her good name
within the professional welfare community. Job after job, including her position at Chapin Hall, she owed to recommendations from people like
Susanne Schulze, people who were authorities in the field. Bouterse's primary loyalties, and her dependencies, did not lead to Chapin Hall's Board
of Managers.

But while the downtown professionals wanted to redirect staff loyalties
inside Chapin Hall, this was not disconnected to the care of children. For if
women like Connie Fish, Ethel Verry, and Susanne Schulze presumed
shared interests with Chapin Hall's professionals, they continued to worry
about competence. Private reports duly noted the "atmosphere" of the institution and the character of the staff. Connie Fish's 1951 internal Welfare Council memo on Adrianna Bouterse was typical:

> I was well impressed with the superintendent on my visit. While she and I
> sat on the lawn before supper a number of the children came over freely and
> talked with her. One sat on her lap, and at bedtime as she took me through
> the dormitories one of the little girls asked for a piggy back ride, and every
> child in turn in this entire dormitory was taken for a piggy back ride. Mar-
> garet Stiel, consultant of the Division of Child Welfare, advised me that
> on her visit every staff member interviewed by her spoke highly of Miss
> Bouterse and particularly of her fairness.[61]

While Community Fund and Welfare Council staffers wanted a "professional" staff at Chapin Hall, this should not be taken to mean that they
thought crudely in terms of credentials and degrees. And because they
now conceptualized Chapin Hall as an institution for group living instead
of a surrogate home, this should not be taken to mean they wanted a cold,
unfeeling place. Their unwavering support for Bouterse depended upon

their sense that tenderness was not divorced from professionalism, indeed, that tenderness was one critical aspect of professional social work.

What was left for the managing board to do? First, the Executive Committee was brought into all deliberations about major policy and personnel changes. If there was a new executive director to hire, key managers took part from beginning to end. They interviewed applicants and evaluated résumés, although they were often guided by Welfare Council staffers and Susanne Schulze. The Executive Committe was very active in all discussions on the major remodeling of 1956 and the hiring of a new psychiatrist in 1953.

Board members were consulted because they retained formal control over Chapin Hall. Given that Chapin Hall could withdraw from Community Fund at any time and that the original 1865 charter from the state legislature was still intact, the professional community had to wield its power gently. Chapin Hall's managing board retained legal control over the institution, and this translated into effective veto power. So while the Welfare Council pushed Chapin Hall to merge the male and female boards, it did not happen. The women found the proposal distasteful, the men were indifferent. And while pressure to integrate began as early as 1943, it was not until after *Brown v. The Board of Education* that the boards seriously rethought their position. (This was one of the few decisions thought weighty enough to bring the men's board into the consultations. It was virtually the only nonfinancial decision the directors were involved in during Chapin Hall's one-hundred-and-twenty-year history.) Only in January 1956 did the boards vote to integrate, and it wasn't until several years later that an African-American child actually entered Chapin Hall.[62]

Agencies like the Community Fund and the Welfare Council were the most active proponents of integration in the city's white welfare establishment. Yet even they did not press the issue. During the extensive negotiations between the board and the professional community in the winter of 1948–49, integration was never mentioned, despite the known and rather desperate need for institutions that served black children. Far above on the professionals' priority list was creating a "group home." The Welfare Council and Community Fund were intent on patiently "educating" the staffs and directors of the agencies, apparently even if it took years. As late as January 1953, there was still *no* Protestant group home in the city that took African-American children.[63]

Integration was an enormously explosive issue and even if the downtown agencies had pressed there is no reason to assume they would have gotten what they wanted. Professionals in the Chicago Housing Authority who vigorously fought for integrated public housing lost their jobs in the early 1950s.[64] This is not the place to go into the complexities of this; no doubt readers' opinions will in part reflect their own political perspectives and evaluations of the possible. Still, integration was a distinctly second-level priority among the welfare professionals who dealt with Chapin Hall in the forties and fifties. In a system where the volunteer board retained ultimate decision-making power, the downtown agencies could rule smoothly only if they weren't too aggressive on controversial issues. And in the 1950s, they wanted to rule smoothly.

If the managers discussed and voted on major issues, that was not their main business. Most of the managers' time went into more mundane activities—helping with interior decorating, working in a resale shop to raise money, and minor sorts of public relations work, and organizing the yearly fashion shows. The managers also ran a yearly fundraising campaign. Every spring, they devised brochures, wrote letters, addressed envelopes, licked stamps, and did all the other tasks involved in the drive.

While fundraising involved a lot of time and was more substantial than some of the other work, even here the scale was far different than before. In the nineteenth century, the women had raised all the money for the institution. As late as 1929, Julia Thompson had led a massive campaign drive to build the boys' cottage. There was nothing close to this scale in the 1950s. The postwar yearly fundraising drive accounted for but a small percentage of the yearly budget.

Shifting basic managerial responsibility to peripheral fundraising was central to the marginalization of the Board of Managers and was actively encouraged by the welfare professionals. It was Connie Fish, for example, who suggested that Chapin Hall join with four other agencies in 1957 and open a resale shop, where donated clothing, furniture, and appliances were sold with proceeds going to the member agencies. Chapin Hall women helped staff the shop. Yet this encouragement in itself suggests what the Welfare Council wanted from volunteer women. The amount of time involved was considerable; the amount of income generated never exceeded a few thousand dollars. Increasingly, the managers' time and energy were devoted to smaller tasks.

Of course, this in part was simply the logical result of the declining participation of volunteer women, something apparent from the 1930s. But more was at work than that. The 1950s changes reduced the role of an Executive Committee which had retained its energy and drive right up to that time. Clarissa Haffner, Kay Milliken, Nancy Rich, and Julia McNulty were no less capable than any of the nineteenth-century managers. The whole volunteer system had not collapsed in the 1930s. What had disappeared was the support that maintained and implemented the work of the Executive Committee.

This was not a distinction recognized by the welfare professionals, who actively worked to marginalize even the Executive Committee. And they were successful. By the 1960s, even the Executive Committee would have to call on Clarissa Haffner, the knowledgeable elder stateswoman, for advice. In past generations, women without that managerial know-how would never have been let on the Executive Committee. The Welfare Council staff people, even as they recognized the talents of people like Haffner, also edged them away from active involvement with the agency. Caught in the lure of professionalism, the umbrella agencies did not think about retraining active volunteers to a new and significant role. Instead, they urged that the institution be handed to the staff.

The active managers knew exactly what was happening. Some of the older women resisted efforts to have the staff take over admissions in 1949 because they knew it would lead to decreased board involvement. Milliken and Haffner were all too aware that the best-attended board meetings were those connected to a fashion show and lunch. And when these women discussed among themselves why attendance was lagging, they came back to the obvious—the staff was doing more and more.[65] In the 1950s, some of the younger board members, like Julia McNulty, could also understand the shift. Nevertheless, there was little resistance to this process. The post–World War II managers accepted the professionals' direction and no longer had the confidence to resist, as a Julia Thompson had in the 1920s.

That Clarissa Haffner and Kay Milliken were themselves so captivated by professionalism augured ill for the future of any sort of active volunteerism. On the other hand, to resist, given what was happening in the late forties around the city, could very well have meant the death of Chapin Hall. By that time, the professional welfare community had grabbed enough clout to engineer policies that by 1960 would make once mighty volunteer managers a marginal presence. Haffner and Milliken saved the agency in the only way possible.

Some variation of these changes took place at practically every non-Catholic children's institution in the postwar years. The marginalization of the managers effectively choked the last remnant of the nineteenth-century system of Protestant child welfare in Chicago. Whatever would happen in the future would be a matter of managerial welfare professionals dealing with agency welfare professionals. The volunteers were no longer a force in the agency.

As central as these changes were, however, they occurred in such a way as to flatter all involved. The new system built a perverse kind of hall of mirrors in which everyone, if they looked from just the right angle, could see themselves from their best side. The managers and directors, while ceding all effective control of the institution, could still see the agency as "theirs," and the professional staff as "hired help." The professional staff, in turn, could "know" that they were the heart of the institution and that the managers were to be tolerated although never overtly patronized. And the downtown professionals could also see the whole system as "theirs," due to their own increasingly successful management of Chicago's social welfare. For the time being, everyone was happy.

THE MONEY

Ironically, the financial crisis that spurred all the changes of the early 1950s soon disappeared. By the middle of the decade, Chapin Hall didn't need a nickel of the Community Fund money it so desperately wanted in 1948. By the mid-fifties, Chapin Hall's financial picture looked very healthy indeed. Just as in the late 1890s, what mattered was a series of bequests. Chapin Hall did not feel short of money again until the late 1970s.

This is especially striking when considering the increased cost of maintaining an institution like Chapin Hall in the 1950s. Professionalization cost money. Of course Adrianna Bouterse was more expensive than Mabel Morrow. The psychiatrist had to be paid, and there were, by mid-decade, three social workers instead of one, each with a better income than Blanche Robertson had during World War II. Between 1947 and 1960 salaries rose about 80 percent, from about $48,000 to roughly $84,000.[66]

Salaries comprised the only significant change in the institution's budget. In 1947, expenses were just under $93,000. By 1960, it cost $133,000 to maintain Chapin Hall. Fully 90 percent of the difference is accounted for by the increase in salaries.

In 1948 Chapin Hall managers and directors were worried about financing a budget of under $100,000. Yet in 1960, they were fully confident that they could manage a budget about 40 percent larger without any help from the Community Fund. One change lay behind this. Chapin Hall had been the recipient of some key bequests. By 1956, income from the endowment financed more of Chapin Hall's budget than at any other time in the institution's history.

No one had foreseen this in the 1940s, or at least no one had seen how such bequests would alter the institution's financial picture. Yet during the early 1950s the endowment rose significantly. In 1947, endowment income totaled just under $40,000, about 43 percent of total costs. In 1956, on the other hand, the endowment brought in just under $74,000, a full 60 percent of the operating budget.

The largest single gift was from Thomas E. Donnelley, and that points out something significant about the bequests. The flurry of bequests coming around 1890 came from downtown businessmen at large; the 1950s legacies were from families with deep connections to Chapin Hall. The Donnelley family had been giving money to the Chicago Nursery and Half-Orphan Asylum since the 1870s. Several family members served on both male and female boards. Clarissa Haffner was a Donnelley. In the 1950s, key families with a sense of obligation to the institution played a major role in fattening the endowment.

The strength of the endowment—a strength, it should be pointed out, that was atypical rather than the norm in the orphanage's history—meant that Community Fund money was not forthcoming. Community Fund gave to institutions by projecting each agency's income and expenses at the beginning of the calendar year. On the basis of this a certain amount of money was set aside. But if the agency actually spent less money than the projected budget called for, or if there was added income beyond the projected budget, then Community Fund donations were altered accordingly.

Through most of the 1950s, Chapin Hall had the bad luck of having enough money on hand to meet its estimated needs. For a full seven of ten years after entry into the Community Fund, Chapin Hall got no money at all. In 1954, the Fund gave $42 to the agency. From 1955 to 1960, average donations from the Community Fund were $2,000. Despite all the paperwork, and all the monitoring, Chapin Hall did not get any significant financial benefit from Community Fund. In August 1961, Community Fund asked for, and got, a refund of nearly $7,000 from Chapin Hall.[67]

By the late 1950s, then, and despite membership in the Community Fund, Chapin Hall was not financed much differently than during World War II. There was the basic reliance on parental fees, yearly donations, endowment income, and a bit from the county. The numbers were rearranged slightly from before the war—investment income accounted for more of the budget, parents' payments for less—but the basic orientation was the same. Community Fund had not changed the story.

It is not surprising, then, that both staff and managers grew weary of Community Fund's regulation. Practically nothing had been coming in return for the whole decade. In 1961, citing the crush of paperwork involved in membership, Chapin Hall withdrew from the fund.[68]

Yet at that moment there were changes underway that would radically alter Chapin Hall's finances, making it far more dependent upon the public sector. More and more referrals were coming from the State of Illinois and from private agencies in the years after 1958. Also, in 1962 state law was changed so that the state's Department of Children and Family Services would be the most generous supporter of individual children. In the late fifties, the amount of money Chapin Hall got from public sources began rising for the first time since the early forties. But, unlike then, in the 1960s it would just continue to grow.

This money, as in the 1930s, came in to fill the gap left by declining parental support. Parental support of children in Chapin Hall had fallen steadily from the late forties on. This was no longer due to the parents' unwillingness to pay, but to the changed clientele at the institution. While the change was gradual until the late fifties, after that point there was a giant drop. By 1962, parental payments only made up 2 percent of Chapin Hall's budget, down from 25 percent in 1948 and 15 percent in 1956.

The end of involvement in the Community Fund also occasioned a sharp rise in fundraising efforts and, for a short time, the amount of money able to be generated by fundraising increased. From $18,600 in 1956, the managers raised $33,100 in 1962. Yet this was deceptive. If costs kept escalating, fundraising would never be able to cover all increases. They would eventually hit a limit. More ominously, endowment income leveled off in the early 1960s. There would be limits to what the agency could do on its own. If costs rose, and they would, the question would be where the money would come from, and where the dependency would lie. The answer, in the late sixties, was the State of Illinois.

CHAPTER SIX

The Rise and Fall of a Residential Treatment Center, 1963–1984

ETWEEN THE MIDDLE OF THE 1960s AND THE END of the 1970s, Chapin Hall went on a roller-coaster ride that raced from the heights of prosperity and promise to the depths of financial despair. At the outset, the institution, supported by new forms of government funding, dramatically modernized its program. New services were provided; more social workers hired. Increased psychiatric help allowed more problematic children to be cared for. The physical plant was overhauled. By the middle of the 1960s, Chapin Hall was referring to itself as a full-fledged "residential treatment center," a sign that it was in the vanguard of professional care for disturbed children.

In 1973, however, problems began to surface, problems that quickly multiplied. Within a few years the agency was fighting for its life. At the center of Chapin Hall's difficulties was changed public policy. The State of Illinois, following federal guidelines, altered its ideas about child welfare. It referred fewer children to the agency. It began to ask that Chapin Hall take psychotic children. Money became tighter. In the late seventies, Chapin Hall began running rather stunning deficits. Despite various efforts to ameliorate the situation, not much could be done. The residential treatment center, the product of so much enthusiastic hope just twenty years before, closed its doors in 1984. The next year, Chapin Hall reopened as a research institute affiliated with the University of Chicago.

Nothing was more new or more critical to this chapter of Chapin Hall's history than its massive financial dependence upon the State of Illinois, particularly the state's Department of Children and Family Services (DCFS). In the space of a few short years in the late sixties, DCFS became the single most important financial backer of the institution. Suddenly, money was available to do things unthinkable with the endowment. But when that money became tight, Chapin Hall found itself with a staff, plant, and program that it could not support.

Chapin Hall's history in these decades once again reflected much larger patterns. Behind the increased state funding available in the 1960s were changes in federal social security laws (DCFS was primarily administering federal money). Similarly, in the 1960s many Chicago children's institutions were, like Chapin Hall, turning themselves into residential treatment centers. This was, in fact, a nationwide trend.[1] And the problems Chapin Hall faced by the late 1970s were the by-product of new public policy affecting all of Chicago's homes for emotionally disturbed children. As we shall see, this policy once again reflected changed images about children, family life, and institutions. The "new" ideas, in fact, reflected a revival of those progressive anti-institutional notions set aside during the 1940s.

All of Chicago's children's institutions had to come to terms with the new climate. Chapin Hall was not unique. Yet almost no other agency in the city closed. Unlike other children's institutions in Chicago, after 1979 Chapin Hall tried to keep younger children and a large number of girls. In a very literal sense, it no longer could afford to do that. State policy wouldn't allow it.

A RESIDENTIAL TREATMENT CENTER

In the early sixties, however, there was nothing but optimism and hope. In 1963 Adrianna Bouterse stepped down as Chapin Hall's executive director. While she had ably guided the institution through the 1950s, she was hesitant about moving Chapin Hall in new directions. She disliked having to care for the problem children that public agencies increasingly pushed on the private institutions. She had let the population of Chapin Hall dwindle to less than fifty. There was a general sense among the active board members that it was time for new blood. When Bouterse decided to leave, Julia McNulty of the Board of Managers and Wyndham Hasler of the Board of Directors began looking for a new executive director, aided by Clarissa Haffner, Connie Fish of the Metropolitan Council, Susanne Schulze of the University of Chicago, and Seymour Steinhorn, Chapin Hall's consulting psychiatrist.[2] After a nationwide search they hired George Headley, an energetic social worker with big plans for change. The first man to run the institution since it had opened in 1860, Headley's mission was clear. His goal, he announced, was to develop "a children's home program unrivaled in the Chicago area," a full-service psychiatric group home for emotionally disturbed children. He would build a state-of-the-art residential treatment center.[3]

It appeared to be a good time to start. Between the late fifties and the middle of the sixties, residential treatment centers were at their peak status within the professional welfare community.[4] And in the 1960s, money began flooding into agencies like Chapin Hall in sums previously unheard of. Critically important to these changes were modifications in federal law. In 1961, money from the Aid to Families with Dependent Children (AFDC) program was made temporarily available to children in foster care. The next year Congress made this change permanent, and extended it to cover children in nonprofit foster care institutions such as Chapin Hall. This money was to be funneled through state agencies. One reason the Illinois state legislature created the Department of Children and Family Services (DCFS) in 1964 was to administer the social security funds now available.[5]

For Headley and his professional staff at Chapin Hall, the increased money meant that the institution could develop more varied and high-level programs; it aspired to become a leading institution in the field. Chapin Hall would accept more disturbed and older children than it had under Adrianna Bouterse, and it would provide them with better care. The managers and directors had no reason to think otherwise.

What exactly was a residential treatment center? All sorts of institutions claimed the name for themselves.[6] Welfare theorists, however, generally agreed that residential treatment centers should be places where the most seriously maladjusted children could learn to adapt to everyday life. They would be highly structured settings in which children with deep and disabling problems vis-à-vis parents, teachers, or peers would learn how to relate to authority.

One thing that had changed by the 1960s was how troubled a child had to be for placement. In 1948, when the Welfare Council of Metropolitan Chicago defined "emotionally disturbed child," it listed such symptoms as "stealing, truancy, fire setting, exaggerated fears, excessive shyness, feeding difficulties, sleep disturbances, bed wetting." For Susanne Schulze, it was important that only a few seriously disturbed children be in any single group home. And even the most disturbed were expected to manage in public schools. By 1969, when the council made a new attempt to define the term, it cited children with "severe mental, neurological, behavioral and / or emotional disorders," children "so disturbed, disorganized, handicapped, and / or withdrawn, they can not adapt to the needs, expectations, or demands of family, school, and community."[7]

The nature of the therapy was something else often used to define the residential treatment center. More services and more staff were needed. Children were to be in constant contact with caring and trained personnel. More careful diagnosis was mandatory before admittance. This meant more psychoanalytic evaluation and better-trained social workers. Seriously disturbed children needed total professional supervision. That meant better-trained houseparents, houseparents who would know how to understand the bizarre behavior of damaged children. Every single bit of the child's stay should be a "corrective emotional experience," as one writer put it.[8]

The vogue for residential treatment centers was part of the booming national interest in mental health issues. Governmental concern had begun in the mid-fifties, when Dwight D. Eisenhower publicly connected juvenile delinquency with emotional illness and helped pass the Mental Health Study Act of 1955. Although Eisenhower's own support proved tepid, in the late fifties interest in the mental health of youngsters grew, peaking in the early 1960s. In 1961, Congress passed legislation to create test programs in the field of adolescent mental health. In that same year, John F. Kennedy created the President's Committee on Juvenile Delinquency and Youth Crime, another effort to deal with the problem. And also in 1961, the Joint Commission on Mental Illness and Health published the very influential *Action for Mental Health*, a three-hundred-page survey commissioned by Congress in 1955. Among the commission's major recommendations was a plea that "clinics providing intensive psychotherapy for children . . . should be fostered and, where they exist, expanded."[9]

Interest in the issue spread to the state and local level. In 1960, the Welfare Council of Metropolitan Chicago did a major survey of children's institutions in Cook County. Again and again social workers in the area spoke of the shortage of mental health services, especially for the young.[10] In the same year, the Illinois Commission on Children began a major study of family and child welfare in the state, an outgrowth of recommendations from the 1960 White House Conference on Children and Youth. Eventually out of this came the legislation creating the Illinois Department of Children and Family Services which began operation on January 1, 1964. Expanding mental health care was a central concern of the new agency.[11]

Residential treatment centers, with their heightened sense of what therapeutic help might accomplish, were simply one part of the larger struggle for improved mental health facilities. The changes within Chapin Hall on the northwest side of Chicago were really just one small example of a wave of national interest in children's emotional well-being.

During the 1960s, a good number of Chicago children's institutions were redefining themselves as agencies devoted to the mental health of children. Places like Lawrence Hall, Uhlich Children's Home, the Arden Shore Home for Boys, and the Allendale School for Boys all underwent the same sort of transformation that Chapin Hall did. During that decade the last two huge industrial schools (both Catholic) disappeared from the city. The number of institutions defining themselves as homes for dependent children, leftovers from the pre–World War II era, dropped from thirteen to six. More telling, agencies claiming to be group homes for the emotionally disturbed (Chapin Hall's self-definition in 1961) moved from five to four. That was no longer a growth area. But while in 1961 there were only six institutions with the very elaborate psychiatric care denoting "residential treatment center," by 1971 there were fifteen.[12]

Surprisingly, however, these changes did not reduce the number of children living in institutions. As in the 1920s, the increase in the number of children entering the system canceled out any move toward deinstitutionalization. Between 1965 and 1970 the number of Illinois children living in institutions jumped from 1,683 to 4,127. And, in relative terms, a higher percentage of dependent children were living in institutions in 1970 than were five years earlier.[13] While welfare professionals envisioned the residential treatment center, a small unit for deeply troubled children, as the only sort of institution that should remain, and while there was considerable movement in that direction, some larger institutions continued to lumber along as they had in the past.[14]

In the middle of the 1960s, just as had happened several times before in Chapin Hall's history, there was a flurry of activity designed to move the home in a new direction. The changes were many, the staff being expanded, the program broadened, the physical plant remade. In October 1965 George Headley proudly wrote to Ellis Ballard of the Welfare Council that Chapin Hall was in "the midst of a dramatic growth period." By the end of 1967, the institution's promotional literature announced that Chapin Hall was a "residential treatment center."[15]

One sign of Chapin Hall's new direction was its December 1964 merger with Ridge Farm, a residential treatment center that was having financial difficulties. The Ridge Farm plant was sold, the seven children remaining moved to Chapin Hall, and the two boards merged. Viewed from one direction, the merger was just part of the post–World War II drive by downtown welfare professionals to streamline the city's welfare system, the tail of their effort to reduce the number of agencies actually housing children.[16] From another direction, however, the merger signaled Chapin Hall's move toward residential treatment status. There would be older and more troubled children than before. Headley thought the merger one sign of "a bright future" for the institution.[17]

What went on in Chapin Hall gives a hint of what the new orientation entailed for all the residential treatment centers. The professional staff grew significantly. A second consulting psychiatrist was added in late 1963. The next year a group worker was hired to develop more organized activities for the children both within the institution and in the neighborhood. The ad for the position was written by Mary Lou Somers, a professor of group work at the University of Chicago. In 1965 Chapin Hall received a grant from the Wiebolt Foundation to support a group work consultant. They turned to Charles Garvin of the University of Chicago School of Social Service Administration who set the direction of Chapin Hall's group work program for the rest of the decade.[18]

Additional caseworkers were hired to help children on an individual level. In 1963, when Headley took over, Chapin Hall had only two trained caseworkers, himself and Elsie Blumberg. By the end of 1963, however, there were five caseworkers and, by January 1968, there were eight. The ratio of caseworker to child shrank from roughly 1:25 to 1:8. And the change was not only in quantity. All caseworkers had master's degrees in social work. All were conversant with psychoanalytic theory. The gender composition of the staff also changed. Until the 1960s, there had never been a male caseworker on staff at Chapin Hall. In January 1965, Headley, hoping to provide male role models for the boys living at the institution, told the boards that a male caseworker was "desperately" needed. That year he hired two male social workers, one of whom was Tom Libby, who would become executive director of Chapin Hall fourteen years later. By 1968 there was an even mix of male and female caseworkers.[19]

Turning Chapin Hall into a full-service residential treatment center also required some major changes in the physical plant. A new cottage, the first major construction at Chapin Hall since the end of the 1920s, was built in 1965–66. This building, the "Ridge Farm Cottage," housed the older high school boys who had come from Ridge Farm. At the same time, classrooms were built to accommodate the more troubled youngsters now living in the institution. Up until 1964, Chapin Hall would not accept children who could not function in a standard public school classroom. Headley wanted to change that. In 1965, after negotiations between Chapin Hall board members and staff at the Chicago Board of Education, the latter agreed to set up special education classes for children too emotionally disturbed to attend regular school. These classes began in fall 1965 using the new building at Chapin Hall built for the purpose. Although Headley was soon grumbling about the difficulties of dealing with the Board of Education, at the outset he was enthusiastic, calling the new schoolrooms "a tremendous stride forward in our plans to serve these children."[20]

What was happening inside Chapin Hall (and the other agencies rushing to residential treatment status) cannot be disconnected from other changes in the bureaucratic network managing child welfare in Chicago. At the end of the 1960s, the State of Illinois pushed aside the private umbrella agencies that had been created at the turn of the century to organize Chicago's charities. (In fact, the help that Connie Fish and Susanne Schulze gave in the hiring of Headley might be seen as one of the last acts of the old regime.) The Welfare Council of Metropolitan Chicago and the Community Fund were displaced as the central coordinating agencies; the Illinois Department of Children and Family Services took their place. The old notion of "private power for the public good" fell by the wayside. By the early 1970s, Chapin Hall was under the de facto control of DCFS. Two very specific reforms underlie the change. DCFS took control of intake and it took control of finances. The combination was potent.

As late as the mid-1950s, state and county authorities sent very few children to Chapin Hall. In the last years of the decade, however, that started to change. By the early sixties somewhere around one-half of Chapin Hall's children came from public agencies, a figure that remained stable till the end of the decade. As late as 1969, just under 50 percent of Chapin Hall's residents continued to come from either parents or private agencies.[21]

With one dramatic move, however, it was all different. In the summer of 1969, the Department of Children and Family Services managed to collect all Cook County child-placing under its own auspices. In part this was done in response to further expansion of federal social security coverage.[22] DCFS was originally created in 1964 to coordinate all child and family work previously done by the old Department of Public Welfare, the Department of Mental Health, and by the various counties. Until 1969, however, both DCFS and the Cook County Family Court continued to operate side by side. But the historic "children's division transfer" of 1969 made the state bureau the sole child-placing agency for the whole of Chicago and suburbs. In one day, DCFS's foster care caseload doubled and the number of Cook County children receiving some sort of service jumped from 12,000 to 20,000. Over two hundred employees moved from the county to the state payroll.[23]

The change touched Chapin Hall immediately. Within a year, Elsie Blumberg, the caseworker who managed intake, noted that "the bulk of referrals" now came from the state. By 1972 DCFS had placed every child then living in Chapin Hall.[24] That became the norm. The United Way noted in 1981 that with "one or two exceptions at any point in time, all children [at Chapin Hall] are wards of the state whose care is being purchased by DCFS."[25] In the space of a few short years, between 1969 and 1972, the State of Illinois became practically the sole source of referrals to Chapin Hall.

In the nineteenth century, most children were brought to the Half-Orphan Asylum by their parents. In the 1920s, through the Social Service Exchange of the Council of Social Agencies (later the Welfare Council of Metropolitan Chicago) a group of private agencies began to coordinate intake, but their success was limited. In the 1930s, when Cook County's Juvenile Court began paying for children to stay at Chapin Hall, public agencies began contributing. Still, parents continued to place large numbers of children, at least half. Only after the children's division transfer in 1969 did public authorities actually establish a unified system with effective control over intake. Through this move, for the first time, Catholic agencies were brought into an integrated welfare system. Only a few of the city's more than thirty children's agencies sidestepped the system.

No one forced George Headley and Elsie Blumberg to take wards of DCFS. No one forced the Catholic agencies or other nonsectarian agencies to do so. They all wanted to. In the 1960s, Chapin Hall's professionals were keenly enthusiastic about the state's increasing presence. The reason was simple—money. From the late fifties into the late seventies, the State of Illinois grew more and more generous with agencies like Chapin Hall. During the four years between 1966 and 1970 the state took over as the major funder of Chapin Hall, bringing about the most important shift in philanthropic support in the institution's history.

The shift in financing paralleled the shift in admission referrals. There was a gradual increase in public support between 1958 and 1962 and an explosion late in the decade. Public funding for Chapin Hall actually dropped after World War II. By 1956 only 7 percent of all money came from the state, down from 14 percent in the 1940s. But in the late fifties, the percentage of Chapin Hall's income generated by the state started to steadily increase.

Government worked by purchasing services from private agencies like Chapin Hall, paying a fixed per diem sum to Chapin Hall for each ward of the state cared for. The state, in other words, paid by the head. In the late 1950s, such a practice was a disincentive for Chapin Hall to take children from the public sector, for the Cook County Juvenile Court and the State Department of Mental Health did not pay as well as private agencies or parents. But starting in 1958, state rates began steadily climbing. In 1962, with federal social security money now available, the balance tipped. For the first time, Chapin Hall received more money for a child referred and paid for by the State of Illinois than for a child from the county, a private agency, or parents.

Even before the Department of Children and Family Services was created in 1964, then, the state was paying more for care than any other source. And in the next decade and a half, it kept raising the amount of compensation for each child. Each year brought a new increase. It is no wonder that in the mid-1960s Headley and Blumberg began looking for ways to get more children from the state. And if by the late 1970s they had become disenchanted with DCFS, there still was no better source of income.

Once the state paid better than anyone else, it naturally followed that more children would be accepted from DCFS. And that in turn meant that the state would provide an increasing amount of Chapin Hall's income. In 1956, public funds made up 7.2 percent of Chapin Hall's income. By 1962, public money paid for twenty-one out of the forty-five children and accounted for 17.2 percent of the agency's budget. In real terms public money coming to Chapin Hall rose from $8,900 in 1956 to $25,000 in 1962, a leap of nearly 300 percent.

But much more soon followed. Between 1966 and 1972, the floodgates opened and Chapin Hall became hugely dependent upon public money. It was changing federal law that provided most of the difference. The income generated by public sources jumped from 20 percent to 70 percent of Chapin Hall's budget. The money completely changed the scale of the agency. For not only was the state a better source of income than parents, it had become the largest supporter of Chapin Hall, bar none. For the first time since the 1890s, there was a source of income that produced more, far more, than the endowment.

In real terms the change was staggering, easily the single most important shift in Chapin Hall's philanthropic base since the institution's birth in the mid-nineteenth century. In 1962, the state and county gave $25,000; in 1966, $60,000; in 1972, $492,000. Nor did it end there. In 1974 state support was at $668,000; in 1977, $716,000. In the 1980–81 fiscal year, the state, through DCFS, for the first time gave Chapin Hall more than a million dollars.

By the late 1960s the state was supplying so much money that Headley and Blumberg no longer wanted parents to come directly to Chapin Hall. The state paid better and was more reliable. Why spend energy fighting quarrelsome parents for back payments when the DCFS supplied so much more money without any trouble? By the 1970s, three-quarters of Chapin Hall's operating income came from DCFS payments for children's services. In a few short years, Chapin Hall itself had become a ward of the state.

In the 1970s, particularly after 1973, Chapin Hall board members and professionals showed increasing impatience with DCFS. By the 1980s, there was often bitter resentment. In the sixties, however, the relationship was all sweetness and light. Headley and Blumberg were enthusiastic. The more conservative board expressed no opposition. This was quite normal in agencies such as Chapin Hall. One study done by the Child Welfare League of America in 1964 suggested that both professional staff and more conservative board members throughout the nation were looking to the public sector to finance residential treatment for emotionally disturbed children. The state seemed to be the best way to enhance revenue and improve services.[26]

As a result of changes in philanthropy and intake, in the last half of the 1960s, the state, through its Department of Children and Family Services, established a very powerful grip on Chapin Hall. DCFS adapted its regulatory style from the Welfare Council and Community Fund. It worked indirectly, not so much demanding compliance as creating dependence. DCFS did not legally force Chapin Hall to do much. It did, however, define how much money it would receive and what it would receive it for. By the early 1970s, DCFS had de facto become Chapin Hall's regulator. For the first time in its history, Chapin Hall had a strong public agency watching over it.

DCFS's takeover of intake and financing radically altered the whole city. After 1972, there were only a couple of nonsectarian children's homes that were not dependent upon DCFS.[27] Notably, this shift brought most Catholic orphanages under the sway of the state, orphanages that had quite successfully resisted Community Fund pressure over the years. But the money dangled by DCFS was of a different magnitude. Without anyone realizing it, in the space of a few years, DCFS took control of child welfare in Chicago.

THE CHILDREN AND THEIR THERAPY

The children who came to Chapin Hall from the 1960s through the 1980s were more troubled than at any time before in the institution's history. These were children who were neglected at home, who often had major difficulties with friends, parents, or school. Many, probably most, had been abused. The professional staff commented on this regularly.[28] In 1975, DCFS spoke of the "sophisticated" care at Chapin Hall, observing that "the facility is willing to accept increasingly difficult children." Three years later, Thomas Libby pointed out that "we have continued to be open in our intake policy to types of children never before served by this agency." In 1978, DCFS social workers told Libby that Chapin Hall was considered one of the best residential treatment centers in the state.[29]

Overwhelmingly, these children came from the poorest areas of the city. Increasingly they were people of color. Even in the early 1960s, most children came from families where the parent had a steady job. This was especially true of the mothers. But by the 1970s the children coming to Chapin Hall were from very, very unsettled families. Often, these children had been born to mothers who themselves were only fifteen or sixteen years old. Many of these mothers had never worked and were deeply emotionally needy themselves. Fathers, who had historically been the guardians of about one out of three children coming to Chapin Hall, come very close to disappearing in the 1970s and 1980s. They were rarely even remotely involved with the children. For both parents drug use was common. In the case records of these years we can see the beginnings of what has come to be called, by the 1990s, the "no-parent" family. Between the early 1960s and the 1970s, the family background of children at Chapin Hall shifted from the very troubled working class to the underclass.

By the 1970s, the children at Chapin Hall were often violent, sexually active even at ages nine and ten, and completely incapable of maintaining the decorum needed to sit in a standard public school classroom. At the same time, these children often had less external support, coming from families so disorganized that no emotional sustenance was forthcoming. And while children with relatively "simple" problems continued to live at Chapin Hall after 1975, the more unsteady children came in greater numbers.

Louis provides a very good example. He was admitted in 1966, suffering from what was termed "serious maladjustment at school." His mother was also seriously phobic. Once in Chapin Hall, therapists decided that he was "more damaged" than originally thought. In the institution, he alternated between uncontrollable temper tantrums and deep withdrawal. On the one hand, he could explode "in an incoherent display of temper" and run from the building screaming "Nobody loves me." On the other hand, he might sit in a corner sucking his thumb for hours at a stretch if left to his own devices. At times therapists saw him visibly struggling to control himself, often failing in the end. The behavior was threatening to himself and others. During one rage he ran into a busy street: "A car travelling at a high rate of speed was approaching the child and Louis angrily raised his arm, as though this would stop the vehicle. The boy was almost struck." When enraged, Louis would also pick up rocks and fling them at whomever was around. A year after being admitted, when he was ten years old, he threw a butter knife at one of the housemothers. The caseworker noted that "this houseparent and his teacher both admit to being physically afraid of him."[30]

William was another example of the more troubled sort of youngster that came to Chapin Hall. DCFS referred him in 1966. He was eight years old. William's parents had grossly abused him; foster parenting had not worked out because William's acting out was so extreme, including "sex play, compulsive talking and questioning, seeming to be in a daze." Hyperactivity was also a problem. In his last foster home he cut up furniture and clothing with a razor blade, and burned a two-year-old with a hot pan.

Inside Chapin Hall William was "extremely nervous" and depressed, crying at the least provocation. He longed for physical affection and would sit in the housemother's lap for hours. William stayed eight years at Chapin Hall. For a time he did better but new problems arose with adolescence. He was caught setting fires in the stairwell and began using drugs. He also started having sex with other boys. While William did well in a vocational program, when he was sixteen he asked to leave Chapin Hall because no other boys his age were living there. Several years later, he was arrested for producing child pornography.[31]

Judy provides a glimpse of the new sort of girl coming to Chapin Hall in the 1960s. She came in 1969, nine years old. Her mother was insane and her father had committed suicide the year before. Two foster placements had not worked out—she derided her foster parents as hopelessly "low brow," forced herself into such violent coughing fits that she vomited, and, most disturbing, regularly tried to seduce her last foster father. She tried to get into the shower with him, to climb into his bed, and continually "cuddled" him in a sexually provocative way. These sad cries for affection hinted at the loss she felt for her biological father. Nevertheless, the foster father was literally afraid of the girl. DCFS suggested Chapin Hall.[32]

At the end of the decade, these problems were compounded by the general temper of the times. Drinking and drugs appeared. There was a general perception among the staff that the girls were more sexually active. Some kids rebelled against the institutional mentality of Chapin Hall, making it all the more difficult to constructively work with them.

In the late 1970s, these troubled children were joined by even tougher cases. Boys who constantly and brutally fought, girls who wantonly acted out sexually, kids who had been grossly neglected or abused by their parents—these were common. In the 1970s and 1980s there were more children diagnosed as psychotic in the institution, and in 1977 developmentally disabled children were accepted for the first time. There was the girl who regularly pulled her eyebrows and pubic hair off. Or the boy who refused to eat and sat in the corner just drooling.

Increasingly, these were children whose whole lives were chaotic. Tom came to Chapin Hall in 1977 at age twelve. A boy with a good sense of humor, Tom nonetheless was a mass of personality disorders, diagnosed as "borderline psychotic." He had extremely poor judgment and constantly found himself in binds "potentially dangerous to his physical well-being." He failed everything, *everything*, in school. In three years at Chapin Hall he made no friends. "He has no knowledge of what it takes to appropriately establish or maintain relationships," the case worker reported. "He desperately craves any form of attention and longs for a sense of being loved." Yet Tom had no family he could count on. His mother had abandoned him, his father and stepmother refused to care. No aunts or uncles would help. Tom lived for three years in Chapin Hall, making no progress, before he moved on to another institution.[33]

For children like Tom, it was made clear that the staff was not a substitute family. This was a therapeutic institution for emotionally troubled youth. This self-definition of Chapin Hall continued the impulse dating back to the 1940s, when institutions were redefined with a new purpose, as places for disturbed youngsters. This itself was a rejection of the "progressive" orphanage, which was premised on the idea that children's institutions should try to resemble a home. That Chapin Hall was now a residential treatment center did not alter the fact that it saw itself in nonfamilial terms.

A number of things reinforced the message. The formal title—residential treatment center—was deliberate. It conveyed no false sense of "home." It rather evoked the medical model that drove the institution. Similarly, those employees who lived with the children were no longer called "houseparents." They now were "child care workers." But most important, the staff actively tried to avoid letting the children overidentify with them. These children in many cases had absolutely no familial adults maintaining steady contact with them. It was not unusual at all for such youngsters to try to latch onto caseworkers or child care workers, often the only adults expressing interest in their lives. Yet, the "Child Care Workers' Manual" of the early 1970s admonished the staff that they "cannot and must not take the place of a parent."[34] And case records are dotted with examples of employees discouraging such identification, of caseworkers making absolutely clear to children that the adults at Chapin Hall were not family. Such incidents often evoked heartbreak for all involved.

The therapy was intense. There was not a moment of the day that was not supposed to be aimed at molding a balanced ego. The children and adolescents underwent intensive psychotherapy in an effort to uncover the deeper roots of their problems. There were consulting psychiatrists who made evaluations and set direction. Psychoanalytically trained caseworkers had more sustained contact with the children, trying to talk out their difficulties and the deeper problems underlying them. They met with the children once or twice a week. The child care workers who lived with the children also contributed, going to staffings to learn what the professionals thought about each child, bringing back reports on the children's behavior and helping assess what the children were thinking.

At the same time, there was corresponding "milieu therapy" to teach children how to cope with everyday life. Many of these kids could not sit still in school, could not relate at all to peers, had trouble getting back and forth to the store, would often break out into uncontrollable rages. Milieu therapists patiently tried to help children move beyond such behavior, hopefully giving them some of the basic skills needed to survive outside Chapin Hall. Milieu therapy tried to teach children how to sit still in school, how to get back and forth from the store, how to control their fury.

At times psychotherapeutic and milieu therapy came into conflict. For while psychoanalysis emphasized the talking cure, milieu therapy emphasized practical life skills. But children struggling to get control over their emotions could be thrown into new turmoil when confronted with some realization of the deep familial conflicts that led them to Chapin Hall. Gradually over the years, milieu therapy took on more importance in the overall therapy of Chapin Hall. Certainly in the late seventies there was more emphasis than before. The program as a whole, however, even in the 1980s remained heavily psychoanalytic.

By that time, psychoanalysis was no longer commanding the prestige it had in the 1960s. The sort of child who came to an institution by the 1980s was so heavily damaged, and often so uncommunicative, that the "talking cure" was felt to be of limited use. Moreover, Freud had argued that the family was an obstacle to therapy, while social work theorists in the 1980s were arguing that treatment had to center on whole families instead of just emotionally troubled children.[35] This shift away from psychoanalysis had already begun in the 1970s. And while Chapin Hall added milieu therapy, it did not move fast enough to meet changing opinion. What in 1970 appeared to be a wonderful program by 1980 appeared dated.

THE UNRAVELING

In 1973, Daniel Walker became governor of Illinois. Walker was an independent Democrat who had run against the Democratic machine of Chicago Mayor Richard J. Daley. Like many local independent Democrats of the time, one of Walker's major campaign themes was waste in government, a refrain common to antimachine Chicago Democrats like Leon De-Pres and William Singer. Walker brought the message to the state level.

The new governor also hunted for policy ideas from a new breed of liberals, men and women affected by the politics of the sixties but who still remained inside the mainstream political system. They were Democrats more likely to be supporters of George McGovern than Hubert Humphrey. To reform the welfare system, a number of them were advocating a policy that had come to be known rather clumsily as deinstitutionalization. It was the beginning of the end for Chapin Hall's residential treatment program. In the next decade it would visibly alter all of Chicago's child welfare.

Deinstitutionalization referred to a broad effort to get as many people out of long-term institutional care as possible. It touched all sorts of clienteles—the mentally ill, the elderly, the delinquent, the physically and emotionally disabled.[36] Children were also a target. In the second half of the sixties, certain (not all) experts in child care began to question the value of residential treatment centers. Restatements of older anti-institutional ideas were at the core of the movement. Institutions were suspect, thought to be creating problems rather than solving them. The whole use of medical categories to describe troubled children was called into question. The vagueness of the terms "emotionally disturbed" and "residential treatment center" (something known for a long time) was discussed with renewed fervor. That no good empirical research existed showing that residential treatment actually did any good also fed the attack. And the costs involved were still another issue. Residential treatment was by far the most expensive care possible for emotionally damaged children. Deinstitutionalization would save money.[37]

Deinstitutionalization was a rejection of welfare policy as conceived since the 1940s. It marked still another historic shift in attitudes about social welfare and family. Susanne Schulze had argued that institutions benefited certain groups of emotionally disturbed children, herself overturning the Progressive Era notion that family settings were always preferable, although not always possible. The sense that Chapin Hall was not a surrogate family informed both its group home and residential treatment stages. On this issue, advocates of deinstitutionalization basically returned to the progressive attitude. The natural home was absolute first choice, a foster home second. Only the most violent and difficult children should remain in institutions.

Such arguments were at first buried in academic journals. By 1970, however, policy professionals were divided into those defending the system as it had evolved and those loosely associated with the deinstitutionalization movement. The opinions of the latter group were diverse, ranging from emptying all children's institutions *now* to simply having fewer children institutionalized and shorter stays when there. Another suggestion was to move institutionalized children to homes scattered in neighborhoods, creating a kind of anti-institutional institution. This reconfiguration of the cottage ideal proved very attractive in the seventies and eighties. Instead of fifty children in one institution (as in Chapin Hall) there would be seven to ten children in neighborhood homes. (Note the scaling down of size: Progressive "cottages" were meant to contain about twenty-five children.) Such operations came to be called "community-based" programs or "group homes," a usage not to be confused with that of the 1950s, when "group home" referred to places like Chapin Hall.[38]

Deinstitutionalization advocates returned to earlier notions of where children should be; but unlike during the Progressive Era, this was occurring largely *after* the nineteenth-century orphanage had disappeared, largely after foster home care had become the norm for dependent children. As I've been noting, the number of available beds in institutions for males and females under eighteen was steadily shrinking from the late 1940s through the 1960s. Deinstitutionalization conjured up older images of "large, impersonal institutions," but such language was directed as much at residential treatment centers as at the few remaining orphanages left in the city.

In the early seventies, state after state adopted some sort of deinstitutionalization program. In 1975, Title XX of the amended Social Security Act proclaimed that all federal service funds should as far as possible prevent "inappropriate institutional care by providing for community-based care [or] home-based care." Institutionalization must only be "a last resort." Five years later another amendment (this time to the "Title IV-B Program") granted additional funds to states whose foster care programs had services designed to try and keep children at home and to quickly reunify separated families. Thus federal law in the 1970s repeated the exact same message of the 1909 President's Conference on Dependent Children —the biological home was the best place for a child, foster homes were next, and institutions should be avoided as much as possible. Since most state welfare programs depended very heavily on federal funding (Illinois for more than 60 percent in 1976), these changes were generally interpreted as a legal mandate for some sort of deinstitutionalization.[39]

In 1973, the new governor hired Jerome Miller to run the Illinois Department of Children and Family Services. For the previous two years,

DCFS had been wracked by scandal, charged with warehousing children in out-of-state institutions and being unresponsive to abused children. Miller had served as commissioner of the Massachusetts Department of Youth Services, making his reputation by closing down all of Massachusetts' state-run institutions for delinquents, one of the most dramatic acts of the whole deinstitutionalization movement. Miller arrived abrasive, openly damning Illinois practice, brusquely pushing ahead with reform. Once in office, he struck on a number of fronts at once. He immediately began reorganizing the DCFS bureaucracy. He openly expressed distrust of the psychotherapeutic models that dominated residential treatment centers like Chapin Hall. He instituted a host of new child advocacy programs, especially expanded child abuse programs and increased efforts to better serve black children. Miller also actively began searching for African-Americans to hire at DCFS. And he began pulling kids out of institutions. Between May 1973 and June 1974, the number of children that DCFS subsidized in institutions fell by 34 percent. Miller had brought deinstitutionalization to Illinois.[40]

An immediate result of Miller's campaign was that the remaining huge Catholic orphanages fell. Angel Guardian, which during the Depression housed up to 1,200 children at times, and even in the late 1960s had a capacity of 400, closed its doors in 1974. The Catholic orphanages had become dependent upon DCFS for intake and income right around 1970, the same time Chapin Hall did. The large Catholic orphanage, as a real vestige of the early-twentieth-century orphanage, the sort of institution Chapin Hall was in the 1930s (only larger and therefore worse, as the welfare administrators saw it), was the first target of the new DCFS. With no intake, and therefore no funding, it could no longer maintain its program. By 1981, there were only a few institutions in Chicago that might be called "orphanages," mostly nonsectarian institutions that had sidestepped DCFS domination in the early 1970s.

At least some of Miller's suggestions might have been better received if not for his style. His aggressive, shoot-from-the-hip approach upset service-agency social workers all over the state. Miller had come in speaking about the antiquated and cruel welfare system in Illinois. And his overnight reorganization of DCFS robbed agency professionals of steady contacts. Organizations representing social workers soon began a counterattack, loudly attacking Miller in the press, quietly grumbling about him to state legislators. By the spring of 1974 there was open warfare.[41]

For Chapin Hall, the first problem was the confusion created by DCFS reorganization. Elsie Blumberg, the social worker in charge of intake at Chapin Hall, spoke of the "mayhem" inside the state agency. Key liaison personnel disappeared, phone calls went unreturned, offices moved without notice, phone numbers changed without warning. "In the State's search for economy and quick change," Blumberg argued, "it seemed they threw out the baby with the bath water. This was done by transferring cases, decentralizing, then centralizing, then decentralizing again, changing workers with frightening speed, changing offices and phone numbers, and generally being incredibly chaotic."[42]

DCFS also began making multiple referrals (sending the same application materials to several agencies) thus forcing Chapin Hall to compete with other institutions for new children. This complicated Blumberg's job enormously, in her mind replacing a system that worked via cooperation with one that was competitive and market-driven.[43] Blumberg now had to act immediately on all referrals, hoping to beat out other agencies. Confirming letters and phone calls to DCFS had to happen instantly. There were increasingly hurried efforts to find Chapin Hall's consulting psychiatrist for the entrance evaluation. Similar dispatch was necessary in contacting parents or guardians. Blumberg now spent hours on the phone. Even with the best efforts, however, children were often lost. Other agencies, of course, were adopting the same procedures as Chapin Hall and so, if the psychiatrist happened to be away from the phone, or the parents not at home when a call was made, children might be placed elsewhere. Especially frustrating was the confusion inside DCFS. Eight months into Miller's reign Blumberg feared that her job had become "something of a nightmare." "This was my twentieth year at Chapin Hall," she told the boards in January 1974, "and my most difficult."[44]

Miller's general skepticism about the system at large surfaced in other ways. Chapin Hall was one of nineteen private agencies that DCFS sued in 1973 for discrimination against African-American applicants. The suit was thrown out of court. Miller also ordered an inspection of all private agencies. Investigators came to Chapin Hall in January 1974. Headley and Blumberg thought the whole tone inquisitional. Blumberg noted that the investigators "apparently surprised themselves and us by liking what they saw."[45]

Blumberg was distressed by the turmoil and disorder inside DCFS. But she also distrusted the new liberalism that underlay the reforms. They were not separate in her mind. Here is how she began her 1974 annual report:

Farewell to 1973! Farewell to Affirmative Action! Farewell to Evaluation Review! Farewell to the inconceivable confusion that masqueraded as "Child Welfare in 1973"!

Blumberg complained about the new child abuse procedures of DCFS (not realizing that they were mandated by legislation), and the whole effort to reduce the number of children in institutions. She was put off by Miller's skepticism about traditional labels such as "delinquent," or "psychotic." And such opinions were certainly not hers alone. Like most of Chicago's service agency–based social workers, Chapin Hall's whole professional staff greeted deinstitutionalization with rousing skepticism.[46]

Miller proved too controversial and was forced out of DCFS in August 1974. "May he rest in peace professionally speaking," Elsie Blumberg opined. Miller's exit was "our happiest moment in 1974," said Headley. Such were the sentiments of agency social workers around the state. Miller's demise ushered in a short period of uncertainty. Within the year, however, Headley and Blumberg realized that reducing the number of children in institutions was the governor's policy regardless of who ran DCFS. Even if the new director, Mary Leahy, dealt with agencies more rationally than Miller, she still pursued many of his goals. There remained many staffers at DCFS who were, as Headley put it, "plodding along in Miller fashion and are still very difficult." Elsie Blumberg noted that Miller's "body was gone, but so far his spirit lives on." "Institutions," she added, "have become *persona non grata*." Securing new admissions from a suspicious state bureaucracy remained a painful, time-consuming process. Intake, Blumberg noted in 1975, "is fraught with frustration, exasperation, disappointment, and pure unadulterated fatigue. I sometimes think it is like swimming against the tide."[47]

Hopes rose again at the end of 1976 when James Thompson, a Republican, was elected governor. Rumors flew that he was favorably disposed to residential treatment centers. Deinstitutionalization, it was thought, might prove to be just a Democratic policy. Headley noted how establishment Republicans feared that government could not solve all problems and will be looking "to the private sector for solutions." And he was not unaware that a number of the Republicans on Chapin Hall's Board of Directors were personally acquainted with the new governor. Elsie Blumberg noted a changed atmosphere in DCFS in the last days of 1976, which she speculated was due to Thompson's election in November.[48]

In the short term, the Republican administration did appear to make a difference. For the rest of the decade, referrals were better. The number of children in institutional care in Illinois rose modestly in the second half of the 1970s.[49] But in the end hopes were dashed here too. The relative cheapness of foster over residential care was attractive to the fiscally conservative governor. As important, the 1975 change in federal law was interpreted as explicitly mandating a turn to noninstitutional forms of help.

Indeed, in the late seventies, DCFS never wavered from the basic goal of trying to reduce the number of children in institutions, of trying to implement Title XX of the Social Security Act.[50]

Chapin Hall's ability to find placements in the late 1970s was due more to fortuitous causes than any shift in basic state aims. For one thing, DCFS was a mess in those years. In fact, it is probably best to see the agency as in a perpetual state of crisis between 1971 and 1978. DCFS had six different directors in those seven years and was constantly embroiled in public fights over its alleged incompetence, racism, and neglect. Jerome Miller was only the most dramatic example of a larger phenomenon. The constant political turf battles and ever-present journalistic exposés kept the agency off balance, on the defensive. Whatever goals DCFS might have, all the bickering made implementation depressingly difficult.

Even when Gregory Coler took over as director in 1978 and returned some stability to the agency (Coler remained until 1983), short-term goals benefited Chapin Hall. DCFS announced in July 1977 that the number of children in residential care would stabilize in 1979 precisely because it wanted to close the Soldiers' and Sailors' Children's School, the old state orphanage (formerly the Soldiers' Orphans' Home). Between May and September of that year, as the Children's School was emptied, DCFS shifted sixty-five children to private agencies.[51]

This by no means signaled a renewed respect for institutions. Once the state had cleaned its own house, it turned back on the private sector. DCFS planning reports in the early 1980s all called attention to the desire to reduce the institutional population. Indeed, one way the department statistically measured its own success was by the decline in the numbers of children in residential treatment centers. Between 1980 and 1983, the number of dependent Illinois children in institutions dropped 30 percent, from 2,399 to 1,672.[52]

This second wave of deinstitutionalization proceeded without the fanfare of the more dramatic efforts of 1973–75. It had, however, consequences just as important. Among other things, it demolished Chapin Hall's referral base. Largely through aggressive searching, Chapin Hall had maintained a steady population until the end of the seventies. But after that, filling space proved to be an impossible problem. Between 1980 and 1984 the number of resident children plummeted, falling from sixty-one to forty-four, a change roughly paralleling the drop of numbers in the system at large. The decline in numbers was so important because over 70 percent of the agency's income now came from DCFS. Fewer children meant fewer dollars. Chapin Hall was in big trouble.

While the decline in the number of children at Chapin Hall was at the center of its financial woes, the full story is far more complicated. In fact, the financial difficulties first surfaced in 1976, before the second wave of deinstitutionalization. In that year, for the first time in decades, the agency ran a deficit. Each year after that, until the residential treament center closed in 1984, the deficits continued. And they were not small ones. By 1980, the gap between income and outlay was running to more than $150,000 each year.

It was not that in any absolute sense income fell. Quite the opposite. The steady increases in the amount DCFS paid for each child meant that the income Chapin Hall brought in rose to what seemed to be quite handsome amounts even given the drop in population. What was happening was that costs were climbing at an even more phenomenal pace.

Rising costs were a constant for Chapin Hall from the early fifties to the middle eighties. The increase of the 1950s has been discussed in the last chapter. When George Headley was hired in 1963 and Chapin Hall moved to become a residential treatment center, it was no surprise that more money was involved. In 1964, the budget was just under $200,000. Five years later, it cost $416,631 to run Chapin Hall, a jump of over 100 percent. But even with the new program in place, expenses did not stop climbing. During the seventies costs nearly tripled. In 1977 it took over one million dollars to run the agency; in 1980 more than $1,700,000, a stunning 70 percent jump in three years. And it did not end there. Each year, without a break, expenses rose with a depressing predictability. By fiscal year 1982–83, the last full year the residential treatment center was open, the operation cost $2,036,079. Critics were not kidding when pointing out how expensive residential treatment centers were. And if they were expensive in 1964, they were quite literally more than 1000 percent more expensive twenty years later.

The size of these increases should put to rest any vague idea that inflation was the core of the problem. Inflation accounted for only the most minimal part of increased expenditures. In fact, between 1967 and 1983, the cost of running Chapin Hall rose 211 percent more than the Consumer Price Index.[53]

As in the 1950s, the rising costs primarily boiled down to one item—salaries. Between 1967 and 1983, salaries jumped from roughly $220,000 to more than $1,500,000.[54] Salary increases accounted for 77.8 percent of all new expenses in those years. Again, these increases far outpaced the Consumer Price Index. Wages and benefits climbed even a bit more quickly than total costs—233 percent more than the rate of inflation.

Why did salaries outstrip inflation by so much? Most simply, the professionalization of the agency dictated large changes in staffing. For one thing, the number of professionals working at Chapin Hall steadily climbed during the 1960s and 1970s. The decision to become a residential treatment center meant that more trained workers were necessary, bringing staff to patient ratios down to "professional" levels. Accepting ever more difficult children meant adding more and more staff. The mid-seventies decision to accept psychotic children also meant more staff. In 1977, for the first time, a child entered who needed round the clock one-on-one care. In 1963, there were two employees with master's degrees in social work; by the 1980s there were ten. The number of consulting psychiatrists jumped from one to three, and the amount of time they worked for Chapin Hall rose as well.

The professionalization of Chapin Hall also meant, beginning in the 1960s, the increased presence of men. For the first time in the agency's history, male employees were being hired for more than handiwork and maintenance. George Headley, who was the first male ever to run the institution, was also the man who led the push to create a residential treatment center. The increased presence of males at Chapin Hall contributed to the upward spiral of salaries, as men continued to be paid more than women.

Keeping Chapin Hall a professionally respectable agency also meant an increasing division of labor, which again required more staff. Due to the new state attitude toward institutions in the mid-seventies, intake became a full-time job at Chapin Hall. Never before had there been an employee whose sole job was finding new children. Similarly, in the hopes of winning favor with DCFS officials in the late seventies, a series of new initiatives were begun, all of which meant bringing in more staff. In 1976, for example, Chapin Hall opened a foster program, something which both won the praise of state officials but also raised agency costs. In 1980 a business manager was hired, freeing the executive director from any concern with day-to-day financial matters and allowing him to concentrate on the program. It added still another professional salary to the budget.

Professionalization increased salaries in other ways as well. In 1969, largely through state initiative, it was decided to raise the quality of child care workers, those employees who lived with the children. Salaries climbed. At this level too men began to be hired for the first time, again contributing to the upward pull of income. Finally, after a lengthy dispute, the federal Department of Labor informed Chapin Hall in 1979 that there had to be three shifts of child care workers. No longer could workers live with the children, working round the clock. Now it had to be arranged via eight-hour shifts.

The key to the problem, then, was not inflation but the changing standards of what a "professional" institution consisted of. The public sector was behind many of the changes. Whether it was more professional staff, better pensions, or eight-hour days, the hand of government was strong. But probably the most important state intervention was a subtle one—the state had been sending tougher and tougher children to institutions like Chapin Hall since the middle of the 1950s. By the mid-eighties, there had already been a steady thirty-year push by public authorities to have Chapin Hall take only the hardest children to control. Over the years the frontier of what constituted the degree of emotional disturbance that should result in institutionalization was gradually pushed back. And after the state took effective control of the intake system in 1969, it proceeded to reroute many of those children who were, relatively speaking, less emotionally scarred. And since DCFS for all practical purposes controlled Chapin Hall's finances, there was little for Chapin Hall to do except move with the state's program. Its program would be tailored to state needs or else it would die.

The state made increasing demands on Chapin Hall at the same time it was trying to cut costs. The deinstitutionalization push of the early eighties owed as much to efforts to reduce costs as to new thinking about institutions. From the first deficit in 1976, it was a shortage of DCFS-sponsored children *in relation to costs* that caused the deficit. And as the number of children shrank after 1979, the deficits only grew worse. Moreover, although the state was theoretically committed to covering 100 percent of the costs of institutional care, this was not the case. State funding only paid about 75 percent of the actual costs of Chapin Hall. The per diem never paid the total costs of the children. Finally, in 1979, in an effort to save money, DCFS locked the rates for agencies. This wound up to be a crippling blow for Chapin Hall.

Couple all this with the dropping number of children and we have the cause of the deficit. Between 1969 and 1972 Chapin Hall locked itself into a system dependent heavily on state money and state children. It was the only way that money was available to support the expensive therapeutic program. But once state policy changed, and fewer children were deemed suitable for a place like Chapin Hall, it became very difficult to financially support the sort of program that Chapin Hall had.

THE END OF A RESIDENTIAL TREATMENT CENTER

After 1976, the staff could not find enough children to keep Chapin Hall in the black. A full explanation, however, has to move beyond references to deinstitutionalization and the DCFS budget crunch. Numerous private agencies did survive these years. And, after 1983, the number of children in institutional care leveled off. Since that time, in fact, a very slight increase has occurred in the number of children in institutions.[55] Moreover, the falling numbers of institutionalized children between 1980 and 1983 did not affect all agencies equally. Just as in the past, some suffered more than others. In fact, despite the declining number of children in institutions, in the 1970s and 1980s there was actually an increase in the number of institutions. The big Catholic and state orphanages disappeared in the 1970s but the number of residential treatment centers actually rose. The most important institutional change in that decade was the explosion of small (seven to twelve children), neighborhood-based group homes for adolescents. The *Social Service Directory* of the Welfare Council listed three such institutions in 1971 and fifty-three of them in 1981. This shift was not merely local; it was happening across the nation.[56]

The 1980s, the decade that Chapin Hall closed, saw no significant changes in this institutional spread. By that time, the old orphanage and industrial schools of the nineteenth century were gone (leaving aside those few institutions that had circumvented DCFS control). The post–World War II version of the "group home," what Chapin Hall became after 1949, was also gone. By the 1970s, almost every dependent child was routed to foster home care. And if institutionalization was decided upon, the choices were residential treatment centers or neighborhood group homes. When many private agencies closed their doors in the 1950s, Chapin Hall had been on the winning side. With this round of deinstitutionalization, however, it was not so lucky. Since the close of Chapin Hall was not part of a larger attack on the existence of residential treatment centers per se, we have to look more precisely at why intake collapsed after 1980.

In the 1970s, staff and directors began trying to halt the slide. The image of private agencies as hidebound and conservative (an image often drawn by contemporary policy professionals) was as much a half-truth in the 1970s and 1980s as it was during the Progressive Era. Chapin Hall did its best to accommodate the shifting climate, actively struggling both to adjust to changing circumstances and to maintain a good professional standing.

As early as 1974 Headley observed that given the "anti-institutional psychology" now dominating American welfare, Chapin Hall would have to change. "I can foresee the time when we might have only six departments in our present [residential] program," Headley argued, "and the rest of our facilities . . . used for community programs including day care, day school, parent–child groups, and emergency placement for abused children."[57]

In the next few years the staff experimented with a variety of supplementary programs. In 1974, Chapin Hall joined a consortium of private agencies to plan with DCFS about how services might be modified. With another group of private children's institutions, including Children's Memorial Hospital, the agency used a $1.6 million grant to develop a comprehensive child abuse program. In 1975 Chapin Hall opened a foster care program and an emergency care unit for abused and neglected children. In 1977, Chapin Hall accepted developmentally disabled children for the first time. In 1982–83, staff explored turning part of Chapin Hall into a shelter for battered women and children.[58]

All of these efforts were discussed in terms of how they might change the image of Chapin Hall with DCFS bureaucrats and increase the number of children referred by the state. All had problems. Joint efforts foundered on the general instability of the times. Things changed so much and so quickly that it was hard to plan anything. Chapin Hall's in-house efforts, on the other hand, were timidly planned and poorly executed. They were conceived on too small a scale. The emergency care unit was always a tiny program; the foster care program, after hobbling along for several years, was discontinued in 1980.

Probably the most important effort made by Chapin Hall to accommodate new state priorities was to take ever more emotionally damaged children. There is no question that the children and adolescents entering Chapin Hall in the early eighties were significantly different from those that came earlier. Here, too, facile images about the truculence and conservatism of Chapin Hall staff, if not completely jettisoned, need to be seriously modified. The children got a bit older over time. After 1973, the agency routinely accepted psychotic children. In the course of the 1970s, the number of children who were not welcome in Chicago public schools climbed. By the 1980s, nine out of ten new children had to be in some sort of special education program.

Nor did Chapin Hall avoid taking African-American children. One of the marked changes inside the agency during the 1970s was the changing color of the children. In this respect Chapin Hall rather effortlessly adapted DCFS's new priorities. From a handful of black children in 1970, the agency had a black population of 29 percent in 1975 and 58 percent in 1981. By the eighties, Chapin Hall served more African-American children than private agencies in general. A 1983 study of six Chicago private residential programs showed that Chapin Hall was accepting far more minority children than several other well-known homes for emotionally disturbed children.[59]

The same study reveals something else, however, that does indicate why Chapin Hall had severe problems maintaining its population in the 1980s. It was the only agency in the study still trying to balance males and females. In the 1983 study, however, 92 percent of the children living at the six institutions were boys.[60]

At the end of the 1970s, private institutions in Illinois devoted just under 40 percent of their space to females; in 1987 that was down to under 35 percent. In Chicago it was even less.[61] There was a very real move away from an equal balance of the sexes. In part this was conscious policy, in part it simply reflected a basic reality—as institutions came to be viewed as places for only the most troublesome adolescents (which should not necessarily be equated with the most *troubled* adolescents), that meant more boys than girls.

As early as 1967, George Headley had noticed declining referrals for girls. And he also committed himself to bucking the trend. Headley theorized that young girls (nine years old or so) were as emotionally damaged as boys but they tended to withdraw rather than act out. The new policy, he thought, confused mild surface symptoms with genuine emotional health. If not treated early on, Headley thought, there would be more trouble when girls got older—particularly with drugs and sexual promiscuity. Headley's message was repeated a number of times over the years by Chapin Hall professionals. In 1977, Tom Libby sounded the same theme, pointing out that boys were being favored not because they were really more damaged but because their acting out was aggressive rather than sexual.[62]

Indeed, changing the gender balance of a residential program was not a simple matter. A more male staff was needed to relate to boys and living quarters had to be refigured (and sometimes remodeled) to accommodate the different mix. Still, while Chapin Hall did close one girls' cottage in the late seventies, it never really attempted to change. This put the agency sharply at odds with the wants of the welfare system as a whole. By 1983, Chapin Hall could go for months at a time without a single referral of a girl.[63] It was looking for many more girls than DCFS wanted to institutionalize.

If gender was one way the agency fell out of step with DCFS policy, age was another. Although Chapin Hall was very ready to take more troubled children, it remained reticent about accepting adolescents. To be sure, over the years the age of children living inside Chapin Hall rose. The median age of an entering child rose from seven to nine during the 1960s. And after the turn toward residential treatment, Chapin Hall kept more and more adolescents.

But in 1978, DCFS moved to keep children under the age of thirteen out of institutions. Within a year, more than half the children DCFS referred to Chapin Hall were thirteen to fifteen years old. And another 10 percent were sixteen to eighteen. The staff at Chapin Hall did not want these children, something which goes a long way toward explaining why so many beds were empty during the early eighties.

Only rarely were there hints that the staff understood the problem in these terms. In 1980, George Headley complained about how "sluggish" referrals of younger children were. Two years later Tom Libby enthusiastically jumped at the chance to accept a six-year-old girl. Overall, however, these men did not focus on this growing age discrepancy. Chapin Hall kept no statistics on children's ages at this time (a sharp break from historical practice). The staff generally talked about the declining referrals in other, vaguer terms—DCFS once again had it in for private institutions. The more specific issue of age was not remarked on. Although when an outside review of the agency was made in November 1983 the problem was fully discussed, it was certainly too late at that point.[64]

The failure to shift to a male population and the refusal to take older children eventually pushed Chapin Hall away from the mainstream of residential care. These very specific issues suggest the ways that Chapin Hall failed to keep apace of DCFS policy. They also suggest why Chapin Hall had trouble in the 1980s. For it was only after 1978 that the age of children rose beyond what Chapin Hall staff was willing to accept.

Once again we return to the vagueness of the phrase "emotionally disturbed." Policy professionals have used the term since the 1940s (and indeed continue to use it today). Yet its meaning, when describing what sort of child needs institutional help, has varied enormously. And in the 1970s, the meaning changed very rapidly, something which helps explain Chapin Hall's problems after 1980. When Jerome Miller came to DCFS in 1973, he asked rhetorically: "Should an eight-year-old be in an institution unless he has a severe mental disorder or is self-destructive?"[65] Six years later, however, the state was trying to keep all children under the age of thirteen out of institutions. When Jerome Miller issued his challenge, the staff at Chapin Hall could respond. The average age of the entering child rose from seven to nine, hence the state could praise the agency in 1975 for accepting older, more difficult children than ever before; three years later, state social workers could call Chapin Hall a model program. But when the next round of deinstitutionalization came between 1979 and 1983, Chapin Hall did not keep up. The same words were used ("more disturbed children," "tougher children") but they had a different meaning, relating now to children thirteen and over instead of eight. Over the years, then, Chapin Hall had continued to accept "tougher" children, but after 1979 it still did not accept "tough" enough children.

The deficits had begun in 1976, but it was the collapse of intake after

1980 that made them so debilitating. And this collapse was due to very specific shifts in DCFS referrals. More and older male adolescents now defined that notoriously vague phrase "more troubled children."

As the new wave of deinstitutionalization hit, Chapin Hall's ability to effectively respond was hurt in other ways. In 1979, the agency was charged with child abuse. A former resident had claimed that a child care worker had sexually molested him. The state investigation went on for almost a year, enormously draining the staff's energy. And while DCFS cleared Chapin Hall of all charges, the lingering effects of the scandal hurt. Typically, the city's newspapers had reported the charges but not mentioned the acquittal. Nor were DCFS's internal communications any better. Nearly two years after investigators cleared Chapin Hall, not all DCFS caseworkers were aware of the outcome. They were continuing to steer referrals away from Chapin Hall. The problems seemed to feed on each other. In 1981, in an effort to find new sources of income, the board applied to rejoin United Way. It was turned down the next year. By that time, Chapin Hall was generally seen as out of step with the times.

Morale sank at Chapin Hall after 1979. The charges of abuse, declining referrals, burgeoning deficit, and United Way rejection—it all added up. Wages had to be frozen in 1982, further dispiriting the staff. And that the post-1979 policy of DCFS to further reduce the number of institutionalized children was the work of a friendly Republican governor also hurt. The staff saw the writing on the wall. Deinstitutionalization was now an uncontroversial, bipartisan goal. It saved money and in the apogee of the Reagan years—the early eighties—it seemed a given that public money for agencies like Chapin Hall would continue to decline. Indeed, in 1983, the last full year that Chapin Hall was open, DCFS suffered a major budget crunch of its own and announced a 7 percent cut in the amount of money earmarked for children's institutions. It appeared that in the next years even fewer children would be referred to Chapin Hall.

It was not only the staff that was hurt by sagging morale. The board suffered as well. The deficits of the late seventies led to a revival of the boards. In 1979, Jay Buck, a downtown banker, became president of the board. He hoped to create a much more active managing board, one that could steer Chapin Hall's residential program through tough times. In the next few years, he and most other board members came to believe that a more drastic change was necessary.

Buck came to the board in 1964 when Chapin Hall had merged with Ridge Farm. He replaced Wyndham Hasler, who had served for fifteen years as president. During the flush times of the 1960s, the Board of Directors had little to do. It was a moribund operation by 1979. But the deficit had convinced Buck that a more energetic board was necessary.

In large part, Chapin Hall was a victim of good times. The Board of Managers had gradually lost effective control over the institution. Staff now ran everything. And George Headley had very much run a sort of vest-pocket operation. He kept details to himself. Until the late seventies, the boards were quite content with this arrangement.

Buck hoped that a reinvigorated board could manage the problems facing Chapin Hall. In September 1980, when he first took over as president, he was relatively confident that the operation could continue. Buck's strategy was to find ways to get a more active board—this to both keep better watch over the institution and also to get a group of active fund raisers.[66]

Within a year, the board decided to try a major fundraising drive. They would go to United Way, get matching grant funds, and begin a major drive to refurbish the endowment. This plan was derailed, however, when United Way refused to support the idea. In January of 1982, Chapin Hall was turned down.

After the matching grant was denied, Buck gently prodded United Way officials for the reasons. Eventually, Bruce Newman told him that Community Trust officials just did not believe that Chapin Hall would survive. The place was not at the cutting edge of child welfare. It did not take enough "problem" children to please DCFS and without the state there was no way the agency would last.[67]

Although the board would not have put it this way, its strategy was to try to edge Chapin Hall back toward an earlier system of welfare management. Both advice and money were to come from the downtown umbrella agencies and not the state. The plan did not work, however, because DCFS had become such a key and unavoidable player. The state welfare bureaucracy had become the six-hundred-pound gorilla.

It seems that bad morale had touched the board by that time as well. Although the board, by all standards, included some extraordinarily wealthy people, none proposed giving a huge gift to save Chapin Hall. Even if not always articulated, the problems of the agency had subtly affected the board's mood. The traditional family commitments that had been so important in raising money at Chapin Hall from the beginning of the century had dried up.

Buck himself says that it was after the United Way turned down the matching grant that he seriously began thinking about the need to close Chapin Hall.[68] In 1982, a year Tom Libby called "a year of survival" for the agency, Buck got the men's and women's boards to agree to merge, creating one, efficient governing body. Finally Chapin Hall had done what the Council of Social Agencies had first asked them to do in 1935. Also in the spring of 1982, the board began a major fundraising drive, one undertaken without the help of United Way. It had limited success.

Buck did still another thing to rethink the course of Chapin Hall. He asked Bruce Newman of Community Trust to find someone from the outside who could evaluate the program. Newman suggested Harold Richman of the University of Chicago School of Social Service Administration. Richman thus became one of a long string of University of Chicago experts to give advice to Chapin Hall. His study was funded by Community Trust.

When Richman delivered his results in November 1983, he suggested a series of options to the Board. Chapin Hall might reorient itself to take still harder children. It could diversify its program in a variety of ways. Another possibility was to merge with another agency. Finally, it could use its endowment to fund some sort of research or advocacy center. Whatever the option taken, Richman made clear, Chapin Hall could not go on as it had been. There was simply no longer the referral base for the agency to succeed in its present state.[69]

The month after Richman's presentation, the Executive and Finance Committees of the board voted to eliminate further discussion of taking older, harder case referrals from DCFS. In January of the next year, these committees voted to shut down the current operation and look into the research and development option Richman had discussed. At a special board meeting on February 28, the full board voted to close the residential treatment center. The decision was not unanimous. Some voted against, others were unhappy with the decision. One director, Julia McNulty, stood and resigned immediately after the vote. McNulty was the granddaughter of Julia Thompson, the manager who had put decades of work into Chapin Hall, capped by her 1929 fund drive to erect Chapin Hall's second cottage.

Why did Chapin Hall's residential treatment program close? Again, we must emphasize that almost all agencies survived, that deinstitutionalization did not end residential treatment for emotionally disturbed children. Nor did it, after 1983, mean any more decrease in the number of institutionalized children. By the time Chapin Hall closed in 1984, the practical results of deinstitutionalization were complete.

Chapin Hall closed, first of all, because the situation itself was all so confusing. There was a sustained period, probably dating back to the late sixties, when Illinois welfare fell into a flux that did not really settle down until the middle of the eighties. For a long time, Chapin Hall heard contradictory opinions from policy professionals. For much of the seventies it appeared to be a war of two ideas about institutional care. Committees of notables were producing reports during this time suggesting that deinstitutionalization was not the panacea that others thought it to be. It was only in the early 1980s, with the second wave of deinstitutionalization, that it became apparent that even a Republican administration was committed to reducing institutional care.

Moreover, the language used by policy professionals did not help clarify the situation. Vague references to "tougher" children and to "harder" cases only confused agencies that thought they *were* taking "tougher," "harder" wards. The language actually masked more concrete changes in DCFS referrals.

But if the general confusion of the times was a factor, the second and far more critical factor was that the staff in several respects did fall out of step with the mainstream. Headley, Blumberg, and Libby had grown up and supported residential treatment in its "glory days," those years in the 1960s when it appeared that Chapin Hall was moving into the forefront of therapeutic treatment. The institution never completely adapted to the changed climate of the late 1970s and 1980s, with its innate distrust of psychotherapy and of institutionalizing preadolescent children. A gap arose between those who ran Chapin Hall and the DCFS administrators who managed the system. This gap explains why the deficits were so crushing after 1979.

But even that is not a sufficient answer. For similar gaps between the agency staff and managerial social workers had occurred before—in the Progressive Era, in the 1940s. Why could it not be mediated in the 1980s? In large part, it was because the downtown professionals had done such a good job of marginalizing the volunteer managers. By the 1970s, Chapin Hall was no longer "their" institution, it was someplace they helped out at. The staff was in total control. With the managers and directors relatively passive during those years, no one was left to look at the big picture.

Moreover, the entrance of the state had displaced the Welfare Council and Community Fund. From the 1920s through the 1960s, the gap between system managers and Chapin Hall had been mediated by the volunteer women taking advice from the downtown professionals and the downtown professionals negotiating partial compliance with Chapin Hall. In the late 1970s this did not happen because the older system of "private power for the public good" had disappeared. Not only had the women managers become marginalized. In 1979, there was no longer any Susanne

Schulze or Connie Fish to give advice. This change helps explain the poor morale of Chapin Hall after 1979 and marks a third major reason why the agency closed in 1984.

The way the system had broken down can be seen by contrasting how George Headley was hired in 1963 with how Tom Libby was hired in 1980. Headley was hired after a nationwide search. Ads were placed in the appropriate professional journals. Board members Wyndham Hasler and Julia McNulty carefully screened applicants. Susanne Schulze of the University of Chicago and Connie Fish of the Welfare Council gave extensive advice, as did Dr. Seymour Steinhorn, Chapin Hall's consulting psychiatrist. It all reflected the intersection of care-providing agencies and downtown umbrella organizations designed to manage the system. It reflected the ethos of "private power for the public good."

In 1980, however, there was no national search. There was no expert advice. There was, indeed, no input from the boards. Instead, George Headley pulled Tom Libby aside one day and asked him if he wanted to take over as executive director. Libby agreed. After several months of silence, Libby became nervous and asked Headley about the board. Headley told him not to worry. A few weeks later a letter turned up from Wyndham Hasler congratulating Libby on his new post.[70]

At the very end, the most interesting gap at Chapin Hall was one between two different assumptions about what the priorities of child welfare should be.[71] On one side were those who emphasized helping children one at a time, on a very personal basis. As long as Chapin Hall could be seen to be actually benefiting some needy children, this group reasoned, it was doing something right. Adhering to this position were the leading staff professionals and most of the women on the Board of Managers.

On the other side were those who talked in terms of systemic needs, who reasoned statistically, who thought about budgets and what kind of institution the state actually would support. On this side were most of the men on the Board of Managers, including Jay Buck, and Harold Richman who was brought in to evaluate the program.

One side kept alluding to "hands-on care," the other to "perspective." Neither of the groups ignored the other's concerns, and even on the Board of Directors these divisions did not completely define the final vote.[72] They did, however, mark distinctly different emphases in tone and language. To those who thought about personal contact, Chapin Hall, whatever its problems, was doing something right. It was helping children in trouble. If there was any possibility, problems should be weathered, perhaps by tinkering with the program, perhaps by hunkering down till the storm passed. Most of all, they spoke of Chapin Hall as being buffeted by a merciless and soulless bureaucracy, one not only of DCFS employees but of the welfare establishment in general.

To those who spoke in terms of systemic needs of Chicago child welfare, Chapin Hall was clearly in need of serious reorganization. It did not meet the contemporary needs of troubled youth. It refused to accept the fact that younger boys and girls would only rarely be institutionalized. It did not see that the budget deficit would not be turned around with an antiquated program. Chapin Hall must once again become part of the system.

These fault lines reflect an intriguing continuation of earlier debates about the relationship of policy professionals to care-providing agencies. In the late 1940s, when Chapin Hall underwent an earlier rearrangement, downtown policy professionals like Connie Fish and Susanne Schulze assumed that staffing Chapin Hall with women with master's degrees in social work would create a natural alliance between policy professionals like themselves and agency professionals. While that worked for several decades, by the 1980s social workers at Chapin Hall used language quite different from that of the University of Chicago policy professionals brought in to assess the institution. Tom Libby spoke of wanting to help kids, of wanting to work with children. Harold Richman, on the other hand, spoke of the statistical needs of the city. In the long run, Susanne Schulze and Connie Fish were wrong. The agency professionals did not necessarily think like the policy pros.

These differences were duplicated on the Board of Directors, with a basic division between the men and women. Indeed, the men thought in terms of how Chapin Hall could fill the needs of the whole system of Chicago child welfare, while the women, on the whole, kept speaking about how actual flesh-and-blood children could be helped. Thus, at the end, the staff's *mentalité* was far closer to that of the women volunteers than to that of the outside social work professionals. The men on the Board of Managers, on the other hand, spoke in an idiom that resembled that of the policy professionals far more than that of either the staff or the women.

This alliance reflected the coming to fruition of the dreams of 1930s policy professionals. It was the initial goal of the Council of Social Agencies to marginalize the women and deal with the men on the board because they assumed the men would think more like the welfare experts. They would put the needs of Chicago above the interests of a particular agency. That goal proved elusive in 1935, but not in 1984. Indeed, one key proposal in the 1930s was that the male and female boards merge, a change assumed to give more power to the men. When that merger finally happened in 1982, it did in fact give more power to the men. It is possible at least to theorize that if the women still ran the board in 1984, Chapin Hall would not be closed today.

But if it remained open, some large change in the program would have had to have occurred. And in 1984, there was not enough will to continue.

THE NEXT CHAPIN HALL

Chapin Hall closed as a residential treatment center in June 1984. It reopened the next year as a reseach center on children's issues affiliated with the University of Chicago. Harold Richman of the University of Chicago, who had done the 1983 study of Chapin Hall's residential program, became the agency's executive director. In the years since 1985, the Chapin Hall Center for Children, as it is now known, has once again entered a growth phase. From 1986 to 1991 the number of employees jumped from fifteen to seventy. Annual revenue leapt from about $500,000 to over $4,000,000. Money for research has come from many sources, among them the Chicago Community Trust, the Illinois Department of Children and Family Services, the U.S. Department of Health and Human Services, Los Angeles County, the U.S. Government Accounting Office, and the Rockefeller and Ford Foundations.

The current Chapin Hall Center for Children is in many ways far removed from the pre-1984 institution. It does research, not provide services. But in many ways this is just the logical next step in the story I've been telling. Chapin Hall has, in fact, transformed itself into one of the monitoring agencies that the orphanage sparred with over the years. The research now conducted at Chapin Hall is part of local and national efforts to manage child welfare services currently being delivered. Much of the work is done in tandem with state and federal authorities. Research at Chapin Hall often has immediate policy ramifications. Much of the new Chapin Hall's research recalls older issues of child welfare. One interest at the center is understanding how services currently being delivered to troubled families and children can be improved. Chapin Hall has sponsored studies of how state authorities make placement decisions about neglected or abused children, how a number of state programs designed to reunite families actually work, and what the various ramifications of annulled adoptions are, when children are removed from adoptive homes. In all this research, the new Chapin Hall continues the postwar institution's commitment to troubled children, simply shifting its expression from service-providing to research.

Other research interests reflect the revival of even older welfare goals.

The center is beginning to explore the ways that policy might not just react to problems but "enhance child development and family functioning."[73] Chapin Hall has done a major study, funded by the Ford Foundation, surveying what sort of services supportive communities provide for children. In this context, what happens to troubled youth is important, but so are institutions like day care and after-school programs, organized sports, youth volunteer opportunities, parent support and educational programs, libraries, parks, community centers. All these need to be studied to understand how neighborhoods and cities can nurture their young.

This broad array of specifics, as well as the basic theme of how a community helps children along, is very reminiscent of the range of interests that progressives developed in child welfare at the turn of the century. The progressive concern with "prevention" translated into a concern for libraries, parks, the Boy and Girl Scouts, settlement houses, and public health, much of which was highlighted at the 1911 Child Welfare Exhibit I discussed in chapter two. Chapin Hall's community interest echoes earlier reformers.

While certain research translates older themes into contemporary idioms, other projects hint at specifically late-twentieth-century problems. One of the guiding premises of the new Chapin Hall is that in "the last 25 years the world for children has changed dramatically."[74] Divorce, single parent households, working mothers, economic hardships, school problems are all unalterable and unavoidable facts of life. Chapin Hall's recall of the progressive community building theme is part of an effort to address very contemporary issues.

There are more subtle ways that Chapin Hall's interests are clearly rooted in the late twentieth century. One important research goal of Chapin Hall is collecting and making use of large data sets generated by numerous public service agencies around the nation. Chapin Hall wants to accumulate the information, then rework it "into a format that is accessible to policymakers, service providers, and others concerned about the welfare of children." Here is a very new managerial task, absolutely unimaginable for most of the century. Previous generations worried about the dearth of data; Chapin Hall now presumes the opposite. And it does so by addressing one of the key realities of contemporary bureaucratic life—that collection of information does not necessarily guarantee informed decisions. Chapin Hall has moved into what might be called a "postmodern" phase, thinking about how to manage the data that lies strewn all about us, of trying to make sure that we are able to digest our information instead of choke on it.[75]

Still another interest that calls to mind very recent concerns is Chapin

Hall's commitment to community-based planning, to figuring out how to bring about "fruitful collaboration among service providers and local consumers."[76] Behind this is a sense that top-down programs, by themselves, are clumsy; that the best services are based on a good respect for what specific communities want. Implied too is that models devised earlier in the century, models that assumed the managers had the best handle on the situation, need to be revised. Chapin Hall now advocates more cooperation between program administrators and local communities. Here is a another late-twentieth-century fear—state administrative bodies, which are absolutely necessary, need some policing as well.

The new Chapin Hall's respect for community and fear of community dissolution both sound very much like early-twentieth-century Progressive Era reform. On the other hand, the felt sense that random data needs supervision and that centralized service providers do not have all the answers suggest a post-progressive point of view. In its most recent manifestation, the Chapin Hall Center for Children recasts key progressive goals, but with a healthy skepticism about the naivety of progressive means and a pragmatic commitment to closing the gap.

∽ EPILOGUE ∽

Child Saving at the
Fin de Siècle

IN DECEMBER 1994, AS I WAS PUTTING THE FINISH-
ing touches on this manuscript, orphanages suddenly became the
talk of the nation. In the November elections, Republicans gained control
over both houses of Congress for the first time in forty years. Shortly
thereafter, the incoming Speaker of the House, Newt Gingrich, suggested
that the nation consider refusing welfare to unwed mothers under the age
of eighteen and putting their children in orphanages.

The uproar was enormous. Orphanages were discussed on the morning
news shows, the evening news shows, on *Nightline*, on the Sunday morning
talk shows, on news magazines like *Dateline*, on local news around the
country, on C-Span. The orphanage made the cover of *Newsweek* and was
extensively discussed in other print media. Hundreds of newspaper stories
were published on the subject in the space of a few weeks. There had not
been so much concentrated talk about orphanages since the first decades of
the century.

Yet the discussion was depressingly thin. Too much of it polarized
around the controversial new Speaker, Gingrich, and took on a "pro-
Newt" or "anti-Newt" cast. If you liked Gingrich, you were for orphanages. If you didn't, you were against. I've never heard so many well-
educated people pronounce so assuredly on something they knew nothing
about in my life, including some good friends. In part because of the polarized atmosphere, in part due to the way mass media simplifies all politics, stereotypes took center stage. For those hostile to the orphanage,
Dickens' *Oliver Twist* was conjured up. Those favorably disposed, on the
other hand, invoked the avuncular Spencer Tracy and the movie *Boys
Town*. Gingrich himself introduced a showing of *Boys Town* on one of the
major cable networks. George Stephanopoulos, one of President Bill Clin-

ton's most important advisors, dismissed all the orphanage talk with a reference to the Dickens novel.[1]

Yet framing the debate in this way sadly ignored the context that made it possible in the first place. Consequently, this national "discussion" did almost no service to the thousands of children now tangled in our social welfare system. In the 1980s, the number of children without a stable home exploded, much of this due to the destructiveness of crack cocaine. Among those working in the field of child welfare, the phrase "no-parent family" was coined, referring to children who effectively had no one raising them. We have seen the beginning of this development in the new sort of child who came to Chapin Hall by the 1970s. Such children explain much of the dramatic rise in out-of-home care, from 262,000 children in 1982 to 442,000 a decade later. This, in turn, entailed massive increases in the amount of money being funneled through the child welfare system. Popular stereotypes to the contrary, the Reagan-Bush years did not mean less aggregate money spent on welfare. In Illinois, the budget of the Department of Children and Family Services (DCFS) went from $199.3 million in 1983 to $725 million in 1993. Projected spending for 1994 was $897 million.[2]

But although jumps in aggregate spending outpaced the rise in the number of children in out-of-home care, this did not translate into smoothly delivered social services. Instead, during the 1980s, the foster care system was simply overwhelmed. Some eight months before the "Great Orphanage Debate of 1994" began, a series of articles appeared in the *Chicago Tribune* on the chaos of contemporary child welfare in the city. The series, entitled "Saving the Children," chronicled the failure of DCFS to develop long-term plans for the infants, children, and adolescents who came under its auspices. The paper reported on the increasing alienation of foster parents from DCFS bureaucracy, the depressing number of children who floated from foster home to foster home, going for years without any long-term stability, and on kids sleeping in DCFS offices because the agency had neither enough emergency shelters to house them nor a foster care system efficient enough to immediately find them homes. "Records are so disorganized," the paper noted, "that, at any given moment, DCFS can't locate all its children or figure out which foster homes have room and which don't. Occasionally, the agency even loses track of children for weeks or months. Basic information about their health or how to care for them is routinely missing from their files."[3] Perhaps most important of all, however, the *Tribune* noted the seemingly ever-increasing number of children in need. In 1978, the two judges at Cook

County Juvenile Court each handled 718 cases. In 1993, each of the six Juvenile Court judges had a caseload of 3,799.[4]

Once again, the system was under seige. In 1988, the Illinois ACLU filed suit against DCFS for mismanagement of the children under its care. A judgment against the state came in 1991; three years later it was clear that the agency was not going to be able to fulfill all the terms of the court decree. At one point, when it was revealed that children were sleeping in DCFS offices, the agency was further embarrassed when a swarm of foster parents descended upon the agency and just took a number of children home with them. And to add more insult to it all, DCFS then couldn't figure out exactly how many children, or exactly which children, were taken by these foster parents. Then there were the stories of children living in filth, of children dying from abuse, all supposedly being monitored by DCFS caseworkers. Story after story appeared in Chicago's press and television news revealing the latest DCFS outrage. Not surprisingly, the agency admitted at the end of March 1993 that it was finding it impossible to get beyond "crisis management."[5]

This was the background that made the orphanage debate possible at the close of 1994. The problems in Cook County, Illinois, were by no means only local ones. By the 1990s, the crisis in child welfare was national. Between 1985 and 1990, according to the National Foster Parent Association of America, there was a 27 percent drop in the number of families willing to serve as foster parents.[6] All over the country there was talk of overwhelmed welfare bureaucracies unable to handle the flood of children; of the gross mismatch between services delivered and real needs; of lawsuits against state agencies. To take but one of dozens of examples, in the summer of 1991 then-Governor Bill Clinton worked fervently to settle a suit charging that Arkansas child welfare agencies were not doing their job, a suit filed after several children under state guardianship were either severely beaten or died. This was exactly the sort of suit filed in Illinois against DCFS in 1988. Clinton managed to settle the suit without it going to trial, something he wanted to do to avoid bad publicity before he began his run for the Presidency.[7]

It all had a familiar ring. Many of the current complaints might well have been voiced at almost any time in the past one hundred years. It was in this setting that the 1994 orphanage debate opened up. But given the absence of context in so much of this debate, few people around the country realized that Gingrich did not come up with the idea of reviving orphanages himself, that he was simply repeating ideas that had circulated since the close of the 1980s.

The first call for the revival of orphanages came in 1988, four years after Chapin Hall had closed its residential program in Chicago, in an article published in the *Washington Monthly* by Lois Forer, a retired judge of the Court of Common Pleas in Philadelphia. Forer's argument was entirely practical and did not lack context. Given the flood of horribly abused children who were becoming wards of the state, she argued, and given the well-documented inadequacies of the foster care system, the way to do better was to bring back the orphanage.[8]

Forer's essay by itself created no big stir. But in the next few years, scattered voices around the nation, both black and white, called for a rethinking of the orphanage. Those who championed the new orphanage often defined it against the "bad" old orphanages of the 1940s. And there was a key difference. The model for the new orphanage was a series of homes, set next to each other, each housing six to ten children. The most commonly cited model was a set of homes called The Villages, in Topeka, Kansas.[9]

This bore no relationship to the orphanage of the nineteenth century, but in at least some ways it actually did look like the progressive orphanage of the 1920s and 1930s. For one thing, it marked a turn away from the therapeutic model that had dominated children's institutions since the 1950s. In the new orphanage of the 1990s, each child was expected to think of those living in his home as his "family." The adults were to be thought of as "parents." The stay was to be conceived of as long-term. These were not institutions for children with deep and debilitating emotional problems. They were for neglected and abused children. Just as in the early twentieth century, the institution was supposed to be a surrogate home. The new orphanage was a direct descendant of the progressive cottage ideal and bore a number of similarities to the Chapin Hall of the 1930s.[10]

By the 1990s, there were small signs of movement although there were also signs of growing opposition. In February 1994, Jim Edgar, the governor of Illinois, decided to utilize some state money for orphanages. DCFS began preparing to send children to the newly built SOS Children's Village, a new-style orphanage.[11]

In April 1994, however, another turn came in the orphanage discussion. Republican Senators and Congressman made the orphanage idea part of a much broader package of welfare reform. The legislation proposed that unwed mothers under the age of twenty-one be refused AFDC, food stamps, and money for public housing. The money saved from such cutbacks would be sent to the states to manage welfare as each saw fit. Orphanages were mentioned as one way this money might be used.[12]

This changed the whole scale in which orphanages were discussed. Instead of being a practical possibility for a part of that half million children in out-of-home care, those children who came from "no-parent house-holds," the call for orphanages was tied to a complete overhaul of the welfare system, something that conceivably could tear millions of poor children away from their parents (overwhelmingly these being single mothers). It also, in a way that had not been done in the recent past, tied the revival to a very partisan politics. In the Democratic-run Congress, this idea went nowhere. But it was substantially what Newt Gingrich suggested seven months later.

In the years prior to 1994, orphanages were not the only proposed solution for an overwhelmed foster care system. Others called for massively increasing family preservation services. Indeed, researchers correctly noted that while huge amounts of money were being expended on the management of a hobbling foster care system, almost nothing was being spent to try to keep families together. In 1990, congressional Democrats, citing the "extraordinary failings" of foster care around the nation, proposed legislation that would earmark $4.5 billion for drug rehabilitation programs, parenting classes, and assorted other services all in the hope of keeping more children with their biological parents and out of foster care. The price tag was considered too high, however, and there were questions about whether it would work. The legislation did not come close to passing.[13]

Here was the same impasse that the orphanage would face four years later—money. The prospect for massive numbers of new orphanages was as dim in 1994 as expanded family preservation services were in 1990. Almost no one was willing to spend more money on unproven programs.

Behind this was a seemingly ingrained distrust of welfare state managerialism. This is the heart of the current impasse. Too much of the public does not believe that the state can be trusted to do a capable job. What is surprising in the realm of child welfare is how much liberal activists have helped, however inadvertently, to foster that image.

For the first two-thirds of the century, the forces of managerialism viewed themselves as the saviors of children, those who would bring order and efficiency to urban child welfare. State agencies were sometimes attacked for lacking the enlightened leadership of the managerial class and being too beholden to political interests, but the state actually controlled relatively few dependent children. Right into the 1960s, the champions of managerial efficiency most commonly saw the problem as being centered in the antiquated private service-providing agencies (like Chapin Hall) that had been created in the nineteenth and early twentieth centuries. Managerial rationalization was the answer. A figure like Grace Abbott would argue in the 1930s that the public sector was the only unit potentially strong and financially secure enough to effectively manage child welfare.[14] The "historic transfer" of 1969, in which DCFS took over the placement of practically every dependent child in Cook County, was perhaps the last major act informed by such a belief.

But by 1994, the *Tribune* no longer aimed its muckraking at recalcitrant private agencies like Chapin Hall. Now the animus was aimed at DCFS. It was the state that was screwing up. By the 1990s, the institutions invented in the middle of the century to solve the problems of the older urban welfare had themselves come to be seen as central to the problem.

Contemporary cynicism about major institutions is not something new in the 1990s but in fact dates back to the 1970s.[15] Ronald Reagan rode to the presidency on this distrust. While some measure of relative optimism accompanied the election of Bill Clinton, by 1994 the distrust returned, and in a furious form.

Distrust of the state had always been a part of conservative culture. What was new in the 1970s was that liberals and even radicals were developing their own versions of this distrust.[16] In the progressive version, skepticism about welfare managers did not mean that the state should do less. On the contrary, criticism of existing arrangements was meant to generate support for more humane and vigorous action. Yet by the 1990s, huge segments of the public had apparently only heard the critical half of the message. A wave of skepticism about the state had washed over the nation.

From the 1970s, in the realm of child welfare, increasingly it was liberal voices who told the public that the welfare bureaucracy was not doing a good job. Calls for better protection of children's rights were widely sounded by that time. They were buttressed by the claim that welfare managers could not be trusted to work in the child's best interest. In 1973, Hillary Rodham Clinton, in an article clarifying what sorts of legal rights children should be granted, spoke of "the state's poor record in caring for children removed from their families" and cited Anthony Platt's revisionist history, *The Child Savers*, to argue that earlier child welfare advocates worked from misguided motives.[17]

The state responded to such arguments by institutionalizing the means of critiquing itself. The establishment of the Cook County Public Guardian's Office in the 1960s provides one example. For the next several decades that office, charged with protecting the interests of children, became a central player in the public critiques of DCFS. The new federal Legal Services Corporation, begun as an experiment in 1965 and made permanent in 1974, had the same effect. For legal aid lawyers, working to protect the rights of the indigent often meant attacking the bureaucracies of the state, including DCFS. Two of the groups filing the lawsuit Governor Bill Clinton had to contend with in 1991 were Central Arkansas Legal Services, an organization that Hillary Rodham Clinton had chaired in the late seventies, and Ozark Legal Services, an organization she had actually helped found.[18]

In Illinois, perhaps 1973 should be seen as an important turning point in this regard. It was in that year that Jerome Miller began his stint as director of DCFS. He was the first major welfare system-manager in twentieth-century Chicago to enter his job fighting not only the private service-providing agencies but also his own employees. From this point on, it was no longer just the managerial forces attacking the Chapin Halls of the city, the most common pattern of the first seventy years of the century. The new welfare state was developing an adversarial relationship with itself.

Increased impatience with the state stemmed not only from new forces within the state such as the Public Guardian's Office or the Legal Services Corporation. The ACLU's Children's Rights Project was born in New York in 1973, becoming national in 1979. It has often tangled with state agencies. It was the Illinois chapter of the ACLU Children's Rights Project that filed the 1988 lawsuit against DCFS that resulted in a 1991 judgment mandating changes that the agency, even three years later, could not put into practice. All this turned up on the evening news.

Since the 1970s, legal activists, the mass media, and the state itself have all begun harping on the managerial failures—at times the gross managerial failures—of the state's handling of child welfare. Many of these critics were quite liberal, often wishing for significant expansions to child welfare services. But they did not trust the good will or efficiency of welfare managers. And they often presented to the public a message of inefficiency and managerial bungling. Much in the twelve-page pamphlet *A Force for Change: Children's Rights Project of the ACLU* (1993) is interchangeable with any conservative Republican screed. This is from the first paragraph: "Child welfare agencies often turn into overburdened bureaucracies that resist change. Officials pervert child confidentiality laws to shield their records from scrutiny and keep their actions unaccountable to the public that funds them. Children who enter these systems become lost and drift for years in foster care, with no one to meet their needs and no chance for a healthy childhood."[19]

Of course, large numbers of conservatives also made antistatist claims over the years. Yet what is striking when following Chicago's child welfare debates is how little conservatives were a presence. Instead, for several decades citizens have heard from muckraking television and newspapers, from the ACLU, from legal aid lawyers and from the Public Guardian's Office that the child welfare system didn't work. They have heard, most importantly, the tone of perpetual distrust.

Even if the intent of such critiques were to create a better system of child welfare, it is not at all clear that anything beyond the criticism got through. The mass media, after all, simplifies everything it touches. By the mid-1990s, large segments of the public had come to believe that welfare managers couldn't do anything right.

Yet to understand the new situation, it is very important to add something else. While there was a growing sense that managerialism was problematic, there was no sense at all that the system had to be smashed, that an alternative to state management was available. Certainly no serious political forces arose suggesting that the state get out of the business of managing the fate of Chicago's dependent children. No one of consequence dreamed of a pre-1969 solution. Instead, there was an ongoing commitment to manage a system that stubbornly defied management. The state would continue to run the system of child welfare even as it suffered frequent reminders of its inadequacy to the task. It had become a welfare state with no optimism but no alternative.

These changes throw light on the post-1984 Chapin Hall described at the close of the last chapter. Chapin Hall now devotes much energy to studying and monitoring the public sector. The research Chapin Hall does is vital to a system that no longer pretends to be "efficient," no longer thinks that just accumulating the information will suffice. Instead, those that oversee need to be overseen themselves. That the new Chapin Hall, a private agency designed in large part to help monitor public agencies, has grown so dramatically in the past decade hints at the way that the late-twentieth-century welfare state has come to view itself. As the newspaper headline put it: "Besieged DCFS concedes it needs outside help."[20]

The emergence of a post-1970 welfare state also helps explain the emphasis on community/professional interaction at the new Chapin Hall. This dream of getting communities constructively involved in defining the delivery of local social services must be seen as a response to the felt limits of managerialism and the realities of the contemporary state. Instead of relying on the decisions of public authorities or Community Fund managers, as Chapin Hall the orphanage did from the 1940s through the 1970s, the current Chapin Hall research center urges a much more active interchange between local community and professional community. The managers need help in deciding what should be done.

This same unease also fueled the dramatic orphanage talk at the end of 1994. At its most expansive, this talk imagined overturning the whole universe of public welfare. It is certainly still unlikely that the new orphanage will sweep the nation. Such institutions are far too expensive to be attractive to many conservatives. Most progressives, on the other hand, remain suspicious that orphanages would not serve children well. Still, the interest that has been expressed should be read as one more sign of the fin de siècle frustration with the management of child welfare. Frustration, however, is not a policy. Unless enough political will can be mobilized to move beyond our current skepticism, too many children will continue to be caught in the tangle of very imperfect child welfare systems. Only time will tell.

NOTES

Introduction

1. For examples of scholarship that do focus on the point of contact between those using the system and those staffing the system, see Linda Gordon, *Heroes of Their Own Lives: The Politics and History of Family Violence, Boston, 1880–1960* (New York: Viking-Penguin, 1988); Barbara Brenzel, *Daughters of the State: A Social Portrait of the First Reform School for Girls in North America, 1865–1905* (Cambridge, Mass.: MIT Press, 1983); Nurith Zmora, *Orphanages Reconsidered: Child Care Institutions in Progressive Era Baltimore* (Philadelphia: Temple University Press, 1994). Zmora's fine book was published too recently for me to make adequate use of her findings. If readers look to n. 48 in my first chapter, however, they will see at least one place where her work kept me from saying something silly.

2. Judith Ann Trolander, *Professionalism and Social Change: From the Settlement House Movement to Neighborhood Centers, 1886 to the Present* (New York: Columbia University Press, 1987); James Gilbert, *A Cycle of Outrage: America's Reaction to the Juvenile Delinquent in the 1950s* (New York, 1986); John Ehrenreich, *The Altruistic Imagination: A History of Social Work and Social Policy in the United States* (Ithaca, N.Y.: Cornell University Press, 1985); Gordon, *Heroes of Their Own Lives.*

3. See Walter Trattner, *From Poor Law to Welfare State: A History of Social Welfare in America,* 4th ed. (New York: Free Press, 1989), 103–28; James Leiby, *A History of Social Welfare and Social Work in the United States* (New York: Columbia University Press, 1978); Michael Katz, *In the Shadow of the Poorhouse: A Social History of Welfare in America* (New York: Basic Books, 1986), 113–45.

4. For example, Daniel Levine's *Poverty and Society: The Growth of the American Welfare State in International Comparison* (New Brunswick, N.J.: Rutgers University Press, 1988).

5. Ellis W. Hawley, *The Great War and the Search for a Modern Order: A History of the American People and Their Institutions, 1917–1933* (New York: St. Martin's Press, 1979); Barry D. Karl, *The Uneasy State: The United States from 1915 to 1945* (Chicago: University of Chicago Press, 1983); Guy Alchon, *The Invisible Hand of Planning: Capitalism, Social Science and the State in the 1920s* (Princeton: Princeton University Press, 1985).

6. That there is still no good synthetic history of foster care in the United States is just one example of how dependency has been neglected. The first survey of child placing is very recent. Marilyn Irvin Holt, *The Orphan Trains: Placing Out in America* (Lincoln, Nebr.: University of Nebraska Press, 1992). "Placing out" was the nineteenth-century precursor to foster care. Orphans were sent from eastern and midwestern cities to work and live on farms in midwestern and western states.

Chapter One

1. The earliest accounts of the origins of the Half-Orphan Asylum date from the late 1880s. They differ on specifics. Some claim that the institution was started by Mrs. Samuel Howe in the winter of 1859, others say that Howe, Miss Catherine West, and Mrs. Elizabeth Blakie started the nursery in the spring of 1860.

2. Mary Linehan, "Vicious Circle: Prostitution, Reform, and Public Policy in Chicago, 1830–1930," (Ph.D. diss., University of Notre Dame, 1991), 29, 41–42.

3. *Chicago Tribune*, April 21, 1857.

4. *Chicago Tribune*, April 25, 1860.

5. *Chicago Tribune*, October 24, 1861.

6. A copy of the charter is in the Chapin Hall Collection (CHC) at the Chicago Historical Society, box 19, folder 1.

7. Bessie L. Pierce, *A History of Chicago*, 3 vols. (New York: Alfred A. Knopf, 1940), 2:482.

8. These histories were designed to celebrate the legal, political, and especially the commercial elite who created the city. They recorded male contributions, so it is not surprising that the founders of the asylum do not appear. But the fact that their husbands are not mentioned indicates a marginal place within the city's elite. See David Ward Wood, ed., *Chicago and Its Distinguished Citizens, or the Progress of Forty Years* (Chicago: M. George & Co., 1881); John Moses, *History of Chicago*, 2 vols. (Chicago and New York: Munsell & Co., 1895); J. Seymour Currey, *Chicago: Its History and Its Builders: A Century of Marvelous Growth*, 4 vols. (Chicago: S. J. Clarke Pub. Co., 1912); Paul Gilbert and Charles Lee Bryson, *Chicago and Its Makers* (Chicago: F. Mendelsohn, 1929). Wood's book even includes a chapter on famous grain elevators in Chicago (pp. 381–86) but without mention of Samuel Howe. The one history that mentions Howe and Blakie is A. T. Andreas, *History of Chicago*, 3 vols. (Chicago: A. T. Andreas, 1886).

9. Gunthar Barth, *Instant Cities: Urbanization and the Rise of San Francisco and Denver* (New York: Oxford University Press, 1975).

10. *Chicago Tribune*, October 24, 1861.

11. Quoted in Naomi Harwood, "The History and Care of Dependent Children in Cook County to 1899" (Field study, School of Social Service Administration, University of Chicago, 1941), 44.

12. Robert Bremner, *The Public Good: Philanthropy and Welfare in the Civil War Era* (New York: Alfred A. Knopf, 1980), 85–87.

13. For the best discussions of nineteenth-century environmentalism as applied to child welfare, see Barbara Brenzel, *Daughters of the State: A Social Portrait of the First Reform School for Girls in North America, 1856–1905* (Cambridge, Mass.: MIT Press,

1983), 23–26; Steven L. Schlossman, *Love and the American Delinquent: The Theory and Practice of "Progressive" Juvenile Justice, 1825–1920* (Chicago: University of Chicago Press, 1977), 49–53.

14. Robert Bremner, ed., *Children and Youth in America: A Documentary History*, vol. 1, *1600–1865* (Cambridge, Mass.: Harvard University Presss, 1970), 655.

15. Robert Bremner, ed., *Children and Youth in America: A Documentary History*, vol. 2, *1866–1932* (Cambridge, Mass.: Harvard University Press, 1971), 269.

16. *Thirty-Fourth Annual Report of the Chicago Relief and Aid Society, 1891*, 53–55.

17. Day-to-day life was not dramatically different in industrial schools than in orphanages. They were, in some ways, "boarding schools" for poor children. They were much larger, on average, than orphanages. And they did have a mix of dependent and mildly delinquent children.

18. *Thirty-Fourth Annual Report of the Chicago Relief and Aid Society, 1891*, 53–55. Harwood, "History and Care," 108–11.

19. Harwood, "History and Care," 94–96, 147–49. Mothers wanted to use the almshouse because they saw it as a way of not losing their children.

20. Ibid., 121–22.

21. *Chicago Nursery and Half-Orphan Asylum Annual Report* (hereafter *Annual Report*), *1869*, 11; also see *Chicago Tribune*, October 24, 1861; Board of Managers Minutes, CHC, February 7, 1871.

22. Laura L. Houghteling Reynolds, "Reminiscences of the War of the Rebellion" (unpublished manuscript), 2–3. This manuscript is at the Chicago Historical Society. On other Chicago philanthropists of the time, see Kathleen D. McCarthy, *Noblesse Oblige: Charity and Cultural Philanthropy in Chicago, 1849–1929* (Chicago: University of Chicago Press, 1982), 3–24.

23. Most of the women managers in the 1860s lived either in what is today downtown Chicago or else in the mile just north of the Chicago River. On the comingling of economic strata in those areas, see Vivian M. Palmer, "Study of the Development of Chicago's Northside" (unpublished paper written for the United Charities of Chicago, 1932), 42. The paper is available at the Chicago Historical Society.

24. *Annual Report, 1869*, 10–12.

25. From the ragged school on the sands, the asylum moved to 151 North Market Street in the fall of 1860. The next spring, "owing to the increase in applicants," the institution moved to a home on Ohio Street. In 1862, a large building on Michigan and Pine was rented. Finally, in 1865, another house, on Wisconsin and Clark, was rented. This remained the home of the asylum until 1871. *Annual Report, 1869*, 10.

26. *Chicago Tribune*, July 28, 1860.

27. *Chicago Tribune*, January 16, 1867.

28. McCarthy, *Noblesse Oblige*, 18–20.

29. Board of Managers Minutes, CHC, May 28, 1867; November 27, 1867; March 24, 1868.

30. The official address of the asylum was 175 Burling Street. This was the old address system of Chicago. The asylum's front entrance was on Burling and the back entrance on Halsted. Even in the 1870s Halsted was a far more recognizable street, and in the asylum's literature the address 855 North Halsted is mentioned above (and in larger print than) the "official" address. In 1909, the city council rationalized Chicago's

street numbering system and the exact address of the asylum became 1932 North Burling. The building still stands today. Its current occupant is the Infant Welfare Society.

31. In the 1860s, this area, which reached to Fullerton, was the northernmost
neighborhood in the city. North of Fullerton was sparsely settled and remained so until
after the Chicago fire. See Palmer, "Chicago's Northside," 84, 88–89.

32. Reynolds, "Reminiscences," 3.

33. This is based on a sample of admitting records of the asylum. I looked at all
children admitted between 1865 and 1890 whose last name began with the letters A, C,
G, N, R, T. (Records of admission were first kept in 1865.) The sample totaled 361
families who brought six hundred children to the institution.

	ADULT WHO BROUGHT CHILD TO THE ASYLUM			
	1860s	1870s	1880s	Total
Father	9	23	40	72
Mother	10	40	101	151
Other	0	3	9	12
Unknown	24	73	29	126
Total	43	139	179	361

Note: The numbers prior to 1880 are unreliable because lax record
keeping led to such large numbers in the "Unknown" category.
Source: CHC, box 11, folder 1.

34. For the examples of women's wages, see Board of Managers Minutes, September 21, 1880; May 6, 1879; May 21, 1878; CHC, box 4, folder 1. See also Edith Abbott,
Women in Industry (New York: D. Appleton & Co., 1909), 291. Alice Kessler-Harris
touches on wage differentials in the late nineteenth century, but she does not explore
them. See Kessler-Harris, *Out to Work: A History of Wage Earning Women in the United
States* (New York: Oxford University Press, 1982), 143, 155–56.

35. David Montgomery, *The Fall of the House of Labor: The Workplace, the State,
and American Labor Activism, 1865–1925* (Cambridge: Cambridge University Press,
1987), 135–36.

36. No comprehensive records were kept on this. Still, the anecdotal evidence in
the Board of Managers Minutes suggests that a very large number of children in the
asylum had both parents living. Briefly in 1898 and 1899, the managers listed each new
child admitted to the asylum in their minutes. Of the forty-eight children with cause
for entry listed, only nineteen of them were half-orphans.

REASON FOR ENTRY TO ASYLUM	
Parent died	19
Parents separated	11
Parent deserted	8
Father does not support	5
Parent insane	3

Parent ill	1
Parents divorced	1
Total	48

Source: Board of Managers Minutes, CHC, 1898–1899.

37. For the Chicago Orphan Asylum, see Clare McCausland, *Children of Circumstance: A History of the First 125 Years of the Chicago Child Care Society* (Chicago: Printed by R. R. Donnelly & Sons, 1976) 54; on the Soldiers' Orphans' Home, see Joan Gittens, "Children of the State: Dependent Children in Illinois, 1818–1980s" (Chapin Hall for Children, 1986), 31; on the St. Louis Protestant Orphan Asylum, see Susan Whitelaw Downs and Michael Sherraden, "The Orphan Asylum in the Nineteenth Century," *Social Service Review* 57 (June 1983): 281. For other institutions with similar distributions, see Hyman Bogen, *The Luckiest Orphans: A History of the Hebrew Orphan Asylum of New York* (Urbana: University of Illinois Press, 1992), 96; Gary Edward Polster, *Inside Looking Out: The Cleveland Jewish Orphan Asylum, 1868–1924* (Kent, Ohio: Kent State University Press, 1990), 32; Peter Holloran, *Boston's Wayward Children: Social Services for Homeless Children, 1830–1930* (Cranbury, N.J.: Fairleigh Dickinson University Press, 1989), 131; Elizabeth M. Pruden also notes the small number of full orphans in the Saint Paul Protestant Orphan Asylum and Owatonna State Public School in her unpublished paper, "Four Minnesota Orphanages, 1865–1900," 5, 14. I thank Ms. Pruden for permission to cite her research.

38. Of the sample of six hundred children who entered the asylum between 1865 and 1880 (see n. 33 above), the ages of 181 were recorded in the 1870s and of 261 in the 1880s. (Only 5 of the 70 1860s entries included ages.)

CHILD'S AGE UPON ENTRY TO THE ASYLUM				
Age	1870s	%	1880s	%
<One	6	3.3	16	5.9
One	15	8.3	23	8.5
Two	14	7.7	19	7.1
Three	14	7.7	18	6.7
Four	9	5.0	27	10.0
Five	21	11.6	28	10.4
Six	16	8.8	33	12.3
Seven	17	9.4	30	11.2
Eight	25	13.8	33	12.3
Nine	19	10.5	23	8.5
Ten	19	10.5	11	4.1
Eleven	2	1.1	0	3.0
Twelve	3	1.7	0	0.0
Thirteen	0	0.0	0	0.0
Fourteen	1	0.6	0	0.0
Total	181	100.0	261	100.0

Source: CHC, box 11, folder 1.

39. The nationality of 557 children (out of the sample of 600) was recorded in the admissions records. Note that the "Irish" were Protestant Scotch-Presbyterians, not Irish Catholics. For the percentage of children from the British Isles I have combined the English, Scottish, Welsh, and Irish statistics.

NATIONALITY OF CHILDREN ADMITTED TO THE ASYLUM

Nationality	1860s	1870s	1880s
American	17	63	96
Irish	25	54	43
English	2	24	17
Scottish	11	9	2
Welsh	0	1	0
German	3	26	30
Swedish	0	14	38
Norwegian	7	11	21
Danish	2	1	2
Bohemian	0	4	0
Polish	0	3	5
Italian	0	7	2
French	0	1	4
Canadian	0	3	0
Black	0	0	3
Jewish	0	0	6
Total	67	221	269

Source: CHC, box 11, folder 1.

40. M. S. Barton (Chicago Relief and Aid Society) to George F. Ramsey (Board of Directors, Chicago Nursery and Half-Orphan Asylum), March 30, 1872. CHC, box 19, folder 1.

41. In the 1870s, 3.2 percent of children in the Half-Orphan Asylum were Italian. In the next decade, 2.2 percent were Jewish and 1.9 percent were Polish. (See n. 39 above.) These numbers reflect the new patterns of immigration to the city. These ethnic groups were coming in large numbers, were overloading the established Catholic orphanages, and did not yet have their own, ethnic orphanages that could deal with the problems.

Note also that black children were accepted in the nineteenth-century asylum. In the 1880s they made up 2.2 percent of the inmates (n. 39 above). This reflects, primarily, the small numbers of blacks in the city at this time. It is only when migration to the city became significant in the twentieth century that a white-only policy came into being.

42. In emergencies, however, the Executive Committee of the Board of Managers could temporarily take in children until the character check was completed. This allowed the child to get shelter immediately. This device was not stingily used in the nineteenth century.

43. Maris Vinovskis, "An Epidemic of Adolescent Pregnancy? Some Historical Considerations," *Journal of Family History* 6 (1981): 205–30; Joan Jacobs Brumberg, "Ruined Girls: Changing Community Responses to Illegitimacy in Upstate New York, 1890–1920," *Journal of Social History* 18 (Winter 1984): 248–51.

44. *Report of the Managers, 1869*, 11.

45. Board of Managers Minutes, CHC, September 21 and April 14, 1880.

46. Board of Managers Minutes, CHC, June 26, 1872.

47. Of the admissions records sample (see n. 33 above), the length of stay could be determined for 521 children between 1865 and 1890. The averages do not change appreciably in the twenty-five years.

LENGTH OF STAY IN ASYLUM, 1865–90		
Time in Months	*N* Children	%
under 3	201	38.6
3–6	99	19.0
6–9	55	10.6
9–12	32	6.1
12–15	24	4.6
15–18	18	3.5
18–21	9	1.7
21–24	8	1.5
Over 24	75	14.4

Source: CHC, box 11, folder 1.

48. For short stays, see Downs and Sherraden, "The Orphan Asylum," 281; Holloran, *Boston's Wayward Children*, 90–91; Pruden, "Four Minnesota Orphanages," 5–7, 17–18. There is some reason to be cautious, however, about how many orphanages kept children only a short time. Pruden reports that one of the four orphanages she looked at did seem to keep children for years (personal correspondence with author). Also, Nurith Zmora reports that three orphanages in Baltimore had, in the late 1880s, average stays of 3.56 years, 4.3 years, and 5.8 years. Nurith Zmora, *Orphanages Reconsidered: Child Care Institutions in Progressive Era Baltimore* (Philadelphia: Temple University Press, 1994), 53.

Other evidence can be unearthed to suggest that temporary care was what many of Chicago's Protestant orphanages had in mind. (I found no evidence either way for Catholic institutions.) To take a typical example, the Illinois Industrial Training School, a Cook County home for dependent children established in 1883, claimed it was "designed only for a temporary home until the boys are fitted for homes in private families." *Illinois Industrial Training School, First Annual Report, for the year ending May 15, 1886*, 5. Similarly, the Chicago Home for the Friendless would try to place out children after a relatively brief period of time. Hastings Hart, the head of the Illinois Child's Home and Aid Society, was reported in 1899 as believing that most of Chicago's children's institutions worked "along right lines, transferring their wards to family homes after a comparatively short stay. The field of institutionalism which prevails in New York and California is almost unknown here." *Chicago Tribune*, August 13, 1899.

At the turn of the century, some participants in the debate tried to point out that average stays were short and that children returned to their families. See Rev. D. J. McMahon, "Family Influence," *Proceedings of the Conference on the Care of Dependent Children* (Washington, D.C.: U.S. Government Printing Office, 1909): 98; Sherman Kingsley, "The Substitution of Family Care for Institutional Care for Children," *Charities* 10 (April 18, 1903): 387. Progressives typically ignored such testimony. Charles Henderson, for example, flatly stated that "under the institutional system the dependent child is kept for a long period. . . . After a term of years the youth is apprenticed or finds a home." Charles Henderson, *Introduction to the Study of the Dependent, Defective, and Delinquent Classes*, rev. ed. (Boston: D. C. Heath & Co., 1908), 107.

49. *Chicago Tribune*, August 5, 1883.

50. *Chicago Tribune*, March 20, 1883.

51. *Chicago Inter-Ocean*, November 17, 1883.

52. This image, drawn from the progressive critique of the asylum, is still commonly used by historians. See, for example, Walter I. Trattner, *From Poor Law to Welfare State: A History of Social Welfare in America*, 4th ed. (New York: Free Press, 1989), 108. Michael Katz has a slightly more nuanced view. See his *In the Shadow of the Poorhouse: A Social History of Welfare in America* (New York: Basic Books, 1986), 119–20. My contention here is very specific. I do not see the Half-Orphan Asylum as run in a regimented, military style, totally joyless for the children. I am not saying there weren't other problems with the care provided.

More research on other asylums might uncover other patterns. For example, was the tender care at the Half-Orphan Asylum related to the fact that the institution was run by women? Were orphanages run by men harsher? For a very illuminating exploration of this theme in a related context, see John Cumbler, "The Politics of Charity: Gender and Class in Late 19th Century Charity Policy," *Journal of Social History* 14 (Fall 1980): 99–111. Could it be that institutions for the "worthy" poor were warmer than those for the "unworthy"? Or that Protestant and Catholic charities differed substantially? Only more research into specific institutions will answer such questions.

53. Board of Managers Minutes, CHC, August 7, 1877; July 20, 1880; November 1, 1881; October 5, 1880.

54. *Thirteenth Annual Report, 1874*, 5.

55. In my sample of the 1870s and 1880s, there were twenty-two babies under the age of one admitted (See n. 38 above). Records indicate that twelve of them died.

56. Pierce, *A History of Chicago*, 3:320–23.

57. For example, on January 18, 1881, in the midst of a smallpox epidemic, the managers decided that no more children would be received. Only in the middle of March were children again received. Board of Managers Minutes, CHC, January 18, 1881. Again on December 20, 1881, the Board voted to stop admitting children. The asylum again began receiving children on March 7, 1882.

58. Board of Managers Minutes, CHC, August 7, 1877.

59. Don Kirschner, *The Paradox of Professionalism: Reform and Public Service in Urban America, 1900–1940* (New York, 1986), 3.

60. Board of Managers Minutes, CHC, March 18, 1881, and November 1895.

61. Board of Managers Minutes, CHC, March 18, 1881.

62. Board of Managers Minutes, CHC, February 6, 1882.

63. The short amount of time most children stayed at the orphanage made any effective schooling in bourgeois values rather improbable anyway.

64. I cannot imagine that there weren't sharp differences about issues like the eight-hour day, the right to strike, and so on. And I would also guess there were probably sharply differing voting records between the children's fathers and the managers' husbands. My point here is that there was some overlap, not complete agreement. And in the specific setting of the Half-Orphan Asylum, it was that agreement that was critical.

65. Rosner reports that in the 1870s and 1880s the "worthy" poor were admitted to smaller, private hospitals run by volunteer elites while the "unworthy" were sent to larger, public hospitals. David Rosner, *A Once Charitable Enterprise: Hospitals and Health Care in Brooklyn and New York, 1885–1915* (Cambridge: Cambridge University Press, 1982), 17–19.

66. In its own literature, the Relief and Aid Society declared itself founded "not for the purpose of taking care of the pauper population or of indiscriminate charity, but to furnish temporary relief to those who under ordinary circumstances are self-supporting, but who by some sudden calamity or misfortune have been made destitute and helpless, and who with a little occasional well-directed assistance will be able to maintain their self-respect and again become self-sustaining. . . . It does not attempt to deal with the complex questions of social science or moral reform but confines itself to its original purpose as above stated." All of this could very easily have been said by the managers of the Half-Orphan Asylum. In fact, in the 1880s, several board members of the Relief and Aid Society were either on the Half-Orphan Asylum's board or were married to a manager. The quotation is from *The Twenty-Fifth Annual Report of the Chicago Relief and Aid Society* (1882), 4.

67. To take some obvious examples, the working poor are least likely to have health insurance but are ineligible for Medicaid. And the absence of a coherent family policy means that the unemployed are eligible for AFDC but the working poor are not.

68. Board of Managers Minutes, CHC, February 25, 1868.

69. Board of Managers Minutes, CHC, March 10, 1868.

70. Board of Managers Minutes, CHC, March 20 1869.

71. Board of Managers Minutes, CHC, March 27, 1869.

72. Ibid.; *Annual Report, 1869*, 7–9.

73. Reynolds, "Reminiscences," 3–4.

74. Andreas, *History of Chicago*, 3:606.

75. Board of Directors Minutes, July 3, 1873, CHC, box 3, folder 4. The sums are from a flyer advertising the drive; CHC, box 19, folder 1.

76. *Thirteenth Annual Report, 1874*, 10–11; *Fourteenth Annual Report, 1875*, 10, 23.

77. In 1876, special events raised only 11 percent of income; in 1877 only 10 percent. In 1880, despite the enormous investment of time, special events only raised 6.78 percent of the income. *Seventeenth Annual Report, 1877*, 20; *Eighteenth Annual Report, 1878*, 18; *Twentieth Annual Report, 1881*, 16.

78. *Twentieth Annual Report, 1881,* 13.

79. *Twenty-Eighth Annual Report, 1889,* 32; *Thirty-Second Annual Report, 1893,* 27.

80. *Twenty-Eighth Annual Report, 1889,* 22–32; *Thirty-Second Annual Report, 1893,* 27; *Thirty-Fifth Annual Report, 1896,* 19, 26.

81. The list of the legacies is in the back cover of the notebook containing the minutes of Board of Directors meetings; CHC, box 3, folder 4.

82. For example, no biographical information could be found on Mrs. Clark Tillinghast, a very active and influential member of the board during the late 1860s and early 1870s.

83. The members of the elite men's clubs were listed in the annual social register. By 1882, eleven of the fourteen directors belonged to either the Union Club, the Chicago Club, or the Union League Club, the three most important such institutions in the city. See *Twenty-First Annual Report, 1881,* 5; *Chicago Blue Book of Selected Names of Chicago and Surrounding Towns* (Chicago, 1890).

84. *Twenty-First Annual Report, 1881,* 5; *Chicago Blue Book of Selected Names of Chicago and Surrounding Towns* (Chicago, 1882); *Twenty-Ninth Annual Report, 1889,* 5; *Chicago Blue Book of Selected Names of Chicago and Surrounding Towns* (Chicago, 1890).

85. I found these addresses by looking up the 1881 managers in that year's city directory. Note that the addresses are of the old system. 126 Rush Street would be 662 Rush Street today. 224 Ontario would be 63 East Ontario.

86. The 1880 addresses were listed in the Board of Managers Minutes, CHC, December 1879.

87. In 1850, the Chicago Orphan Asylum had outgrown its home in downtown Chicago. The managers of that institution decided to build at Twenty-second and Michigan, within a few blocks of most of their homes. See McCausland, *Children of Circumstance,* 30–32.

88. The board members who were officers of St. James Episcopal were C. R. Larrabee, F. B. Peabody, J. L. Houghteling, and A. C. McClurg. The Fourth Presbyterian provided an unusually large number of the asylum's officers. Among the members of that congregation were Mrs. Oliver H. Lee, Mrs. H. A. Hurlbut, Mrs. William C. Ewing, Mrs. William Goudy, Mrs. C. H. Mulliken, J. H. Trowbridge, and Henry King. Andreas, *History of Chicago,* 3:782, 798, 804.

89. Board of Directors Minutes, May 3, 1892, CHC, box 3, folder 4.

Chapter Two

1. *Forty-Second Annual Report, 1903* [of the Chicago Nursery and Half-Orphan Asylum], 18; *Forty-Fifth Annual Report, 1906,* 18; *Forty-Ninth Annual Report, 1910,* 21.

2. In 1902, for example, there were 215 applications. Only 117 children could be admitted. *Forty-Second Annual Report, 1903,* 18.

3. *Forty-Second Annual Report, 1903,* 18; *Fiftieth Annual Report, 1911,* 20.

4. *Lakeside Annual Directory of the City of Chicago, 1885–86* (Chicago: The Chicago Directory Co., 1885), 33; *Lakeside Annual Directory of the City of Chicago, 1900–1901* (Chicago: The Chicago Directory Co., 1900), 16–17; *Lakeside Annual Directory of the City of Chicago, 1910–11* (Chicago: The Chicago Directory Co., 1910), 56–57.

5. *Thirty-Fourth Annual Report of the Chicago Relief and Aid Society, 1891,* 53–55; *Chicago Charities Directory, 1906* (Chicago Charities Directory Association, 1905).

6. Chicago Department of Public Welfare, *Social Service Directory* (Chicago: H. G. Adair, 1915) 17–35, 164–68.

7. Both the Ridge Farm Preventorium and the Infant Welfare Society would later connect with the history of the Half-Orphan Society. In 1963, Ridge Farm merged with the asylum. In 1971, the Infant Welfare Society moved its administrative head-quarters into the old building of the Nursery and Half-Orphan Asylum, that is, the structure completed in 1871 and discussed in chapter one.

8. Homer Folks, *The Care of Destitute, Neglected, and Delinquent Children* (New York: Macmillan Co., 1902), 164.

9. Naomi Harwood, "The History and Care of Dependent Children in Cook County to 1899" (Field study, School of Social Service Administration, University of Chicago, 1941), 195–96.

10. *Child in the City: A Handbook of the Child Welfare Exhibit at the Coliseum from May 11 to May 25, 1911* (Privately printed, 1911).

11. Most general histories of welfare acknowledge in some way the persistence of pre-progressive habits in the delivery of welfare services after 1890. But because these histories are organized around national leaders and new public policy instead of how services were actually delivered, they have not recognized that tensions between the old and new were central to Progressive Era welfare. Most historians simply portray a progressive elite ousting a Victorian elite. I offer instead the image of progressives as a "counter-establishment." Before historians think about the failures of progressives, they might ponder how long and trying a task it was for progressives to actually take control of urban welfare systems. With this in mind, looking at a conservative institution like the Half-Orphan Asylum is particularly instructive, as it affords us a hint of just how strong the established charities were and how they interacted with the new reformers.

Standard histories of American welfare that paint a picture of a progressive takeover after 1890 include: James Leiby, *A History of Social Welfare and Social Work in the United States* (New York: Columbia University Press, 1978), 136–62; Michael B. Katz, *In the Shadow of the Poorhouse: A Social History of Welfare in America* (New York: Basic Books, 1986), 113–45. The two basic histories of care for dependent children during the progressive era also portray a progressive takeover: Susan Tiffin, *In Whose Best Interest? Child Welfare Reform in the Progressive Era* (Westport, Conn.: Greenwood Press, 1982); LeRoy Ashby, *Saving the Waifs: Reformers and Dependent Children, 1890–1917* (Philadelphia: Temple University Press, 1984).

12. Of the forty-eight homes for dependent children listed in the Chicago Department of Welfare 1915 directory, thirty-four of them had religious affiliations.

13. Chicago Department of Public Welfare, *Social Service Directory,* 17–35.

14. Mitchell Alan Horwich, *Conflict and Child Care Policy in the Chicago Jewish Community, 1893–1942* (Chicago: Jewish Children's Bureau, 1977).

15. An article that was especially helpful in sorting out the differences in approach to social work was: Donna L. Franklin, "Mary Richmond and Jane Addams: From Moral Certainty to Rational Inquiry in Social Work Practice," *Social Service Review* 60 (December 1986): 504–25. Its influence should be evident throughout the chapter.

16. Katz, *Shadow of the Poorhouse*, 118–21; Leiby, *History of Social Welfare*, 144–46, 150–51; Anthony Platt, *The Child Savers: The Invention of Delinquency*, 2d ed. (Chicago: University of Chicago Press, 1977), 61–66.

17. See Hastings H. Hart, *Cottage and Congregate Institutions for Children* (New York: Charities Publication Committee, 1910).

18. *Proceedings of the Conference on the Care of Dependent Children Held at Washington, D.C., January 25, 26, 1909* (Washington, D.C.: Government Printing Office, 1909), 9, 10, 6. The list of participants is found on pp. 20–31. Seventeen Chicagoans are listed as attending.

19. On the birth of mothers' aid pensions, see Theda Skocpol, *Protecting Soldiers and Mothers: The Political Origins of Social Policy in the United States* (Cambridge, Mass.: Harvard University Press, 1992), 424–79.

20. Jane Addams, *Democracy and Social Ethics* (New York: Macmillan Co., 1902), 13–70.

21. *Fifty-Fifth Annual Report, 1916*, 28–29; Mary E. Richmond, *The Long View: Papers and Addresses* (New York: Russell Sage Foundation, 1930), 43.

22. For a good example of how publicity was used to reform a Chicago institution, and a good sense of how progressive reformers thought of publicity, see Julia C. Lathrop, "The Reform of a City Poorhouse," *The Commons* 9 (February 1904): 40–43.

23. Paul Starr, *The Social Transformation of American Medicine* (New York: Basic Books, 1982), 180–97; Katz, *Shadow of the Poorhouse*, 137–45; Steven J. Diner, *A City and Its Universities: Public Policy in Chicago, 1892–1919* (Chapel Hill, N.C.: University of North Carolina Press, 1980), 133–36.

24. "Doctor's Report," *Thirty-Second Annual Report, 1893*, 17.

25. *Thirty-Third Annual Report, 1894*, 17; *Thirty-Seventh Annual Report, 1898*, 14.

26. *Thirty-Seventh Annual Report, 1898*, 14.

27. Board of Managers Minutes, Chapin Hall Collection (CHC) at the Chicago Historical Society, July 16, 1895; June 16, 1900; July 17, 1906; November 21, 1899.

28. Board of Managers Minutes, CHC, March 18, October 28, 1902.

29. Vivian M. Palmer, "Study of the Development of Chicago's Northside" (unpublished paper written for the United Charities of Chicago, 1932), 85–86; *Annual Report of the United Charities, 1910*, 13. The same report stated of the "lower north district": "Here is the problem of congestion in the highest degree known to Chicago. . . . There is unusual need of prompt giving in food, fuel and medical care" (13).

30. *Forty-First Annual Report, 1902*, 21; also see *Forty-Fifth Annual Report, 1906*, 20.

31. Board of Managers Minutes, CHC, March 19, April 2, May 7, 1901.

32. Board of Managers Minutes, CHC, May 4, 1897; February 15, 1898; January 2, October 16, 1900.

33. Board of Managers Minutes, CHC, December 2, 1902; May 17, 1904; March 15, 1907.

34. *Forty-Fifth Annual Report, 1906*, 19; *Forty-Seventh Annual Report, 1908*, 21; *Forty-Ninth Annual Report, 1910*, 22.

35. The average number of residents was culled from the annual reports of the asylum. For 1898, see *Thirty-Eighth Annual Report, 1899*, 20. For a typical post-1900

statement about the need to increase the population of the asylum, see *Forty-Fourth Annual Report, 1905,* 18.

36. *Fiftieth Annual Report, 1911,* 19.

37. To be precise, between 1910 and 1916, the number of children averaged 142 and the number of staff people living in the building averaged 26. The figures are taken from the annual reports.

38. Charles Henderson, *Introduction to the Study of the Dependent, Defective, and Delinquent Classes,* rev. ed. (Boston: D. C. Heath & Co., 1908), 109. Henderson was a professor of sociology at the University of Chicago and a leading progressive reformer.

39. Board of Managers Minutes, CHC, January 3, 1905; March 17, 1903.

40. Board of Managers Minutes, CHC, March 19; March 7, 25, 1905.

41. Board of Managers Minutes, CHC, June 15, 1897. Rules against such language were distributed to employees from the early 1880s, but this was the first time that records show an employee discharged for such language. This was done at a special Board of Managers meeting called just to consider this incident. Witnesses were called to testify and the employee defended herself as if in a court of law. She did not, however, save her job.

42. Board of Managers Minutes, CHC, August 21, September 4, 1900; December 6, 1904.

43. Board of Managers Minutes, CHC, March 6, 1900.

44. For examples of conflicts over candy, see the Board of Managers Minutes, CHC, February 6, February 13, March 6, April 20, November 20, 1900.

45. For representative examples of worries over unruliness of children, see Board of Managers Minutes, CHC, August 17, 1897; February 5, 1901. On corporal punishment, Board of Managers Minutes, CHC, July 17, November 20, 1900; June 15, 1904. On bread and water, October 2, 1900. The number of switchings is reported each month during much of 1894–95 and 1901 in the "Matron's Report" which is attached to the Board of Managers Minutes.

46. The number of runaways was reported in the "Matron's Report" attached to the Board of Managers Minutes. For the managers' response, see Board of Managers Minutes, CHC, October 16, 1900; June 4, 1901; May 26, 1905.

47. Board of Managers Minutes, CHC, May 19, 1903; November 1, 1904; March 20, 1906.

48. Board of Managers Minutes, CHC, December 4, 1894; April 2, 1900.

49. Board of Managers Minutes, CHC, April 2, July 16, 1901. It appears that the decision to restrict access of neighborhood children came about after some neighborhood children had induced some "asylum boys" to run away.

50. Board of Managers Minutes, CHC, July 17, August 7, 1900.

51. Board of Managers Minutes, CHC, June 4, 1901; *Forty-Third Annual Report, 1904,* 19.

52. *Forty-Fourth Annual Report, 1905,* 19; *Forty-Third Annual Report, 1904,* 19.

53. *Forty-Sixth Annual Report, 1907,* 22.

54. Good citizenship was a common progressive theme. For good examples of how Chicago progressives applied this theme to child welfare, see the essays published by the Chicago School of Civics and Philanthropy, *The Child in the City* (Chicago: Manz Engraving Co., The Hollister Press, 1912).

55. Board of Managers Minutes, CHC, December 1, 1896; April 3, 1900; June 5, 1900; May 6, 1902; December 1, 1914; January 5, 1915.

56. Addams, *Democracy and Social Ethics*, 13–70.

57. *Fiftieth Annual Report, 1911*, 19.

58. Board of Managers Minutes, CHC, August 6, 1901.

59. Board of Managers Minutes, CHC, November 1, 1904.

60. See, to get a flavor of the opposition, Harriette N. Dunn, *Infamous Juvenile Law* (Chicago: H. Dunn, 1912). Dunn and her brother, William Dunn, were prominent crusaders against the court. Dunn was a German-American who owned Dunn Manufacturing Company. This pamphlet is filled with stories about greedy social workers, bad judicial decisions, the collapse of legal rights of both children and parents, and of how the court wantonly made children wards of the state.

61. For the story of how the Chicago Erring Woman's Refuge was changed by becoming dependent on the city for admissions, see Mary Linehan, "Vicious Circle: Prostitution, Reform, and Public Policy in Chicago, 1830–1930" (Ph.D. diss., University of Notre Dame, 1991), 76–94.

62. Board of Managers Minutes, CHC, February 15, 1898; July 17, 1898; May 6, 1902; March 25, 1903; March 15, 1904; March 25, 1905.

63. Board of Managers Minutes, CHC, June 18, July 2, 1901; May 19, 1903; November 1, 1904.

64. Board of Managers Minutes, CHC, December 31, 1906; January 15, 1907.

65. Cyrus Bentley to George Isham, February 25, 1907, CHC, box 19, folder 7.

66. Board of Managers Minutes, CHC, March 15, 1907.

67. In 1901 the crush of applications was such that the managers passed a rule explicitly denying entry to any applicant with a lower-middle-class income. A mother applied who made $60.00 a month. The board voted to exclude all children from families that were this well off. It should be emphasized that the basic reason for this was lack of space. The asylum was sorely overcrowded; there were always too many applications. Board of Managers Minutes, CHC, January 15, 1901.

What was a $60.00 a month salary? Certainly respectable but by no means lavish. At the end of 1902 it was exactly the salary of both the matron and janitor at the Half-Orphan Asylum (the head nurse made $35.00). Board of Managers Minutes, CHC, December 16, 1902.

68. *Fifty-Fifth Annual Report, 1916*, 28–29.

69. *Fiftieth Annual Report, 1911*, 19.

70. For a typical progressive criticism, see Jeffrey R. Brackett, "Provincialism in Charity," *The Commons* 9 (June 1904): 246.

71. Azel Hatch to Ira Geer, January 29, 1900. CHC, box 19, folder 4.

72. See the comments of Hastings Hart of the Illinois Child's Home and Aid Society in the *Chicago Tribune*, August 13, 1899; also Rev. D. J. McMahon, "Family Influence," *Proceedings of the Conference on the Care of Dependent Children*, 98; Sherman Kingsley, "The Substitution of Family Care for Institutional Care for Children," *Charities* 10 (April 18, 1903): 387.

73. We should be careful not to overgeneralize from these bits of information. More research would turn up a more nuanced picture of turn-of-the-century children's homes. Still, it does appear that the progressive picture of institutional life was

probably overdrawn and that there were good reasons for at least some institutions (such as the Half-Orphan Asylum) to resist certain progressive suggestions.

74. *Benevolent Institutions, 1910* (Washington, D.C.: Government Printing Office, 1913), 28–29.

75. Ibid., 96–100.

76. Information on the particular institutions is taken from the *Chicago Charities Directory, 1906*. On the average population of all Illinois institutions, see *Benevolent Institutions*, 27.

77. *Chicago Charities Directory, 1906*.

78. *Caritas Christi Urget Nos: A History of the Offices, Agencies, and Institutions of the Archdiocese of Chicago*, 2 vols. (Chicago: Archdiocese of Chicago, 1981), 2:925–26; Horwich, *Conflict and Child Care Policy in the Chicago Jewish Community, 1893–1942*, 28–29; *The Diamond Jubilee of the Archdiocese of Chicago, 1920* (Des Plaines: St. Mary's Training School Press, 1920), 762.

79. *Caritas Christi*, 2:926.

80. See *Fifty-Seventh Annual Report of the Chicago Home for the Friendless for the Year 1915*, 32. The largest New York agencies that sent children west did not stop the practice until the late 1920s. Marilyn Irvin Holt, *The Orphan Trains: Placing Out in America* (Lincoln, Nebr.: University of Nebraska Press, 1992), 162.

Chapter Three

1. Guy Alchon, *The Invisible Hand of Planning: Capitalism, Social Science, and the State in the 1920s* (Princeton: Princeton University Press, 1985), 167. Also see Ellis W. Hawley, *The Great War and the Search for a Modern Order: A History of the American People and Their Institutions, 1917–1933* (New York: St. Martin's Press, 1979); Barry D. Karl, *The Uneasy State: The United States from 1915 to 1945* (Chicago: University of Chicago Press, 1983).

2. David Rothman, *Conscience and Convenience: The Asylum and Its Alternatives in Progressive America* (Boston: Little, Brown & Co., 1980).

3. See Kathleen D. McCarthy, *Noblesse Oblige: Charity and Cultural Philanthropy in Chicago, 1849–1929* (Chicago: University of Chicago Press, 1982), 140, 148. My disagreement with McCarthy here should not be confused with a disrespect for her work. In fact, it was one of the more useful studies I consulted on Chicago charity.

4. Florence Martin to Azel Hatch, September 27, 1906. Chapin Hall Collection (CHC) at the Chicago Historical Society, box 21, folder 8.

5. *Fifty-First Annual Report, 1912*, 22. Also see, *Fifty-Sixth Annual Report, 1917*, 29; *Fifty-Seventh Annual Report, 1918*, 12; *Special Report: Chicago Nursery and Half-Orphan Asylum, 1860–1913* (Chicago: Privately printed, 1913), 18–19. A copy is in the Chicago Historical Society.

6. Board of Managers Minutes, CHC, September 20, October 18, 1904; Mrs. Florence Martin to Azel Hatch, September 27, 1904, CHC, box 21, folder 8.

7. *Special Report, 1860–1913*, 18–19. This setting is not unique to the edges of the city at this time. This area, for example, looks remarkably like much of Oak Park, Illinois, at the same time. Oak Park was about four miles south and one mile west of the land the Half-Orphan Asylum bought. At the close of the century, trolley lines were

laid decades before anyone had any ideas of building subdivisions on the land. They were meant to connect the urban and nearby rural areas as much as anything.

8. *Fifty-Third Annual Report, 1914,* 20–21; *Fifty-Fourth Annual Report, 1915,* 20.

9. On the Illinois Industrial School for Boys, see *Fifty Years of Boy-Building, 1887–1937* (Glenwood, Ill.: Glenwood Manual Training Center, n.d.), 21; *Thirteenth Annual Report of the Illinois Manual Training School Farm, 1900,* 3; on the school for girls, see *Annual Report of the Illinois Industrial School for Girls, 1908–09,* 15.

10. The women realized that the Half-Orphan Asylum was not as well known as it was twenty years before, but they did little to change the situation. In 1904, for example, the annual report noted that the long-standing policy of no public entertainments had "kept us from being well-known in the community." *Forty-Third Annual Report, 1904,* 18. Public entertainments were ended in 1880 because they raised no substantial amounts of money. By 1904, the managers saw such events not in terms of the income they would directly bring in but in terms of the publicity they would generate. The managers did nothing to follow up on this in these years, but the thought laid the groundwork for the annual fashion shows that began after World War II.

11. William O. Green to Mrs. Carroll H. Sudler, November 11, 1914, CHC, box 19, folder 8; Board of Directors Minutes, CHC, September 27, 1915.

12. At this point, the building was known as "Chapin Hall," the institution as the Chicago Nursery and Half-Orphan Asylum. As we shall see below, in 1930 the managers decided to start referring to the whole institution as Chapin Hall.

13. *Fifty-Sixth Annual Report, 1917,* 27; *Sixty-Ninth Annual Report, 1930,* 16.

14. Board of Managers Minutes, CHC, May 17, 1921; July 18, 1923; *Sixtieth Annual Report, 1921,* 11, 12; *Sixty-Third Annual Report, 1924,* 23; *Fifty-Seventh Annual Report, 1918,* 12.

15. Isabel M. Devine, "Report of Study of the Chicago Nursery and Half-Orphan Asylum" (unpublished report for the Chicago Council of Social Agencies, 1935), 28. A copy of the report is in the Welfare Council of Chicago Papers, Chicago Historical Society, box 259, folder 2.

16. There is no capacity figure in the 1930 *Social Service Directory* for St. Hedwig's Industrial School for Girls, a Polish Catholic institution. In 1920, St. Hedwig's housed 700 girls; in 1946 it still had a capacity of 250. In 1930 it was probably somewhere in between. Thus about 400 more dependents should be added to the number in the text.

17. *Fifty-Second Annual Report, 1913,* 21; *Special Report, 1913,* 16–17.

18. *Fifty-Seventh Annual Report, 1918,* 12.

19. *Fifty-Eighth Annual Report, 1919,* 27. For other comments about the inflationary problems of those years, see *Fifty-Seventh Annual Report, 1918,* 12; *Fifty-Ninth Annual Report, 1920,* 25; *Sixty-First Annual Report, 1922,* 9.

20. *Sixty-Fourth Annual Report, 1925,* 24.

21. See, for example, Francis Tyson, "Family Protection through Supplemental Income," *Annals of the American Academy of Political and Social Science* 121 (September 1925): 27–28; J. Prentice Murphy, "Superficial Character of Child Caring Work," *Proceedings: National Conference on Social Work, 1922* (Chicago: University of Chicago Press, 1922), 39.

22. *Sixty-Sixth Annual Report, 1927,* 14; *Sixty-Seventh Annual Report, 1928,* 17;

Sixty-Eighth Annual Report, 1929, 13. Yet it was not entirely true that the asylum was continuing to provide short-term care (see the next chapter).

23. *Sixty-Eighth Annual Report, 1929,* 16.

24. Fred M. Niemeyer, *A History of Angel Guardian Orphanage* (Privately printed, n.d.), n.p. A copy of this booklet is at the Chicago Historical Society. There appear to be no extant annual reports of Angel Guardian.

25. Board of Managers Minutes, CHC, October 1, 1929.

26. On the girls' meals, see Board of Managers Minutes, CHC, September 3, 1929; on the husband and wife teams and the repairs in the girls' cottage, see *Seventy-First Annual Report, 1932,* 15.

27. *Seventieth Annual Report, 1931,* 16; Minutes of the Annual Meeting, January 21, 1930, CHC, box 9, folder 3.

28. Board of Managers Minutes, CHC, February 7, 1928; Devine, "Study of the Chicago Nursery and Half-Orphan Asylum," 10–11. In 1916, shortly before the initial move to Chapin Hall, it was suggested that the name of the institution be changed and that the term "asylum" be dropped. Only two out of fifteen board members voting wanted a name change. Board of Managers Minutes, CHC, February 15, 1916.

29. Ruth Orton Camp, "Chicago Orphan Asylum, 1849–1949" (Privately printed, n.d.), 107–08; *Seventy-Eighth Annual Report of the Chicago Home for the Friendless for the Year Ending 1936,* 6; William Irvine, *A Tradition of Caring: A History of Family Care Services of Metropolitan Chicago (Chicago Home for the Friendless)* (Privately printed, n.d.), 29–32; Mitchell Alan Horwich, *Conflict and Child Care Policy in the Chicago Jewish Community, 1893–1942* (Chicago: Jewish Children's Bureau, 1977), 41–44; *Caritas Christi Urget Nos: A History of the Offices, Agencies, and Institutions of the Archdiocese of Chicago,* 2 vols. (Chicago: Archdiocese of Chicago, 1981), 2:813–14.

30. Devine, "Study of the Chicago Nursery and Half-Orphan Asylum," 29.

31. *Special Report, 1913,* 14.

32. See, for examples, Board of Managers Minutes, CHC, November 18, 1924; December 7, 1926; January 18, 1927.

33. For example, in 1932, of the 132 children in the asylum only fifteen had been placed by Juvenile Court. See Illinois Department of Public Welfare, "Inspection: Chicago Nursery and Half-Orphan Asylum, 8/15/32," 2. Welfare Council of Metropolitan Chicago Papers, Chicago Historical Society, box 259, folder 2. Also see Devine, "Study of the Chicago Nursery and Half-Orphan Asylum," 27.

34. Sandra Stehno, "Foster Care for Dependent Black Children in Chicago, 1899–1934," (Ph.D. diss., University of Chicago, 1985), 156–57.

35. "Minutes of the Meeting of the Children's Council," October 25, 1923. Welfare Council of Metropolitan Chicago Papers, Chicago Historical Society, box 35, folder 1.

36. It should be quickly added, however, that much more was involved with the decline in the number of applications (see chap. four). For the citywide decline in applications, see Council of Social Agencies, "Minutes of the Meeting of the Section on Institutions for Dependent and Neglected Children of the Child Welfare Division," October 23, 1928, Welfare Council of Metropolitan Chicago Papers, Chicago Historical Society, box 35, folder 2. For another agency experiencing the decline, see *Seventy-Fifth Annual Report of the Chicago Orphan Asylum, 1925,* 11.

37. Devine, "Study of the Chicago Nursery and Half-Orphan Asylum," 88–89.

38. *Special Report, 1913,* 13.

39. On the Association of Commerce, see Board of Managers Minutes, CHC, December 1, 1914; on the creation of the Social Services Committee, see Board of Managers Minutes, CHC, January 2, 1917.

40. For examples, see Board of Managers Minutes, CHC, January 20, August 4, September 1, 1925; March 6, October 5, December 7, 1926.

41. On the problem of letting older girls stay, see Board of Managers Minutes, CHC, September 1, 1925; September 6, 1927; on having the social worker do follow-up work, see Board of Managers Minutes, CHC, June 19, 1928.

42. Board of Managers Minutes, CHC, January 22, 1929.

43. *Special Report, 1913,* 20.

44. McCarthy, *Noblesse Oblige,* 137.

45. Board of Managers Minutes, CHC, May 2, 1922. Until 1926, each child that entered the asylum had a card kept on file with only the most rudimentary information, such as birthdate and parent's address. For every child who entered the institution after 1926, there is a detailed case history, discussing the background of the case, the character of the parent, the difficulties the child might have adjusting to the asylum, and so on.

46. See, for example, Camp, "Chicago Orphan Asylum, 1849–1949," 98; Irvine, *A Tradition of Caring,* 29; *Report of St. Mary's Home for Children, 1941–1942–1943,* 3; *Fifty Years of Boy Building,* 27–28; Horwich, *Conflict and Child Care Policy,* 37. A copy of the St. Mary's report can be found in the Archdiocese Archives, Catholic Archdiocese of Chicago.

47. Board of Managers Minutes, CHC, October 18, 1927.

48. Ibid., January 24, April 3, August 7, December 20, 1928.

49. See chapter two.

50. For the contacts between these agencies and the Half-Orphan Asylum and for the list of board members of the Juvenile Protective Association, see the various letters in CHC, box 19, folder 8.

51. H. Douglas Singer, M.D., to the superintendent of the Chicago Nursery and Half-Orphan Asylum, August 22, 1918, CHC, box 19, folder 8. Dr. Singer at the time was the acting director of the Juvenile Psychopathic Institute.

52. For examples of the disinclination to criticize child care agencies, see "Meeting of Steering Committee [of Child Welfare Committee]," December 4, 1923, and "Minutes of Executive Committee of the Child Welfare Committee," March 28, 1924, Welfare Council of Metropolitan Chicago Papers, Chicago Historical Society, box 35, folder 1.

53. The child welfare committee of the Council of Social Agencies in the 1920s was by no means inactive. It worked to make sure child labor laws were enforced and that young women coming to Chicago could find adequate housing. It tried to soften public attitudes toward illegitimacy. It also attempted to develop reliable citywide statistics on child welfare and to find more adults who would adopt. Finally, the youth committee regularly lobbied the legislature for more funding for Illinois' Department of Public Welfare. See Welfare Council of Metropolitan Chicago Papers, Chicago Historical Society, box 35, folders 1–3.

54. "Minutes of Meeting of the Child Welfare Committee," November 15, 1923; "Meeting of the Steering Committee [of the Child Welfare Committee]," December 4, 1923; "Minutes of the Meeting of the Child Welfare Committee," September 22, 1924; "Minutes of the Meeting of the Section on Institutions for Dependent and Neglected Children," April 19, 1929. Welfare Council of Metropolitan Chicago Papers, Chicago Historical Society, box 35, folders 1–3.

55. The figures here are drawn from the Council of Social Agencies, *1930 Social Services Directory* (Chicago: Chicago Council of Social Agencies, 1930). One reason the distinction broke down was that state law, at least until 1923, only allowed Juvenile Court to support children at industrial schools. This led to a number of orphanages reincorporating themselves as industrial schools. Angel Guardian and the St. Joseph's Bohemian Orphanage, two of the largest Catholic institutions, did so in 1912. The Addison Industrial School for Girls and the Addison Manual Training School for Boys, Lutheran institutions, were both reorganized in 1922 to be able to receive "industrial school" status. The law also encouraged new institutions to define themselves as industrial schools. The Morgan Park Industrial School for Girls and its counterpart for boys (both incorporated in 1920) were really small orphanages, yet they had a training program allowing them to incorporate as industrial schools and thus to be eligible for state funding.

56. For a number of the Catholic orphanages, change would not come until the late thirties or even forties. Yet several Catholic orphanages were clearly making the transition at the same time Chapin Hall was. A 1928 survey of Angel Guardian, complaining about the lack of recreational programs, fired up the priests running the orphanage to develop new play facilities. Margaret Wise, "Survey of the Angel Guardian Orphanage" (1928), chapter eleven. A copy of this report is in the archives of the Archdiocese of Chicago. Similarly, St. Mary's Training School built a gym in 1931, part of a new recreational program. The decision to raise money for the gym was made in 1928. See *Caritas Christi*, 2:926–27.

57. *Sixty-Eighth Annual Report, 1929*, 14.

58. Illinois Department of Public Welfare, "Inspection: Chicago Nursery and Half-Orphan Asylum, 8/15/32," 14. Welfare Council of Metropolitan Chicago Papers, Chicago Historical Society, box 259, folder 2. Devine, "Study of the Chicago Nursery and Half-Orphan Asylum," 48.

59. Joseph Lee, *Play in Education* (New York: Macmillan Co., 1915); Henry Stoddard Curtis, *The Play Movement and Its Significance* (New York: Macmillan Co., 1917); John Gillin, *Wholesome Citizens and Spare Time* (Cleveland: Survey Committee of the Cleveland Foundation, 1918). Also see Henry Stoddard Curtis, *The Practical Conduct of Play* (New York: Macmillan Co., 1915); Henry W. Thurston, *Delinquency and Spare Time* (Cleveland: Survey Committee of the Cleveland Foundation, 1918); and Clarence Rainwater, *The Play Movement in the United States: A Study of Community Recreation* (Chicago: University of Chicago Press, 1922). On Ford, see Henry Ford, *My Philosophy of Industry* (New York: Coward-McCann, 1929).

60. *Sixty-Second Annual Report, 1923*, 23; Board of Managers Minutes, CHC, May 20, June 17, 1924.

61. Board of Managers Minutes, CHC, February 16, March 16, April 20, November 2, 1926; *Sixty-Sixth Annual Report, 1927*, 15.

62. Board of Managers Minutes, CHC, July 17, 1928. No play director was deemed necessary for the girls because there were so many adult women around—both staff and volunteers (i.e., managers)—that the girls would have plenty of direction. The boys, on the other hand, needed handling. It is worth pointing out how overwhelmingly female the management and staff of the institution was from its inception in the 1860s through all changes until the 1960s, when, for the first time, a significant number of men joined the staff.

63. Board of Managers Minutes, CHC, May 19, September 3, December 3, 1929.

64. Board of Managers Minutes, CHC, December 6, 1927; *Sixty-Seventh Annual Report, 1928,* 14; Board of Managers Minutes, CHC, March 3, October 10, 1928; *Sixty-Eighth Annual Report, 1929,* 14.

65. On vacation policy, see Board of Managers Minutes, CHC, May 21, 1929. I found no explicit discussion of haircuts and uniforms in the managers' minutes, but photographs of the 1920s indicate that both changed between 1923 and 1930. For the end to silence at meals, see Board of Managers Minutes, CHC, October 2, 1928.

66. *Sixty-Sixth Annual Report, 1927,* 15; *Sixty-Seventh Annual Report, 1928,* 14–15.

67. On the value of play, see Gerald Mangold, *Problems of Child Welfare,* rev. ed. (New York: Macmillan Co., 1924), 192–95; for a typical contrast of the old and new forms of care, see Henry Thurston, *The Dependent Child: A Story of Changing Aims and Methods in the Care of Dependent Children* (New York: Columbia University Press, 1930), esp. 261–71, 289–92.

68. Mangold, *Problems of Child Welfare,* 193.

69. "Superintendent" of the asylum was the new name given to the matron. After the orphanage opened its first cottage (in 1917), the woman in charge of the cottage was called the matron, while the woman who watched over the whole institution was called the superintendent.

70. Illinois Department of Public Welfare, "Inspection: Chicago Nursery and Half-Orphan Asylum," 15; Devine, "Study of the Chicago Nursery and Half-Orphan Asylum," 45.

71. Devine, "Study of the Chicago Nursery and Half-Orphan Asylum," 49–50. The differences between the "old" Half-Orphan Asylum and the "new" parallel the two different asylums discussed by Eileen Simpson. Simpson lived in two different orphanages in the interwar years. The first was a harsh, religious place. Uniforms were required. The second institution was far more relaxed. She was encouraged to find ways to enjoy herself. See Eileen Simpson, *Orphans: Real and Imaginary* (New York: Weidenfeld & Nicolson, 1987), 20–61.

72. Undated letter [1918?] from Harriet Kemper to staff. CHC, box 21, folder 8.

Chapter Four

1. For one discussion of this, see Marshall Jones, "Crisis of the American Orphanage, 1931–1940," *Social Service Review* 63 (1989): 613–29.

2. Ibid.

3. Between 1934 and 1948, the highest average number of children in the institution was 136 (in 1937) and the lowest was 126 (in 1942). See the Secretary's Reports

for those years, Chapin Hall Collection (CHC), Chicago Historical Society, box 17, folder 1.

4. Between 1923 and 1933, the number of dependent children in institutions in the state of Illinois fell by 8.5 percent, from 11,264 to 10,301. By 1938, the number had been reduced to 9,434, a drop of another 11.1 percent. *Children under Institutional Care, 1923* (Washington, D.C.: Government Printing Office, 1927), 18; and *Children under Institutional Care and in Foster Homes, 1933* (Washington, D.C.: Government Printing Office, 1935), 72; John Kahlert, *Child Dependency in Illinois* (Springfield, Ill.: Illinois Department of Public Welfare, 1940), 36; *Social Service Yearbook, 1939* (Chicago: Council of Social Agencies of Chicago, 1939), 32.

5.	ILLINOIS DEPENDENT CHILDREN	
Year	In Institutions	Under Foster Care
1923	11,264	2,339
1933	10,301	5,151

Sources: Children under Institutional Care, 1923, 18; *Children under Institutional Care and in Foster Homes, 1933,* 72.

6. For how Illinois lagged behind other states, see *Children under Institutional Care and in Foster Homes, 1933,* 5. For the best discussions of the gradual replacement of institutional care by foster care, see Martin Wolins and Irving Piliavin, *Institution or Foster Family: A Century of Debate* (New York: Child Welfare League of America, 1964), 36–47; Paul Lerman, *Deinstitutionalization and the Welfare State* (New Brunswick, N.J.: Rutgers University Press, 1982), 107–24.

7. Chicago Council of Social Agencies, "Study of Child Care Agencies," Isabel Devine, director (1937), 11. A copy of this report is in Regenstein Library at the University of Chicago.

8. This is the obvious conclusion after looking at a study done of twenty-five cities by the U.S. Children's Bureau in 1937. See U.S. Department of Labor, Children's Bureau, "Social-Statistics Project / General Letter of Information / Dependent and Neglected Children," no. 3 (January 4, 1939).

9. *Children under Institutional Care and in Foster Homes, 1933,* 61; *Social Security Bulletin* 3 (December 1940): 56.

10. *Benevolent Institutions, 1910* (Washington, D.C.: Government Printing Office, 1913), 28; *Children under Institutional Care and in Foster Homes, 1933,* 26. The number of children in institutions actually dropped slightly in the 1920s, as noted in the text, but that was offset by a rise in the number of children in institutions between 1910 and 1920. Hence, between 1910 and 1933, the number of children in institutions actually rose, from 9,047 to 10,301.

11. To take one typical example, in 1937, a divorced father brought his daughter to Chapin Hall. The mother, the caseworker later noted, was unable "to accept reponsibility" for the daughter's care. The father, a violinist with the Chicago Symphony

Orchestra, was clearly troubled himself. There are hints of his homosexuality and difficulty coping. Yet the parents were apparently never pressured to think of foster care. The only sentence in the case record about it reveals a remarkable deference to the parents: "The parents are divorced and it is their feeling that neither they nor a foster mother are the satisfactory persons to take care of her." This feeling was never questioned by the social worker. The girl, nine years old, was admitted. Case 1.

Case records will be referred to by number in the notes. Since I have changed the names in the text, these numbers refer to my own ordering system. In my files, in other words, I have the name that "Case 1" refers to.

12. Margo Horn suggests that the new therapeutic sensibility of interwar social work was not as coercive as other scholars have claimed. In fact, Horn argues, social workers dealing with dependent children struggled to keep families together. Chapin Hall's files suggest that Horn is right that the new approach was not coercive, but that this did not always keep families together. Margo Horn, "The Moral Message of Child Guidance, 1925–1945," *Journal of Social History* 18 (Fall 1984): 25–36.

13. The information found in this and the next two paragraphs comes from the 1930 and 1946 *Social Service Directory* of the Council of Social Agencies. On the closing of small orphanages downstate, see Kahlert, *Child Dependency in Illinois,* 35–36.

14. On the number of institutionalized children in Cook County, see Kahlert, *Child Dependency in Illinois,* 39.

15. Between 1934 and 1936, 462 children entered Chapin Hall; 241 of them (52.1 percent) were from parents either divorced, separated, or deserted. Between 1946 and 1968, of the 530 children who lived in Chapin Hall, 320 (60.3 percent) came from such homes.

Year	Illness	Insane	Death	Illegitimate	Divorce	Separation	Desertion	Unfit	Oth.
1934	5	18	48	0	44	10	27	0	2
1935	18	17	51	0	40	12	19	0	3
1936	3	7	49	0	34	33	22	0	0
1937	3	3	37	11	30	10	33	13	3
1942	5	6	39	7	29	49	22	12	2
1943	5	6	56	6	27	46	34	0	3
1944	5	9	44	7	34	41	31	0	6
1945	4	16	35	4	44	30	31	0	3
1946	4	14	37	7	45	39	33	0	1
1947	6	18	32	8	49	38	20	3	5
1948	6	17	31	9	50	34	12	7	5

Source: Secretary's Reports, CHC, box 17, folder 1.

Before 1937, illegitimate children were generally included in other categories. Yet they were accepted into Chapin Hall from the late twenties. The 1931 annual report noted that in 1930, the Half-Orphan Asylum housed eleven children born out of wedlock. *Seventieth Annual Report, 1931,* 13–14.

16. Lawrence C. Cole, "The Plan of a General Bureau of Inquiry," *Proceedings of*

the National Conference of Social Work, 49th Annual Session, June 22–29, 1922 (Chicago, 1922), 150–51; "Sifting the 'Orphans,'" *The Survey* 49 (February 15, 1923): 638–39; Stuart A. Queen, "Are Orphan Asylums Necessary?" *Journal of Social Forces* 2 (March 1924): 384–88.

17. City of Chicago Department of Public Welfare, *Annual Report, 1928–29*, 16.

18. Between 1934 and 1936, a total of 457 children entered Chapin Hall, and 148 of them (32.6 percent) were half-orphans. Between 1946 and 1948, 530 children lived in the institution, but only 100 (18.8 percent) were half-orphans. I have taken the figures from the various Secretary's Reports, CHC, box 17, folder 1.

19. "Orphanhood—A Diminishing Problem," *Social Security Bulletin* 18 (March 1955): 17. In 1920 there were estimated to be 750,000 full orphans. In 1930, only 450,000; and by 1954, only 60,000.

20. Theda Skocpol, *Protecting Soldiers and Mothers: The Political Origins of Social Policy in the United States* (Cambridge, Mass.: Harvard University Press, 1992), 466–67; also see Ann Vanderpol, "Dependent Children, Child Custody, and the Mothers' Pensions: The Transformation of State-Family Relations in the early Twentieth Century," *Social Problems* 29 (February 1982): 231; Mortimer Spiegelman, "The Broken Family—Widowhood and Orphanhood," *The Annals of American Political and Social Science* 188 (November 1936): 117.

21. Council of Social Agencies, *Social Service Year Book, Chicago, 1939* (Chicago: Council of Social Agencies of Chicago), 14.

22. Ibid. Also see Council of Social Agencies, *Social Service Year Book, 1935*, 24.

23. *Sixty-Fourth Annual Report, 1925*, 23; *Sixty-Sixth Annual Report, 1926*, 13.

24. See below for a discussion of this.

25. To take two random samples, from August to December 1932, fifteen mothers brought children to Chapin Hall while five fathers did. Between August and December 1936, nineteen mothers brought their children; seven fathers did. Social Service Reports, CHC, box 17, folder 3.

26. Linda Gordon, *Heroes of Their Own Lives: The Politics and History of Family Violence, Boston, 1880–1960* (New York: Viking-Penguin, 1988), 99–108.

27. Case 2.

28. Case 3.

29. Case 4.

30. Case 5.

31. Casework reports of the 1930s and 1940s that discuss neglectful mothers often note things such as the mother was "flashily made-up" or that she was "expensively, but rather vulgarly dressed." These comments, which again are typical of such mothers, come from Case 6. On the other hand, fathers who neglected their children rarely had such censorious notes in their files.

32. Case 7.

33. In 1929, Julia Thompson noted that about two-fifths of the children stayed less than a year, "proving that we are attaining our object of helping many people temporarily over hard times." In the 1870s and 1880s, however, 74 percent of children left Chapin Hall within a year. The 40 percent figure cited by Thompson did not indicate traditional standards of temporary care as she suggested. It rather indicated just the

opposite. See *Sixty-Eighth Annual Report, 1929*, 13. For other mention of the "temporary" care provided by Chapin Hall, see *Sixty-Fourth Annual Report, 1925*, 24; *Sixty-Fifth Annual Report, 1926*, 14; *Sixty-Seventh Annual Report, 1928*, 17.

Between 1945 and 1948, of the 520 children who left the institution, 145 (27.8 percent) had spent less than a year in Chapin Hall. A total of 250 (48 percent) had resided less than two years in the institution. Figures derived from the Secretary's Reports, CHC, box 17, folder 1. For the nineteenth-century figures, see chapter one.

34. *Proceedings of the Conference on the Care of Dependent Children Held at Washington, D.C., January 25, 26, 1909* (Washington, D.C.: Government Printing Office, 1909), 6. Also see Vanderpol, "Dependent Children, Child Custody, and the Mothers' Pensions," 232.

35. Case 8.

36. Superintendent's Report, August and September, 1940, CHC, box 18, folder 4.

37. *Sixty-Third Annual Report, 1924*, 24.

38. The amounts of money collected from the various sources during the 1915 building campaign and the 1930 building campaign reflect the changes.

SOURCE	AMOUNT	%
1915 Campaign		
Chapin Hall	$96,575.24	61.5
Chicago Near North	36,700.00	23.4
North Shore suburbs	21,700.00	13.8
Downtown	1,000.00	.6
Source unknown	1,150.00	.7
Total	157,125.24	100.0
1930 Campaign		
Chapin Hall	$27,050.00	47.5
Chicago Near North	200.00	.3
North Shore suburbs	22,750.00	39.9
Downtown	150.00	.2
National foundation	5,000.00	8.8
Source unknown	1,850.00	3.2
Total	57,000.00	99.9[*]

*Figures rounded.

The lists of donors for the campaigns are in the CHC, box 22, folder 3. I have devised the above charts by tracing the names on the lists through *Who's Who in Chicago*, the Chicago social register, and Chicago phone books. Of course, a neighbor who gave to Chapin Hall was often a downtown businessman. What is important, though, is that being part of the downtown business community, in itself, was rarely enough to draw a contribution to Chapin Hall. One generally had to be a neighbor as well. Those names with current or traditional connections to the orphanage are listed under "Chapin Hall." These people might be currently active, but might have had a mother, for example, who had long been associated with the institution. The donation, then, was to honor the work of a relative.

39. These figures were based on the figures from the annual reports of 1900, 1904, 1908, 1912, and 1913. The other principal source of income was the balance on hand from the previous year. That made up 6 percent of all income. These figures, of course, have been rounded off.

40. These figures are derived from the 1920, 1924, and 1928 annual reports. The precise distributions are as follows:

	%
Balance from previous year	2.9
Donations	21.8
Parental Board Payments	30.9
Endowment Interest	34.7
Use of Endowment	4.2
Special Events	1.0
Other	4.3
Total	99.8*

*Figures rounded.

41. In making these calculations, I have not included money left from the previous year ("balance from previous year") as transitory income because on the first day of each fiscal year, the managers were aware of how much of this money was available and could plan accordingly. Under transitory income I have included donations, board from parents, money from special events, and that labeled "other." On the first day of each fiscal year, the amount of income each of these sources would produce was unclear. While there might be some variation in the amount the endowment would produce, it provided a steady and dependable income, even during the Depression.

42. Board of Managers Minutes, CHC, February 17, May 5, 1931; April 18, 1933; October 15, 1935.

43. On pay cuts, see Board of Managers Minutes, CHC, March 15, August 16, 1932; also Illinois Department of Public Welfare "Inspection: Chicago Nursery and Half-Orphan Asylum, 8-15-32," 4. A copy of this report is in the Welfare Council of Metropolitan Chicago Papers, Chicago Historical Society, box 259, folder 2. On the cut in sick leave and the firing of the office secretary, see Board of Managers Minutes, CHC, February 2, 1932; on vacations, see Board of Managers Minutes, CHC, August 16, 1932.

44. Board of Managers Minutes, CHC, March 17, June 2, 1931.

45. Board of Managers Minutes, CHC, June 2, 1931.

46. *Seventy-First Annual Report, 1932,* 14.

47. On the infants' nursery, see Isabel M. Devine, "Report of Study of the Chicago

Nursery and Half-Orphan Asylum" (unpublished report for the Chicago Council of Social Agencies, 1935), 91, (a copy of this report is in the Welfare Council of Metropolitan Chicago Papers, Chicago Historical Society, box 259, folder 2); and *Seventy-Second Annual Report, 1933*, 17; on the social worker and nursery school teacher, see Board of Managers Minutes, CHC, November 17, 1931; on the house parents, see *Seventy-First Annual Report, 1932*, 15. The husband had a part-time job elsewhere. The couple was given free room and board but no salary.

48. Board of Managers Minutes, CHC, June 7, 1932.

49. More precisely, aggregate income for 1928 was $75,325.21; for 1934, $50,605.15. *Sixty-Eighth Annual Report, 1929*, 19, 24; Isabel M. Devine, "Study of the Chicago Nursery and Half-Orphan Asylum," 25.

50. In 1928, donations added up to $12,451.31. By 1940, they were $7,787.00. *Sixty-Eighth Annual Report, 1928*, 19, 24; "Annual Report to the State of Illinois Department of Public Welfare for the year ending Dec. 31, 1940," CHC, box 24, folder 3.

51. In 1928, parental board payments totaled $23,964.00. In 1932, they added up to $10,823.59. See *Sixty-Eighth Annual Report, 1929*, 19, 24; *Seventy-Second Annual Report, 1933*, 21.

52. Secretary's Report of 1935, CHC, box 17, folder 1.

53. In 1928, endowment interest added up to $26,498.04. It remained at that point for the next twelve years. In 1940, that income was $26,700.00.

54. The strategy of the 1920s was heavy investment in real estate and comparatively little in stock. The conservative nature of this approach was explicitly discussed in the 1920s.

55. Frank Denman Loomis, *The Chicago Community Trust: A History of Its Development, 1915–1962* (Chicago: Chicago Community Trust, n.d.), 4–7, 16–18.

56. Associated Jewish Charities was organized in 1900; the Federated Orthodox Jewish Charities was created in 1912. On their organization and activities, see the Chicago Council of Social Agencies, *The Financing of Social Agencies* (Chicago: privately printed, 1924), 56 ff. For background on the disputes between Orthodox and Reformed charities, see Mitchell Alan Horwich, *Conflict and Child Care Policy in the Chicago Jewish Community, 1893–1942* (Chicago: Jewish Children's Bureau, 1977).

57. Loomis, *Chicago Community Trust*, 19–20.

58. Ibid., 21.

59. Board of Managers Minutes, CHC, August 4, 1931. The managers (in consultation with the directors) in 1931 made major efforts at fundraising. The end result, however, was that 1931 donations equaled 1930 donations. The added work did not increase income. See Board of Managers Minutes, CHC, May 19, June 2, 16, August 4, 1931. The board also turned to charity benefits, held at the Blackstone Theater in downtown Chicago and in Lake Forest. See Board of Managers Minutes, CHC, August 18, November 17, 1931. Finally, the board tried to tighten up its collection of delinquent board payments and, for the first time in years, charged parents when they took their children on vacation. (This policy was only applied to those parents who had jobs.) Board of Managers Minutes, CHC, May 19, 1931.

All of these measures were being worked out at the same time that the managers were refusing Community Fund money. The strategies of 1931, to redouble efforts for traditional sources of money and to cut costs, in essence failed, something the managers and directors knew by the fall of 1932, when they accepted Community Fund support.

60. Devine, "Study of the Chicago Nursery and Half-Orphan Asylum," 25, 91; *Seventy-Third Annual Report, 1934,* 16; Board of Managers Minutes, CHC, March 20, 1934, box 9, folder 4; *Seventy-Sixth Annual Report, 1937,* 19.

61. Board of Managers Minutes, CHC, December 3, 1940.

62. *Seventy-Second Annual Report, 1933,* 17; *Seventy-Third Annual Report, 1935,* 16, 49.

63. See Council of Social Agencies, *Social Service Year Book, 1935.*

64. On 1941, see "Annual Report to State of Illinois Department of Welfare for year ending Dec. 31, 1941," CHC, box 24, folder 3. For 1948, see "Annual Report to State of Illinois Department of Welfare for year ending Dec. 31, 1948," CHC, box 24, folder 3.

65. By 1937, public money accounted for 21.9 percent of the income of Chicago's Protestant child-care institutions (as opposed to only 6.5 percent for Chapin Hall). See the Council of Social Agencies, "Study of Child Care Agencies" (unpublished manuscript, 1937), 30. A copy is in Regenstein Library at the University of Chicago.

A 1928 study of eight major cities (Chicago excluded) indicated that 25.5 percent of all money for care of dependent children came from the public treasury and that 36.1 percent came from Community Fund. Even in 1937, according to the CSA study cited above, Protestant child-care institutions in Chicago still got only 21.9 percent of their income from public sources and only 15.8 percent from the Community Fund. That is to say, even after the increase in social spending due to the Depression, Chicago institutions relied more heavily on traditional sources of income (endowment, donations, parental payment) than institutions in other cities did before the Depression. Griffith et al., "Receipts and Expenditures of Social Agencies during the Year 1928," *Social Service Review* 4 (September 1930): 354.

66. Joan Gittens, "The Children of the State: Dependent Children in Illinois, 1818–1980s" (Chapin Hall Center for Children, 1986), 71–81, 105–16.

67. Ellen Condliffe Lagemann, *Private Power for the Public Good: A History of the Carnegie Foundation for the Advancement of Teaching* (Middletown, Conn.: Wesleyan University Press, 1983).

68. All twelve directors in 1936 were listed in that year's *Who's Who in Chicago.* Nine were listed as Republicans. Three listed no political allegiance. None said they were Democrats.

69. Board of Managers Minutes, CHC, February 5, 19, 1929.

70. For comments on attendance, see Secretary's Report, January 18, 1949, Secretary's Annual Report, January 28, 1947, CHC, box 17, folder 1.

71. Report [of the Policy Committee, 1940], CHC, box 20, folder 6.

72. Kenneth T. Jackson, *Crabgrass Frontier: The Suburbanization of the United States* (New York: Oxford University Press, 1985), 87–102.

73. Lake Forest's population in 1910 was 3,349; in 1920, it was 3,657. By 1930 it had grown to 6,554, an increase of roughly 80 percent. During the 1930s, the population of Lake Forest only grew by 331, to 6,885. See John Andriot, ed., *Population Abstract of the United States,* (McLean, Va.: Andriot Associates, 1983), 1:191.

Other elite suburbs also grew dramatically during the 1920s. The population of

Scarsdale, N.Y., for example, increased by 176 percent during the 1920s. New York City only grew 21 percent at the same time. See Carol A. O'Connor, *A Sort of Utopia: Scarsdale, 1891–1981* (Albany: State University of New York Press, 1983), 43.

74. In 1900, thirteen of thirty-nine Chicago Orphan Asylum managers lived in Hyde Park and Kenwood, and twenty-three still lived in the South Prairie Avenue district. By 1930, twenty-three of the thirty managers lived in Hyde Park–Kenwood. *Fiftieth Annual Report of the Chicago Orphan Asylum* (Chicago, 1900), 12; *Eightieth Annual Report of the Chicago Orphan Asylum* (Chicago, 1930), 5. Like Chapin Hall, the Chicago Orphan Asylum moved out of the center of the city during the progressive years. Yet the COA was able to move in the 1890s, while the Half-Orphan Asylum did not move until 1916.

75. Jackson, *Crabgrass Frontier*, 102.

76. Thompson, a leader from the Progressive Era and one of the women who led the effort to alter the direction of the asylum in the 1920s, also had her suspicions about the new professionalism. In 1923, she wrote: "In the steady pursuit of better material conditions, however, we must endeavor to emulate the truly charitable purpose which animated the labours of the early workers in this particular field." *Sixty-Second Annual Report, 1923,* 22. And after she led the battle to hire the first social worker and have the agency keep more extensive case records, Thompson again pointed out the ambiguous nature of the gains, referring to them as "possibly more scientific" and stressing the personal caring involved in the old way. See *Sixty-Eighth Annual Report, 1929,* 16–17.

77. Board of Managers Minutes, CHC, September 2, 1930.

78. Board of Managers Minutes, CHC, September 2, 1930; March 3, 17, 1931.

79. One former manager I interviewed reported that Adrianna Bouterse was "not a sophisticated person," and that despite her professional work done at the University of Chicago School of Social Service Administration, she was quite deferential to the board. In the 1930s, the professionals at the Council of Social Agencies, when they evaluated Chapin Hall, reported on Mabel Morrow's passive disposition.

80. Board of Managers Minutes, CHC, August 15, September 19, 1933, April 3, June 5, 1934.

81. Council of Social Agencies, *Social Service Year Book, 1935,* 38–39. The yearbook states that twenty-four agencies will be studied, but in the final 1937 report, only twenty-two agencies were listed as participants.

82. Devine, "Study of the Chicago Nursery and Half-Orphan Asylum," 14.

83. Ibid.

84. Ibid.

85. See the 1-14-38 entry in the Council of Social Agencies file on Chapin Hall in the Welfare Council of Metropolitan Chicago Papers, Chicago Historical Society, box 259, folder 2.

86. One significant change showing the increased traditionalism in the choice of directors is the interconnection of the two boards. In the nineteenth century, very few of the directors were the husbands of managers. The effort was to find the most conscientious people to serve. As late as 1911, only three of the eleven directors were husbands of managers. By 1932, seven of the twelve directors were spouses of managers. More and more the directors were chosen because they were the husbands of other

managers or the sons of previous managers. *Fiftieth Annual Report, 1911,* 3–4; *Seventy-First Annual Report, 1932,* 5–7.

87. "Report of the Realignment Committee of the Council of Social Agencies" (1937), 13, 26. A copy of this report is in Regenstein Library at the University of Chicago.

88. Welfare professionals, welfare educators (including Edith Abbott of the University of Chicago), and business and civic leaders such as Philip Armour were all on the committee. Yet that the proposals came from the professionals suggested the "real" reason that Devine wanted some of the women involved in the policy process. An idea endorsed at the beginning by businessmen, volunteer women and the welfare professionals probably had a better chance of success than one simply proposed by the professionals.

89. The phrase, "died a natural death," is from the 1940 Report of Policy Committee (handwritten and labeled "Report") in the CHC, box 20, folder 6. For the involvement and opposition to the merger movement in the Chicago Orphan Asylum, see Clare McCausland, *Children of Circumstance: A History of the First 125 Years of the Chicago Child Care Society* (Chicago: Printed by R. R. Donnelly & Sons, 1976), 131–38.

Chapter Five

1. Superintendent's Report, February 1942, Chapin Hall Collection (CHC) at the Chicago Historical Society, box 9, folder 7.

2. See Hazel Frederickson, *The Child and His Welfare* (San Francisco: W. H. Freeman, 1948); Cecelia McGovern, *Services to Children in Institutions* (Washington, D.C.: National Conference of Catholic Charities, 1948); Howard Hopkirk, *Institutions Serving Children* (New York: Russell Sage Foundation, 1944). Hopkirk was the executive director of the Child Welfare League of America. Also see Alfred Kadushin, *Child Welfare Services* (New York: Macmillan Co., 1967), 520. Kadushin (writing in the mid-sixties) claimed that the change took place in the 1950s, but it is clear that new ideas were being expressed in the previous decade.

3. Joseph H. Reid, "The Role of the Modern Children's Institution" (1955), in *Child Welfare Perspectives: Selected Papers of Joseph H. Reid* (New York: Child Welfare League of America, 1979), 99–106. Also see Joseph H. Reid and Helen R. Hagen, *Residential Treatment Centers for Emotionally Disturbed Children* (New York: Child Welfare League of America, 1952).

4. Susanne Schulze, "How Does Group Living in the Institution Prepare the Child for Life Outside?" (Paper, United States Department of Labor, Children's Bureau, Washington, D.C., 1944), 3, 5; also see Susanne Schulze, "Group Living and the Dependent Child," *Proceedings of the National Conference of Social Work, May 1946* (New York, 1947), 387–97; Susanne Schulze, ed., *Creative Group Living in a Children's Institution* (New York: Association Press, 1951).

5. Andrew Polsky, *The Rise of the Therapeutic State* (Princeton: Princeton University Press, 1992), 149–56.

6. Elaine Tyler May, *Homeward Bound: American Families in the Cold War Era* (New York: Basic Books, 1988).

7. As I have argued, family maintenance was central to welfare policy from the late nineteenth century. What changed were the strategies used to secure that end. As Linda Gordon notes: "The defend-the-conventional-family policy in social work continued straight through the 1940s and 1950s." See Linda Gordon, *Heroes of Their Own Lives: The Politics and History of Family Violence, Boston, 1880–1960* (New York: Viking-Penguin, 1988), 23.

8. Secretary's Report, 1949, CHC, box 17, folder 1.

9. Helen Hardy, "Policies of Admission to the Protestant and Non-Sectarian Institutions for Dependent Children in Chicago" (1928), Welfare Council of Metropolitan Chicago Papers, box 35, folder 3; Reynolds is quoted in Malcolm Bush, *Families in Distress: Public, Private, and Civic Responses* (Berkeley and Los Angeles: University of California Press, 1988), 34; the Children's Bureau report is quoted in Dorothy Bradbury's unpublished manuscript, "The Children's Advocate: The Story of the Children's Bureau, 1900–1946," 648, Bradbury Papers, Regenstein Library, University of Chicago.

10. Council of Social Agencies, *1930 Social Service Directory.*

11. Sandra Stehno, "Foster Care for Dependent Black Children in Chicago, 1899–1934," (Ph.D. diss., University of Chicago, 1985), 248–55.

12. Board of Managers Minutes, CHC, December 14, 1943; March 21, 1944; October 16, 1945.

13. Superintendent's Report, October 1943, CHC, box 9, folder 8.

14. On the University of Chicago and restrictive covenants, see Arnold Hirsch, *Making the Second Ghetto: Race and Housing in Chicago, 1940–1960* (Cambridge: Cambridge University Press, 1983), 145–46; on Protestant children's homes and minorities, see Connie Fish, "Barriers to Adequate Group Care for Children of Minority Groups," January 15, 1953. Welfare Council of Metropolitan Chicago Papers at the Chicago Historical Society, box 146, folder 3.

15. Board of Managers Minutes, CHC, November 20, December 18, 1945.

16. Board of Managers Minutes, CHC, December 14, 1943.

17. Elizabeth Goddard, "Evaluation Report of Chicago Nursery and Half-Orphan Asylum," April 26, 1948. Chapin Hall Files (CHF) at Chapin Hall Center for Children at the University of Chicago (UC).

18. Board of Managers Minutes, CHC, June 20, 1948.

19. Mrs. Charles C. [Teddy] Haffner to Laurence C. Callahan, April 15, 1948. CHF, UC.

20. On negative evaluation by the state, see Fred DelliQuardi to Mrs. Victor C. [Kay] Milliken, August 4, 1948. CHF, UC. DelliQuardi was the superintendent of Child Welfare of the state's Division of Child Welfare in the Department of Public Welfare. For an account of the Association of Commerce, see Teddy Haffner to Laurence K. Callahan, April 15, 1949. CHF, UC.

The 15 percent figure is based on the 1947 budget. I have included both contributions and benefits in this figure. The budget is attached to Elizabeth Goddard [Council of Social Agencies], "Evaluation Report of the Chicago Nursery and Half-Orphan Asylum," April 28, 1948, in CHF, UC.

21. See the minutes of various meetings in the Chapin Hall file in the Welfare Council of Metropolitan Chicago Papers, Chicago Historical Society, box 259, folder 3.

22. On the truculence of Mabel Morrow, see Teddy Haffner to Laurence Callahan, April 15, 1949, CHF, UC. In February 1949 Morrow argued vigorously against the CSA proposal to cut back the number of nurses at Chapin Hall. She went and found doctors to provide expert support for her position. Notes and reports on this are in CHF, UC.

23. See report of December 8, 1948 by Elizabeth Goddard in Welfare Council of Metropolitan Chicago Papers, Chicago Historical Society, box 259, folder 3.

24. Welfare Council of Metropolitan Chicago, *1946 Social Service Directory; 1961 Social Service Directory*.

25. Ibid.

26. Ibid.

27. Ibid.

28. Welfare Council of Metropolitan Chicago, *Statistics* 28 (April–June 1961): 2.

29. Haffner to Callahan, April 15, 1948. CHF, UC.

30. Board of Managers Minutes, CHC, August 16, 1949.

31. Board of Managers Minutes, CHC, December 6, 1949; April 17, 1950.

32. Report of the Case Committee for 1949, CHC, box 16, folder 1.

33. Board of Managers Minutes, CHC, October 17, 1950.

34. Annual Report of the Secretary for Year Ending Dec. 31, 1949, CHC, box 17, folder 1.

35. Welfare Council of Metropolitan Chicago, *Social Services Year Book, 1947–48*, 29.

36. Welfare Council of Metropolitan Chicago, *Statistics* 29 (January–May 1962): 2.

37. See Seth Low, *America's Children and Youth in Institutions, 1950–1960–1964: A Demographic Analysis* (Washington, D.C.: U.S. Department of Health, Education, and Welfare, 1965), 4–5.

38. Schulze, "Group Living and the Dependent Child," 392–93. The Community Fund and Welfare Council set up similar guidelines. See "Report of Group to Consider Program for Emotionally Disturbed Children," February 17, 1950; and "Criteria for Treatment Programs for Emotionally Disturbed Children in an Institutional Setting," May 31, 1952. Community Fund Collection, University of Illinois at Chicago Circle, Special Collections, box 16, folder 5.

39. Board of Managers Minutes, CHC, October 16, 1945.

40. Policies Relating to the Placement of Children in Chapin Hall [February 1951], CHC, box 10, folder 4.

41. This paragraph is based on a random sample of twenty files of children who entered the institution between 1950 and 1956.

42. Case 9.

43. Case 10.

44. Case 11.

45. For Bouterse, see Board of Managers Minutes, CHC, September 16, 1956. She voiced similar sentiments two years later at the Community Fund, "Minutes of the Meeting of the Child Care Reviewing Committee," February 6, 1958, Community Fund Papers, University of Illinois at Chicago Circle, Special Collections, box 82, folder 1; "Annual Report of Executive Director for 1963," CHF, UC.

46. Cook County Department of Welfare, "Additional Services Needed for Dependent and Neglected Children in Cook County," December 8, 1954; Cook County Department of Welfare, "The New Child Welfare Service for Children in Cook County (Serving Children Who Cannot Be Accepted By Other Agencies)," 1956. Copies of both documents are in the Chicago Historical Society.

47. Case 12.

48. Case 13.

49. Case 14.

50. Case 15.

51. "Through the years we have seen dramatic differences between the children we used to have and those we are asked to take now. Less come to us from private, personal sources, but even those who do, and are placed by their own parent or parents, have considerably advanced emotional problems, for which solutions are sought. As for the rest, they are all children from unbelievably traumatic backgrounds, who can only be hoped to be raised to healthy adulthood, if they get help in a professional, flexible, benign but firm, setting. . . . Generally speaking, we cannot and will not consider any overtly psychotic or such acting out children who need and can use only closed environments, but, at best, our children will be disturbed, and will need care over and above what needs to be provided for any child." "Casework Report for Annual Meeting," January 28, 1964. CHF, UC.

52. Case 16.

53. Roy Lubove, *The Professional Altruist: The Emergence of Social Work as a Career, 1880–1930* (Cambridge, Mass.: Harvard University Press, 1965), esp. 110, 117. Lubove also argues that psychiatric social work emerges in the 1920s. Yet Welfare Council staffers were regularly talking in the 1950s about how few Chicago agencies had psychiatric social work. I can only speculate here that the dominance of the University of Chicago School of Social Service Administration (SSA) as a training ground for the city's social workers has something to do with this. The school remained hostile to psychiatric social work through the 1920s and even into the 1930s. It may be that Chicago agencies continued to do more sociological reporting because so many were trained at SSA. That certainly explains the case of Chapin Hall, at any rate.

54. Gordon, *Heroes of Their Own Lives*, 282–85; Rael Jean Isaac and Virginia C. Armat, *Madness in the Streets: How Psychiatry and the Law Abandoned the Mentally Ill* (New York: Free Press, 1990), 41–43; Robert Castel, *La gestion des risques: De l'antipsychiatrie à l'aprèspsychanalyse* (Paris: Editions de Minuit, 1981).

55. Harold A. Richman and Matthew W. Stagner, "Social Services for Children: Recent Trends and Implications" (Chapin Hall Center for Children, 1987), 10.

56. See report on Chapin Hall in the Welfare Council of Metropolitan Chicago Papers, Chicago Historical Society, box 259, folder 3.

57. Minutes of the conference of representatives of Chicago Nursery & Half Orphan Asylum . . . with representatives of child caring agencies, January 14, 1949, Welfare Council of Metropolitan Chicago Papers, Chicago Historical Society, box 259, folder 3.

58. Report of the Building Committee as Given by Mrs. Rich at the May 17, 1955 Board Meeting, CHC, box 10, folder 7.

59. On the caseworker, see Board of Manager Minutes, CHC, February 15, 1955:

on the fundraising campaign of 1957, see Linn Brandenburg (associate executive director of Community Fund) to Adrianna Bouterse, April 8, 1957, in Welfare Council of Metropolitan Chicago Papers, Chicago Historical Society, box 259, folder 3.

60. Minutes of the conference of representatives of Chicago Nursery & Half Orphan Asylum Board of Directors [sic] with representatives of child care agencies, January 14, 1949, Welfare Council of Metropolitan Chicago Papers, Chicago Historical Society, box 259, folder 3; Board of Managers Meeting, CHC, June 21, 1949; Monthly Meeting, June 19, 1956; Monthly Meeting, June 21, 1955, CHC, box 10, folder 7; "Annual Report of the President for 1963," CHF, UC. Also see "Annual Report of the President for the Year 1962," CHF, UC.

61. Report in Welfare Council of Metropolitan Chicago Papers, Chicago Historical Society, box 259, folder 3.

62. Board of Managers Minutes, CHC, June 19, 1951; December 15, 1953; February 15, June 21, July 19, September 20, December 13, 1955; March 20, September 18, 1956.

63. On the absence of institutional care for blacks, see Connie Fish, "Barriers to Adequate Group Care for Children of Minority Groups," January 15, 1953, Welfare Council of Metropolitan Chicago Papers, Chicago Historical Society, box 146, folder 3. Moreover, all the material in this file, which is on Welfare Council efforts to integrate agencies, reflect the very patient attitude of the professionals. Again and again, education was stressed as a necessary prerequisite to integration. In 1955, after the managers of Chapin Hall simply visited a number of institutions that were integrated, they received a letter from Connie Fish saying she was "heartened" by their efforts. Monthly Meeting, CHC, December 13, 1955.

64. Hirsch, *Making the Second Ghetto,* 234–38.

65. "Why is the attendance at the meetings so bad? Of course much of the business is a matter of routine and we all know and appreciate the fact that we have run smoothly and effectively under Miss Morrow's and Mrs. Robertson's leadership. . . . Let's admit the meetings haven't the glamour that we reserve for the Fashion Benefit." Secretary's Report, CHC, January 18, 1949.

66. Salaries and wages in 1948 were $47,780.71 and in 1960 they were $84,345. Council of Social Agencies, "Evaluation Report of Chicago Nursery and Half Orphan Asylum" [April, 1948], CHF, UC; 1960 figure from Welfare Council of Metropolitan Chicago Papers, Chicago Historical Society, box 259, Folder 3.

67. "Chicago Nursery and Half Orphan Asylum Monthly Meeting 10-21-61," CHF, UC.

68. "Chicago Nursery and Half Orphan Asylum Monthly Meeting 10-21-61," "Chicago Nursery and Half Orphan Asylum Monthly Meeting 12-19-61," CHF, UC. Wyndham Hasler to Mrs. Linn Brandenburg, December 4, 1961. Community Fund Collection, University of Illinois at Chicago Circle, Special Collections, box 7, folder 8.

Chapter Six

1. Andrew Polsky, *The Rise of the Therapeutic State* (Princeton: Princeton University Press, 1991), 179–80.

2. The general sense that new blood was needed at the top I owe to my interview

with Julia McNulty, April 1987; on the job search, see "Annual Report of the President for 1963," 1, Chapin Hall Files (CHF) at the University of Chicago (UC).

3. George Headley, "Annual Report of Executive Director for 1964," 6, CHF, UC; also see George Headley, "Annual Report of the Executive Director for 1965," 7, CHF, UC, where the same sentiment is repeated.

4. Herschel Alt, *Residential Treatment for the Disturbed Child* (New York: International Universities Press, 1960), ix; Council of National Organizations on Children and Youth, *Focus on Children and Youth* (Washington, D.C., 1960), 37, 301; Lydia F. Hylton, *The Residential Treatment Center: Children, Programs, and Costs* (New York: Child Welfare League of America, 1964), ix, 2–3; Committee on Child Health of the American Public Health Association, *Services for Children with Emotional Disturbances* (New York: American Public Health Association, 1961), 71–72; Bert Kruger Smith, *Children of the Night* (Austin, Tex.: Hogg Foundation, 1961); Child Welfare League of America, *Treatment Settings for Children with Emotional Disorders* (New York: Child Welfare League of America, 1962).

5. Committee on Ways and Means, U.S. House of Representatives, *Green Book: Overview of Entitlement Programs* (1990), 755; Brenda McGowan, *Child Welfare: Current Dilemmas, Future Directions* (Itasca, Ill.: F. E. Peacock, 1983), 96; Winford Oliphant, *AFDC Foster Care: Problems and Recommendations* (New York: Child Welfare League of America, 1974), 6.

6. Child Welfare League of America, *Standards for Services of Child Welfare Institutions* (New York: Child Welfare League of America, 1964), 10.

7. "Definition: Emotionally Disturbed Child," January 1948, Welfare Council of Metropolitan Chicago Papers, Chicago Historical Society, box 498, folder 18; "Public Meeting on the Education of Emotionally Disturbed Children," January 16, 1969, Welfare Council of Metropolitan Chicago Papers, Chicago Historical Society, box 500, folder 18.

8. See Alfred Kadushin, *Child Welfare Services* (New York: Macmillan, 1967), esp. 553–54; Jack Adler, "General Concepts in Residential Treatment of Disturbed Children," *Child Welfare* 47 (November 1968): 519–23; Hylton, *The Residential Treatment Center*; Child Welfare League of America, *Treatment Settings for Children with Emotional Disorders* (New York: Child Welfare League of America, 1962).

9. On the interest in mental health, and its connections to the specific issues of youth, see James L. Sundquist, *Politics and Policy: The Eisenhower, Kennedy, and Johnson Years* (Washington, D.C.: Brookings Institution, 1968), 115–21; Joint Commission on Mental Illness and Health, *Action for Mental Health* (New York: Basic Books, 1961), xiv.

10. Research Department, *The Agencies Report on Problems and Prospects, 1960* (manuscript: Welfare Council of Metropolitan Chicago, March 1961). Of 183 respondents, 63 spoke of the inadequacy of psychiatric resources in the city. It was the most common complaint reported. From one children's agency: "Psychiatric facilities are extremely limited and so behind on their scheduling that a referral becomes meaningless." From a leisure-time agency: "Many children in this area have serious emotional handicaps and there is no kind of treatment service available for them. We have worked with several boys . . . but their problems are of such a nature that we could be of no help to them." The authors of the report themselves stated that one commonly noted com-

plaint was the shortage of "specialized institutional care and treatment for children and adolescents with serious personality problems and emotional disorders—this is a problem with respect to all types of children and especially Negro youth." These quotes are from sec. 2, p. 2. A copy of the report is in the library of the Chicago Historical Society.

11. Naomi Hiett, *Thirty Years of Teamwork for Children: A History of the Illinois Commission on Children* (Springfield, Ill.: privately printed, 1982), 33–34, 39, 42–43, 49–50; *The Department of Children and Family Services: A First Report* (Springfield, Ill., 1965).

12. These figures have been compiled by comparing the 1961 and 1971 *Social Services Directory* of the Welfare Council of Metropolitan Chicago.

13. Robert M. George and Susan Smith, "Substitute Care in Illinois: 1977–1988," (Chapin Hall Center for Children Discussion Paper, 1990), 2.

14. Certain huge Catholic institutions remained the most visible dinosaurs. In 1971 Angel Guardian Home for Children still had a capacity of 425; Maryville Academy would hold 650. But the situation was complicated. It was not that Catholic institutions were obstructionist. It was that they were moving in the same direction at a slower pace. Angel Guardian, for example, dropped its industrial school in the 1960s and reduced its population by 400. Similarly, the Chicago Industrial Home for Girls, another Catholic institution, closed during the 1960s. Its capacity had been 400. Catholics were also building residential treatment centers of their own as well, albeit at a slower pace than nonsectarian institutions.

It is also true that there were non-Catholic institutions that resisted the trend. In 1971, the Glenwood School for Boys continued to advertise itself as a place for "normal dependent boys from broken homes." It still housed 240 boys. Splits between Catholic and non-Catholic institutions should be understood to be tendencies rather than hard and fast distinctions. Source: Welfare Council of Metropolitan Chicago, *Social Service Directory, 1971.*

15. George Headley to Ellis A. Ballard, October 15, 1965, Welfare Council of Metropolitan Chicago Papers, Chicago Historical Society, box 703, folder 11.

16. See chapter five on this point.

17. George Headley, "Annual Report of Executive Director for 1964," 6, CHF, UC.

18. On the ad for the group worker, see George Headley to Albert J. Neely [March 3, 1964] in the file entitled "Cook County Children's Division," CHF, UC.

19. George Headley, "Annual Report of Executive Director for 1963," 1, CHF, UC; George Headley, "Annual Report of the Executive Director for 1964," 3, CHF, UC; George Headley, "Annual Report of the Executive Director for 1965," 3, CHF, UC; George Headley, "Annual Report of the Executive Director for 1967," 1, CHF, UC.

20. George Headley, "Annual Report of Executive Director for 1964," 4, CHF, UC; George Headley, "Annual Report of the Executive Director for 1965," 4, CHF, UC; Headley, "Annual Report of the Executive Director for 1967," 4, CHF, UC.

21. In 1963, there were twenty-one public placements (thirteen from the state, eight from the county), while agency placements accounted for thirteen children and private placements for seven. See "Annual Report of Secretary for Year Ending De-

cember 31, 1963," CHF, UC. In 1969, thirty-two children came from the state, seventeen from a private agency, and eleven from private families. George Headley, "Annual Report of the Executive Director for 1969," 2, CHF, UC.

22. Congress in 1967 amended social security law further. These amendments took effect in 1969. Among the provisions, they made it mandatory that all states participate in the federal foster care AFDC program. They also made AFDC money available to children entering foster care without it. Previously, a child had to be receiving AFDC when entering a foster placement in order to have AFDC pay for it. Jessica Pers, *Government as Parent: Administering Foster Care in California* (Berkeley: Institute for Governmental Affairs, 1976), 72–74. The result of these changes is that the number of children in foster care receiving AFDC jumped dramatically, from 16,800 in 1969 to over 100,000 in the mid-1970s. House Ways and Means Committee, *Green Book*, 756.

23. Department of Children and Family Services, *Biennial Report, 1969–1970*, 5–6.

24. Elsie Blumberg, "Annual Report on Intake and Discharge—1970"; George Headley, "Annual Report of the Executive Director for 1972," 2, CHF, UC.

25. United Way of Metropolitan Chicago, "Chapin Hall for Children: Staff Analysis," November 12, 1981, CHF, UC.

26. Hylton, *The Residential Treatment Center*, 189–200.

27. The two institutions that resisted DCFS control continue to do so today. These institutions are the Illinois Masonic Children's Home and the Glenwood School for Boys. By 1991 they were the only agencies listed in the Welfare Council's *Human Care Services Directory of Metropolitan Chicago* as "orphanages" and had policies harking back to the 1940s or 1950s. The Masonic Children's Home, for example, only accepted children who could attend public school. Acceptance at Glenwood continued to be dependent on the parents' ability to pay.

28. Headley, "Annual Report of the Executive Director for 1965," 2, 7.

29. The 1975 state report quoted in George Headley, "Annual Report of the Executive Director for 1975," 1; Thomas Libby, "Annual Report of the Associate Executive Director, 1978," 1, CHF, UC.

30. Case 15.

31. Case 16.

32. Case 19.

33. Case 20.

34. Frank T. Watters and Elsie Blumberg, "Child Care Workers' Manual" (March 1971), 41, CHF, UC.

35. See Philip Barker, "The Future of Residential Treatment for Children," in Charles E. Schaefer and Arthur J. Swanson, eds., *Children in Residential Care: Critical Issues in Treatment* (New York: Van Nostrand Reinhold, 1988), 3–4; Robert Lyman, et al., "Issues in Residential and Inpatient Treatment," in Robert Lyman, Steven Prentice-Dunn, and Stewart Gabel, eds., *Residential and Inpatient Treatment of Children and Adolescents* (New York: Plenum Press, 1989), 9.

36. The best single book on the subject is Paul Lerman, *Deinstitutionalization and the Welfare State* (New Brunswick, N.J., 1982).

37. For samples of the critical literature on residential treatment for emotionally disturbed children, see Gabriel D'Amato, *Residential Treatment for Child Mental*

Health (Springfield, Ill.: Thomas, 1969); William Bolman, "The Future of Residential Care for Children," *Child Welfare* 48 (May 1969): 279–88; Anthony N. Maluccio and Wilma D. Marlow, "Residential Treatment of Emotionally Disturbed Children: A Review of the Literature," *Social Service Review* 46 (June 1972): 230–50. On developmentally disabled youngsters, see James L. Paul, et al., *Deinstitutionalization: Program and Policy Development* (Syracuse, N.Y.: Syracuse University Press, 1977); on delinquents, see Joel Handler and Julie Zatz, eds., *Neither Angels Nor Thieves: Studies in Deinstitutionalization of Status Offenders* (Washington, D.C.: National Academy Press, 1982). For an overview of the movement, see Martha M. Dore and Karen Guberman Kennedy, "Two Decades of Turmoil: Child Welfare Services, 1960–1980," *Child Welfare* 60 (1981): 371–82.

38. For a good introduction to "group homes" as they were understood in the 1970s, see Alan Keith-Lucas and Clifford W. Sanford, *Group Child Care as a Family Service* (Chapel Hill: University of North Carolina Press, 1977). It is important to see that this represented a new meaning of the term "group home." In the 1950s, Chapin Hall itself was called a "group home," reflecting an earlier usage of the term. It then meant an institution of thirty-five to sixty children who, because of difficulties at home, would best thrive in such a setting. Group homes of the fifties were also further characterized by breaking up the larger population into several smaller, cottage-like living units each with roughly ten to twelve children. As discussed in chapter five, this is what Chapin Hall did in the 1950s, reflecting contemporary professional opinion. For a good statement of earlier ideas about group homes, see Susanne Schulze, "Group Living and the Dependent Child," *Proceedings of the National Conference of Social Work, May 1946* (New York, 1947): 387–97.

Both in the 1950s and 1970s, the term "group home" was used in the professional literature to contrast with what were called "large congregate institutions." But just as the meaning of "group home" changed, so too did the meaning of the other term. In the fifties, "large congregate institution" referred to the older orphanages that housed over 100 children—in other words, to what Chapin Hall was prior to 1949. By the seventies, however, "large congregate institution" in the professional literature referred primarily to residential treatment centers. That is, in the 1970s "large congregate institution" became associated with exactly what Chapin Hall had become in the 1950s and 1960s to escape being called a "large congregate institution."

39. Title XX quoted in Sheila Kamerman and Alfred Kahn, *Social Services in the United States* (Philadelphia: Temple University Press, 1976), 202–3. For some helpful comments indicating the range of deinstitutional activities of the early seventies, see 201–3. On the Title IV-B program, see Carol Golubock, "Current Status of Federal 1980 Foster Care Reforms," *Clearinghouse Review* (July 1983): 294–300. DCFS in 1976 drew 68 percent of its budget from federal Title XX funds. See Illinois Department of Children and Family Services, *Framework for the Future: Plan for Children and Family Services, fiscal years 1977–1979* (Springfield, Ill., April 1976), 78.

40. Mark Testa, "Child Placement and Deinstitutionalization: A Case Study of Social Reform in Illinois," in Handler and Zatz, eds., *Neither Angels Nor Thieves*, 829–30. For more on Jerome Miller's reforms, see Illinois Department of Children and Family Services, *Illinois Cares for Kids: New Directions in Child Welfare Services, Annual Report, 1973-74;* for succinct statements of Miller's own views at the time, see

"Miller Explains His Position," *Chicago Tribune*, August 2, 1973; and Jerome Miller, "The Politics of Change: Correctional Reform," in Yitzhak Bakal, ed., *Closing Correctional Institutions: New Strategies for Youth Services* (Lexington, Mass.: Lexington Books, 1973), 3–7; on Miller's Massachusetts experience, see Lloyd E. Ohlin, Robert B. Coates, and Allen D. Miller, "Radical Correctional Reform: A Case Study of the Massachusetts Youth Correctional System," *Harvard Educational Review* 44 (February 1974): 75–111.

41. "The Growing Furor over the State's Children," *Chicago Tribune*, July 25, 1973; Testa, "Deinstitutionalization in Illinois," 831–32. The Illinois chapter of the National Association of Social Workers, who represent agency social workers, was by May of 1974 openly campaigning for Miller's ouster. Also see the *Chicago Tribune*, June 24–30, July 2, 4, 1974. And see the letters to the editor all blasting Miller in *Chicago Tribune*, July 2, 4, 7, 8, 10, 12, 19, 1974.

42. Elsie Blumberg, "Social Service Annual Report—1973," 2–3, CHF, UC.

43. Jerome Miller did not disagree: "Ultimately, I'd like our kids to have the ability to shop for the best care. . . . They take him to X place. If he does well, fine. If not, we get him in somewhere else. . . . The bad places won't stay in business. The good ones will prosper. I see nothing against a little free enterprise in the child care system." "Miller Explains His Position," *Chicago Tribune*, August 2, 1973.

44. Blumberg, "Social Service Annual Report—1973," 1–4, CHF, UC.

45. "Dependent Children's Facilities Face State Probe," *Chicago Tribune*, June 21, 1973; George Headley, "Annual Report of the Executive Director for 1973," 1; Blumberg, "Social Service Annual Report—1973," 2, CHF, UC; also see Illinois, DCFS, *Illinois Cares for Kids*, [5].

46. Blumberg, "Social Service Annual Report—1973," 1, 2, 4–5. Blumberg argued that Miller's "much-trumpeted Child Abuse Section," had "replaced an excellent one, in my opinion" (2). While this is questionable on the face of it, to say the least, it was wrong to blame Miller for this. The state legislature, in September 1973, passed a new child abuse law which mandated a reorganization of DCFS's procedures. See Illinois DCFS, *Illinois Cares for Kids*, [9].

47. George Headley, "Annual Report of the Executive Director for 1974," 2; Elsie Blumberg, "Social Service Report—1974," 1–2; Elsie Blumberg, "Annual Report of the Director of Development and Intake for 1975," 1–2; also see George Headley, "Annual Report of the Executive Director—1976," 1.

48. Headley, "Annual Report of the Executive Director—1976," 1; Elsie Blumberg, "Annual Report of the Director of Development and Intake—1976," 1.

49. In December 1975, DCFS paid for 1,988 children in Illinois institutions. In December of 1979, that number had risen to 2,399. See Department of Children and Family Services, *Annual Report, 1975*, 5; Department of Children and Family Services, *1981 Plan*, 2 vols. (Springfield, Ill., April 1980), 1:63.

50. In an April 1976 report, DCFS spoke of the pressing need to find alternative placements for as many as 50 percent of children currently in institutions. An internal study indicated that 23 percent of institutionalized children had either no behavioral problems or only very minor ones. Numerous other institutionalized children, it was argued, would also benefit from either a home or foster home. DCFS, *Framework for the Future, Fiscal Years 1977–1979* (Springfield, Ill., April 1976), 76. This same report

also spoke of the need to implement Title XX and Title IV-B of the Social Security Act (77). The next two planning reports repeated these themes. See DCFS, *Plan for Children and Family Services, Fiscal Years 1978–1980* (Springfield, Ill., July 1977), 17–18, 20–21, 25; DCFS, *1981 Plan,* 1:59.

51. DCFS, *Plan for Children and Family Services: Fiscal Years 1978–1980* 21; DCFS, *1981 Plan,* 1:75.

52. DCFS, *1981 Plan,* 59; DCFS, *Illinois Human Services Report: Phase I and Phase II,* 2 vols. (August 1982), 1:17, 104, 114; DCFS, *Illinois Human Services Data Report: Phase I,* 2 vols. (June 1983), 1:115. For the statistics on institutionalized children, see *1981 Plan,* 1:63; DCFS, *Human Services Data Report: Phase I* (June 1986), 79.

53.

	Total Expenses	Consumer Price Index	Chapin Hall Expenses
1967	$ 322,060	100.0	100.0
1983	2,036,079	299.3	632.2

Sources: Chapin Hall annual reports; *Economic Report of the President, 1985,* p. 290. In 1979, Chapin Hall switched its fiscal year from January/December to July/June. The Consumer Price Index I have used for 1967 is that of January 1; for 1983 it is July 1.

54. The exact figures were: 1967, $222,692; 1983, $1,557,395.

55. See Matthew Stagner, Sheil Merry, and Clark Peters, "Group Residential Care in the Illinois Department of Children and Family Services: Children and Providers in the 1990s" (Chapin Hall for Children: May 1989), 5–8.

56. See Martha Morrison Dore, Thomas M. Young, and Donnell M. Pappenfort, "Residential Group Care Facilities for Children and Youth in the United States, 1965 and 1981: An Analysis of Change over Time," (School of Social Service Administration, University of Chicago, 1982), 22.

57. Headley, "Annual Report of the Executive Director for 1974," 3–4. CHF, UC.

58. Headley, "Annual Report of the Executive Director for 1974," 3, CHF, UC; Headley, "Annual Report of the Executive Director for 1975," 3–4, CHF, UC; "1977 Annual Report, President of the Board of Managers," 1, CHF, UC.

59. For the 1975 figure, see Elsie Blumberg, "Annual Report of the Director of Development and Intake for 1975," 6; for the 1980 figure see United Way, "Chapin Hall for Children: Staff Analysis," 3. Between July 1976 and June 1979, only 48 percent of children living in Chicago area private institutions were black, lower than the 58 percent figure of Chapin Hall. For the Chicago figure, see Malcolm Bush, *Families in Distress: Public, Private, and Civic Responses* (Berkeley and Los Angeles: University of California Press, 1988), 152. The 1983 study showed that these agencies only had a 38 percent black population. Nearly 60 percent of the children at Chapin Hall, however, were black. Project *COPE,* "Children in Need: A Preliminary Report on Children Entering Residential Child Care (Supplementary Tables)," (November 9, 1983), table 2. A copy of this report is in CHF, UC.

60. On Chapin Hall in 1981, see United Way, "Chapin Hall for Children: Staff Analysis," 4; Project *COPE*, "Children in Need," 1 and supplementary table 1.

61. Stagner, Merry, and Peters, "Group Residential Care," 11.

62. Headley, "Annual Report of the Executive Director for 1967," 5–6; see also Thomas Libby, "Annual Report of the Associate Executive Director, 1977," 1. On numerous other occasions during the 1970s and 1980s, Chapin Hall staff expressed uneasiness over the lack of female referrals. For example, Elsie Blumberg, "Annual Report of Social Service for Year 1971," 1; Blumberg, "Social Service Report—1974," 4; Thomas Libby, "Executive Director's Report for the Board of Directors," June 21, 1983; all in CHF, UC.

63. "Mr. Libby's Report," May 17, 1983, CHF, UC.

64. "Mr. Headley's Minutes," July 16, 1980; "Mr. Libby's Report," September 21, 1982; the outside report was that done by Harold Richman of the University of Chicago School of Social Service Administration, "An Analysis of Options for Chapin Hall for Children" (November 1983), 2 and fig. 1; all in CHF, UC.

65. Illinois DCFS, *Illinois Cares for Kids*, [5].

66. Interview with Jay Buck, May 1987. I have also used a copy of a diary Buck kept of the closing years of Chapin Hall.

67. Interview with Buck; interview with Bruce Newman, July 1989.

68. Interview with Buck.

69. Richman, "An Analysis of Options for Chapin Hall for Children."

70. Interview with Tom Libby, April 1987.

71. The following paragraphs are based on a number of conversations with people involved in the closing as well as scattered records in the Chapin Hall Files.

72. One woman board member I spoke with who voted to close the institution was clearly troubled by it. She blamed her husband (another board member) for not finding a solution that could keep the agency open. This reflected not only the conflicting ways the two thought about the agency, but also an assumed division of labor between men and women. Julia McNulty, the board member who stood and resigned when the vote was taken, told me that all the men voted to close the institution and the women split. McNulty was the first to give me a sense of the shifting gender politics at work in Chapin Hall in the 1960s and beyond. It was she who early on indicated to me the importance of the increasing presence of male professionals and what she considered the gender implications of the merger of the managers and directors. Interview with McNulty, March 1987.

73. Chapin Hall Center for Children at the University of Chicago, "A Guide to Current and Completed Projects" (Autumn 1993): 8.

74. Remarks by Harold Richman at Chapin Hall's 125th anniversary inaugural dinner, 2, CHF, UC.

75. For a parallel analysis that looks at the rise of private think tanks in Washington, D.C., during the 1960s and 1970s as, in part, a means of interpreting waves of statistical information that float through that city, see David Ricci, *The Transformation of American Politics* (New Haven: Yale University Press, 1993).

76. "Report to the Lilly Endowment / The Chapin Hall Center for Children: Present Status, Future Plans / The Field for Children and Youth Services: Needs and Opportunities for Its Advancement" (December 1992), 14. Copy in author's possession.

Epilogue

1. On Stephanopoulos, see "The Orphanage," *Newsweek* (December 12, 1994): 30.

2. "Fixing DCFS Mess Begins with Basic Steps," *Chicago Tribune*, March 11, 1994.

3. *Chicago Tribune*, March 9, 1994.

4. *Chicago Tribune*, December 21, 1993. On June 30, 1993, there were 33,900 children under DCFS care; on June 8, 1994, there were 40,522 children in DCFS custody. *Chicago Tribune*, June 8, 1994.

5. *Chicago Tribune*, April 2, 1994.

6. "The Orphanage," *Newsweek* 30; "Foster Care Crisis," *CQ Researcher* 1 (September 27, 1991): 705–29.

7. Connie Bruck, "Hilary the Pol," *New Yorker* 70 (May 30, 1994): 76–78.

8. Lois G. Forer, "Bring Back the Orphanage," *Washington Monthly* (April 1988): 17–21.

9. Joyce Ladner, professor of social work at Howard University, Op-ed article, *Washington Post*, October 29, 1989; "A Better Way to Provide Foster Care," *Des Moines Register*, September 6, 1990; "The New Orphanages," *U.S. News and World Report* (October 8, 1990): 37–41; Penelope Lemov, "The Return of the Orphanage," *Governing* (May 1991): 31–32; Mary-Lou Weisman, "When Parents Are Not in the Best Interests of the Child," *Atlantic Monthly* 274 (July 1994): 43–63.

10. Not the least important is that it suggests still another shift in the ongoing efforts to think of institutions in relation to family. It is, at least for some proponents, the overturning of the institutional model as developed in the 1940s. Because of the weakness of the foster care system, children's institutions should not only be driven by a medical model. The new orphanage was conceived as providing a surrogate family, just as the earlier cottage ideal did. "In a well-meant effort to recognize the rights of parents and the potential benefits of a family setting, we have consigned infants and youths to a foster care system that, by its design, cannot provide the continuity and care so many children desperately need" (Ladner, *Washington Post*, October 29, 1989).

11. On the governor and the SOS Children's Village, see *Chicago Tribune*, March 11, 1994.

12. The proposed legislation was S. 2134 and H.R. 4566 and was known as "The Real Welfare Reform Act." Among those supporting this legislation were conservative advocacy groups such as Empower America, which included William Bennett, Newt Gingrich, and Jack Kemp on its Board of Directors, and the Family Research Council. Bennett had been advocating more orphanages since 1990. See William J. Bennett, Jack Kemp, Vin Weber (Empower America Co-Directors), "Memorandum to Congressional Republicans," April 13, 1994; and press release from Family Research Council, April 28, 1994. Copies of both in author's possession.

13. "Foster Care Crisis," *CQ Researcher*, 720–21.

14. "Address by Miss Grace Abbott," (January 14, 1935), Abbott Papers, box 25, folder 10, Regenstein Library, University of Chicago.

15. "The Decline of Confidence in American Institutions," *Political Science Quarterly* (Fall 1983): 379–402. According to one study, the number of those expressing

high regard for Congress went from 42 percent in 1966 to 10 percent in 1978. High regard for the presidency went from 41 percent to 14 percent. See James Sundquist, "The Crisis of Competence in our National Government," *Political Science Quarterly* (Summer 1980): 306.

16. In academic writing, the emergence of a "social control" interpretation of the welfare state in the 1960s, which especially took hold in the 1970s, was one sign of the new skepticism of radicals. See Anthony M. Platt, *The Child Savers: The Invention of Delinquency* (Chicago: University of Chicago Press, 1969). Strong distrust of social work was also a theme of the writings of Christopher Lasch. See Christopher Lasch, *Haven in a Heartless World: The Family Besieged* (New York: Basic Books, 1977). More anarchist work inspired by Michel Foucault also contributed to the mood. See Jacques Donzelot, *The Policing of Families* (New York: Pantheon, 1979).

Some recent feminist writing on the welfare state, despite its distance from the social control argument, continues to be skeptical of welfare managers, arguing that a strong adversarial feminist movement outside the state is critical to effective policy and that managers inevitably dilute progressive political thrusts. See Nancy Fraser, "Women, Welfare, and the Politics of Need Interpretation," and "Struggle over Needs: Outline of a Socialist-Feminist Critical Theory of Late Capitalist Political Culture," in *Unruly Practices: Power, Discourse, and Gender in Contemporary Social Theory* (Minneapolis: University of Minnesota Press, 1989).

17. Hilary Rodham, "Children under the Law," *Harvard Educational Review* 43 (November 1973): 513. For her use of Platt, see pp. 491, 494. On Platt's role in changing the image of welfare managers, see n. 16 above.

18. Bruck, "Hilary the Pol," 76.

19. *A Force for Change: Children's Rights Project of the ACLU* (American Civil Liberties Union, 1993), 1.

20. *Chicago Tribune*, April 2, 1994.

INDEX

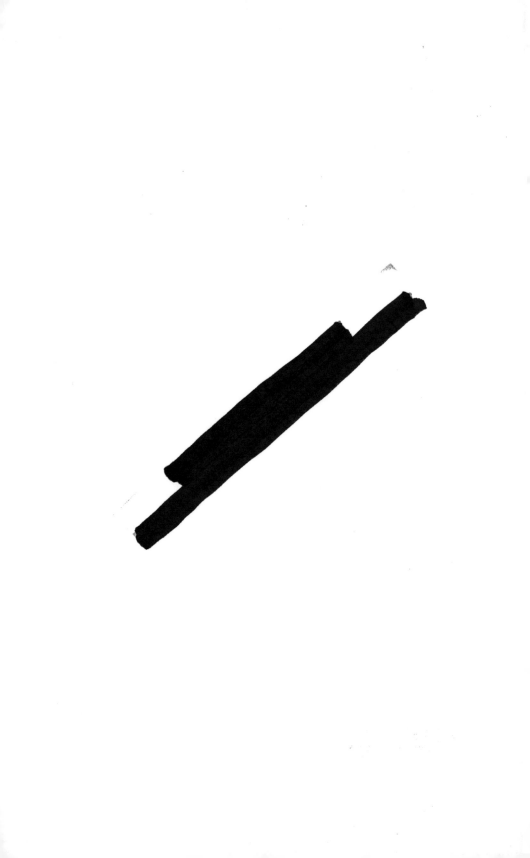